Dr Peter Marshall has established himself over many years as the principal writer of student textbooks on bookkeeping, which is reflected in the accreditation and endorsement of both principal institutes which his books alone have received. He is the author of *Mastering Book-keeping* and *Computerised Book-keeping*.

Other titles from How To Books

MASTERING BOOK-KEEPING
Dr Peter Marshall

COMPUTERISED BOOK-KEEPING
Dr Peter Marshall

SETTING UP AND RUNNING A LIMITED COMPANY
Robert Browning

WRITE YOUR OWN BUSINESS PLAN
Paul Hetherington

Mastering Spreadsheet Book-keeping

Dr Peter Marshall

Constable & Robinson Ltd
55–56 Russell Square
London WC1B 4HP
www.constablerobinson.com

First published in the UK by How To Books,
an imprint of Constable & Robinson Ltd., 2014

A copy of the British Library Cataloguing in Publication
Data is available from the British Library

ISBN 978-1-84528-501-2 (paperback)
ISBN 978-1-84528-556-2 (ebook)

Printed and bound in the UK

1 3 5 7 9 10 8 6 4 2

Contents

Contents

Contents

List of figures

List of figures—cont.

Until recently there has been a dearth of books on the market dealing with computerized bookkeeping. Even now, those there are largely tend to deal with Sage systems. This is reflected in the prevailing neglect of the application of spreadsheets in the setting of exam papers. Not everyone has a Sage package, but more or less everyone who has a computer has Microsoft Excel or something similar. Furthermore, this spreadsheet technology is highly versatile and useful. With the knowledge and skills you can gain from *Mastering Spreadsheet Bookkeeping*, if you have a computer and MS Excel software, you can easily set up your own computerized accounting package.

As a businessperson, you will be aware of the benefits of using computerization in your accounting, but perhaps as the owner of a small business, you are under the impression that it is beyond your economical reach due to the cost of over-the-counter software packages? If so, *Mastering Spreadsheet Bookkeeping* will show you step by step how you too can easily computerize your accounting without splashing out on expensive new software.

If you are currently working as a freelance bookkeeper, you will already have mastered the manual system; if you hadn't, you would not have gained your qualification to operate! *Mastering Spreadsheet Bookkeeping* will help you to get up to speed quickly with a widely used computerized system and gain a thorough knowledge of how to use spreadsheets to their fullest advantage. With this knowledge and skill you will increase your efficiency of operation and, as a result, your earnings potential.

Finally, if you are an accountancy student with a module in bookkeeping, or you are studying for a qualification in bookkeeping (e.g. for Levels I and II Certificate in Computerised Bookkeeping (ICB) and Level III Diploma in Computerised Bookkeeping (ICB)), *Mastering Spreadsheet Bookkeeping* is the ideal learning tool for you. All exam boards now encourage their students to develop skills in computerized bookkeeping. This is what employers demand. Exam boards are beginning to shy away from using specific packages in their syllabi. Their focus is, understandably, on computerization using only widely used operating systems such as MS Excel. With its focus on MS Excel and its clear, step-by-step approach, *Mastering Spreadsheet Bookkeeping* will help you to develop your computerized bookkeeping skills with confidence. In addition, exam-style questions and answers are provided for self-testing so you may consolidate your bookkeeping knowledge as you learn.

Dr Peter Marshall has been a leading authority on bookkeeping for over twenty-five years. His bestselling How To title, *Mastering Book-keeping*, is now in its ninth edition and is endorsed by both the Institute of Certified Bookkeepers and the International Association of Book-keepers.

Bookkeeping has recently become a legally regulated occupation in the UK and certain legal responsibilities have been placed upon those who offer their services for gain. Although *Mastering Spreadsheet Bookkeeping* will give you the knowledge and skill to carry out such work, it is important that you become familiar, especially if you are new to this subject, with the legalities involved.

Acknowledgements

The author and publisher wish to thank the following organizations for their kind permission to reproduce facsimiles of mock examination papers on computerized accounting:

The Institute of Certified Bookkeepers (ICB)
Association of Accounting Technicians (AAT)
City & Guilds

Part One

An Introduction to Spreadsheet Bookkeeping

1 A period of transition

With the increasing globalization of trade and industry at all levels it is becoming necessary to achieve some degree of harmony in accounting practices between countries. The standards that applied in the UK since 1970, i.e. Statements of Standard Accounting Practice (SSAPs) and Financial Reporting Standards (FRSs), are being gradually phased out and replaced by International Accounting Standards (IASs) and International Financial Reporting Standards (IFRSs). All companies listed on European Union (EU) stock exchanges already use the international standards and in time they will be used by all UK businesses.

Here are some examples of the changes in terminology with which you will have to become familiar. In the international standard terminology, instead of turnover the term *revenue* is used; instead of stock the term *inventory* is used; and debtors and creditors are called *accounts receivable* and *accounts payable*. Provisions tend to be referred to as *allowances*; the profit and loss account is known as the *income statement*; and any profit that is brought down to the balance sheet is termed *retained profits*. Debentures are known as *loan notes*; fixed assets are called *non-current assets*; and long-term liabilities are called *non-current liabilities*.

2 The role and significance of professional associations

One of the distinguishing characteristics of all professions is the existence of professional associations. Such bodies maintain and improve the reputation of the profession by the regulation of conduct, the improvement of skills and the validation of qualifications.

The professional associations for bookkeepers are the Institute of Certified Bookkeepers, under the Royal Patronage of His Royal Highness Prince Michael of Kent GCVO, and the International Association of Book-keepers (IAB) (see Further resources).

Bookkeeping became a regulated profession under the Money Laundering Regulations of 2007. As a result of this, bookkeepers now have special legal duties imposed upon them, and failure to comply with them has serious legal consequences. All practising bookkeepers must be registered with a supervisory body. Both of the professional bodies mentioned above are Treasury Appointed Supervisory Bodies under the Money Laundering Act and, as such, will monitor, guide and supervise members to ensure compliance.

In addition, membership also provides proof of proficiency, which is recognized worldwide. Each association offers assistance with career development, not only through the provision of training and qualifications, but also though notification of job vacancies, updates on legislation and advice and guidance on private practice. Members also get the opportunity to meet and associate with others in the same profession in local groups and forums.

Figure 1 www.bookkeepers.org.uk homepage (reproduced by kind permission of the Institute of Certified Bookkeepers)

When a business keeps a substantial number of personal details in computerized accounting records it may be obligated to register with the Information Commissioner's Office, the independent regulatory body that deals with the Data Protection Act 1998 (see Further Resources). The person who decides how data will be used and for what purpose is referred to in the Act as the data controller while a person on whom data is kept is referred to as a data subject. The purpose of registration is essentially so that the data subjects are aware of what information is held and how it is used.

It is not necessary to inform the Information Commissioner if:

- the data controller is only using the data for sending and receiving invoices and statements;
- the data subjects are companies and no individuals can be identified in them;
- the data is only used to process payroll and prepare statutory returns.

However, if a data controller is going to make accounting data available to management or any other department for non-accounting purposes, e.g. marketing, statistical, planning or control purposes, the company must be registered. It must disclose the kind of data held, the purpose for which it will be used and how subjects can access their own data.

Legal obligations in respect of personal data

Businesses registered under the Data Protection Act 1998 must comply with certain standards of practice contained in Schedule 1 of the Act. These require that the personal data shall:

- be obtained only for specified and lawful purposes and must not be used in any manner incompatible with such purposes;
- be relevant and adequate but not excessive for the purpose for which it has been collected;
- be accurate and kept up to date;
- not be kept for any longer than necessary for the purpose for which it was collected;
- only be processed in accordance with the subject's rights under the Act;
- be protected by appropriate organizational and technical measures against unauthorized and unlawful use, or accidental loss or damage;
- not be taken outside of the country to any country where there is not adequate legal protection of the rights and freedom of data subjects in respect of the processing of their personal data.

In most businesses today, accounting information will be used for non-accounting purposes, so it is very likely that anyone who controls such data will need to register and comply with the Act.

4 Double entry bookkeeping

Let's just remind ourselves of the essential principle of double entry bookkeeping because we have to keep this in mind as we construct and use our spreadsheet system.

Debit and credit

Transactions have two sides, a debt and a credit. When a firm sells goods to a customer a debit entry is made in that customer's ledger account because they have become our debtor (for the sake of simplicity, in this example we'll assume the sale was VAT exempt). A credit entry of the same amount has to be made in the nominal ledger because the firm has made a revenue.

Both of these transactions must be recorded separately because we need:

- a total of sales figures for tax computation and management purposes (to make sure the business is working to plan);

- a cumulative total of money owed by each customer.

A check on accuracy

There is another important advantage of double entry bookkeeping. If both sides of each transaction have been recorded then, at any time, if the sums have been done correctly the debit entries will equal the credit entries. It provides a check of accuracy. An example is as follows:

Assets – liabilities = Capital

Having reminded yourself of the crucial importance of maintaining the double entry, keep this in mind as you configure and use your spreadsheet system.

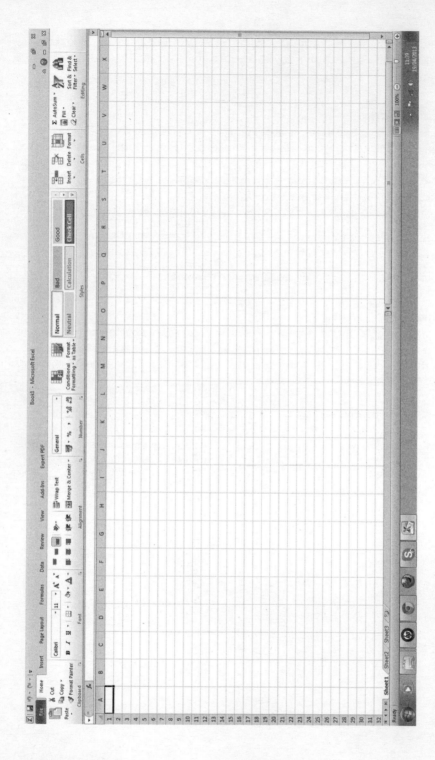

Figure 2 An MS Excel spreadsheet page

Figure 3 The control section of an Excel page known as the ribbon

5 Configuring spreadsheets within the traditional daybook format

This chapter contains guidance for those who are already knowledgeable and skilled in double entry bookkeeping, but not in the use of spreadsheets for the purpose. Chapters 8 to 50 give more comprehensive guidance on the whole subject of double entry bookkeeping and spreadsheet use.

Nowadays, we can use the electronic pages of a spreadsheet program to keep the books of a business. This has great advantages. If you want to stick to the configuration of your manual system, but simply make your work quicker and simpler, then you can simply reconstruct daybook and ledger pages on a spreadsheet to look like the manual versions, and add code and formulae to make the pages sum and balance themselves.

Figures 4 to 14 provide examples of such configurations. Because of the uniformity of structure of all daybooks and ledgers, these examples will serve for all the daybooks, the ledger divisions, the cash book and the petty cash book.

Configuring a spreadsheet page for daybooks

It's easy to configure pages that look like traditional daybooks and that will add themselves up and cross balance. All you have to do is draw in the answer boxes and insert simple formulae in them.

To draw in answer boxes, click on the cells where you want the answers to go and then click on the inverted triangle at the right of the borders button in the fonts group on the ribbon with the 'Home' tab open. This will release a drop-down menu of styles. Select single top and double bottom borders for the grand monthly total box in the main totals column, and single top borders for the totals of the analysis columns.

To enter the appropriate formulae in each, click into the first cell to be added in the column, hold down the shift key and click into the answer box, then click on the sigma icon, near the right of the ribbon when the Home tab is open. There is more than one way to do this, but that is by far the quickest in this case.

Making things easy for yourself

Now you don't have to go through this each month. You can keep this page without any actual monthly figures in it as a template.

Four steps for creating a template

1.   Create a single sheet workbook.
2.   Format it with the titles and formulae.
3.   Save as a template.
4.   Enter the folder in which you wish to store it.

Configuring the ledger divisions

Placing an equals sign (=) into a cell tells the system that what follows will be a formula rather than data. Entering the word 'SUM' tells it that the system is being asked to add some figures up and place the answer in this cell. Immediately you enter the word 'SUM' a pair of brackets will appear, in which the cells to be added are to be placed. You can specify a range of cells by placing a colon between the parameters, e.g. A5:A10, or by separating cells with commas (without spaces), if they are not adjacent, e.g. A5,A10. You can also use a mixture of both, if some cells are adjacent and others are not.

Date 2013	Supplier	Inv no.	Fo.	PURCHASE DAYBOOK Net inv. value	VAT 20%	Stationery	Books	Calculators
Apr 1	Morgan and Baldwyn	4/1	BL6	80.00	16.00	80.00		
3	Morgan and Baldwyn			200.00	40.00			200.00
15	S. Jones	4/2	BL5	70.00			70.00	
21	S. Singh	4/3	BL9	160.00			160.00	
30	Morgan and Baldwyn	4/4	BL6	40.00	8.00	40.00		
				150.00	30.00	150.00		
				700.00	94	270.00	230.00	200.00

Figure 4 Example of a traditional purchase daybook page written up on a spreadsheet

Date 2013	Supplier	Inv no.	Fo.	PURCHASE DAYBOOK Net inv. value	VAT 20%	Stationery	Books	Calculators
Apr 1	Morgan and Baldwyn	4/1	BL6	80	16	80		
3	Morgan and Baldwyn			200	40			200
15	S. Jones	4/2	BL5	70			70	
21	S. Singh	4/3	BL9	160			160	
30	Morgan and Baldwyn	4/4	BL6	40	8	40		
				150	30	150		
				=SUM(F4:F9)	=SUM(G4:G9)	=SUM(H4:H9)	=SUM(I6:I9)	=SUM(J5:J9)

Figure 5 Traditional purchase daybook spreadsheet (Figure 4) with the formulae revealed

SALES DAYBOOK

Date		Customer	Inv. no.	Net inv. value	VAT 20%	Bricklyr supplies	Carptry supplies	Décor supplies	Roofing supplies
2013									
Jan	2	D. Davidson	SO1	415.00	83	40.00	360.00	15.00	
	4	Kahn & Kahn	SO2	30.00	6		30.00		
	5	JBC Roofing	SO3	250.00	50				250.00
				695.00	139	40.00	390.00	15.00	250.00

Figure 6 Example of a traditional sales daybook page written up on a spreadsheet

SALES DAYBOOK

Date		Customer	Inv no.	Net inv value	VAT 20%	Bricklyr supplies	Carptry supplies	Décor supplies	Roofing supplies
2013									
Jan	2	D. Davidson	SO1	415	83	40	360	15	
	4	Kahn & Kahn	SO2	30	6		30		
	5	JBC Roofing	SO3	250	50				250
				=SUM(E17:E19)	=SUM(F17:F19)	=SUM(G17:G19)	=SUM(H17:H19)	=SUM(I17:I19)	=SUM(J18:J19)

Figure 7 Traditional sales daybook spreadsheet (Figure 6) with the formulae revealed

CASH BOOK

(Receipts)

Particulars	Fo	Discount	Cash	Bank
Balance	b/d		50.00	1,750.00
Edwards garage	SL2	2.50		97.50
Cash sales	NL2		7.50	
C. Jones	SL5			12.50
Bank			290.00	
J.B.C. Roofing	SL7	5.00	110.00	
Cash sales	NL2		20.00	
Eliot transport	SL8	5.00		200.00
Morgan & Baldwyn	SL1			42.50
Cash				7.50
		7.50	477.50	2,110.00
			50	1349

(Payments) Cr.

Date	Particulars	Fo	Discount	Cash	Bank
June 1	Razi & Thaung	BL3			40.00
1	D.Davidson	BL5			21
9	A.T. Office supplies	BL4		100.00	
12	Cash				290
14	Wages	NL8		240.00	
14	Petty cash	PCB3		50.00	
20	M. Bandura	BL6		30.00	
22	L. cleaves	BL12	4.87		190
22	Van den Burgh	BL7			200
30	Interest & bank charges				20
30	Bank			7.50	
30	Balance	c/d		50	1349
			4.87	477.50	2,110.00

Figure 8 Example of a traditional cash book page written up on a spreadsheet

CASH BOOK

	Dr.		Date	(Payments)	Cr.
	Cash	Bank		Cash	Bank
	50	1750	June 1		40
	7.5	97.5	1		21
			9	100	
	290	12.5	12		290
	110		14	240	
	20		14	50	
			20	30	
		200	22		190
		42.5	22		200
		7.5	30		20
			30	7.5	
	=IF(N15>E15, N15-15,"")	=IF(P15>G15, P15-15,"")		=IF(E15>N15, E15-15,"")	=IF(G15>P15, G15-15,"")
	=SUM(D4:D14)	=SUM(F4:F14)		=SUM(M4:M14)	=SUM(O4:O14)
	477.5	2110		477.5	2110
	=M15	=O15		=D15	=F15

Figure 9 Traditional cash book spreadsheet (Figure 8) with the formulae revealed
Note: Only those columns that contain formulae are shown in the example.

15

PETTY CASH BOOK

Dr Receipts	Fo.	Date 2013 May	Cr Details	Receipts	Total exp	Analysis	Motor exp	Travelling	Postage	Stationery	Cleaning
50.00	CB5	1	Cash								
		1	Petrol	5/1	10.00		10.00				
		2	Fares	5/2	3.20			3.20			
		5	Petrol	5/3	8.00		8.00				
		8	Postage	5/4	9.00				9.00		
		17	Stationery	5/5	1.30					1.30	
		22	Fares	5/6	1.40			1.40			
		25	Fares	5/7	1.40			1.40			
		26	Petrol	5/8	7.00		7.00				
		31	Cleaning	5/9	4.00						4.00
		31	Fares	5/10	1.40			1.40			
		31	Postage	5/11	1.80				1.80		
					48.50		25.00	7.40	10.80	1.30	4.00
48.50	CB6	31	Cash				NL8	NL9	NL15	NL17	NL18
98.50		31	Balance c/d		98.50	0.00					
98.50					195.50						
98.50		Jun 1	Balance b/d								

Figure 10 Example of a traditional petty cash book page written up on a spreadsheet

PETTY CASH BOOK

Dr Receipts	Fo.	Date 2013	Cr Details	Receipts	Total exp	Motor exp	Travelling	Postage	Stationery	Cleaning
50	CB5	May 1	Cash							
		1	Petrol	5/1	10	10				
		2	Fares	5/2	3.2		3.2			
		5	Petrol	5/3	8	8				
		8	Postage	5/4	9			9		
		17	Stationery	5/5	1.3				1.3	
		22	Fares	5/6	1.4		1.4			
		25	Fares	5/7	1.4		1.4			
		26	Petrol	5/8	7	7				
		31	Cleaning	5/9	4					4
		31	Fares	5/10	1.4		1.4			
		31	Postage	5/11	1.8			1.8		
					=SUM(I7:I17)	=SUM(L7:L17)	=SUM(M7:M17)	=SUM(N7:N17)	=SUM(O7:O17)	=SUM(P8:P17)
						NL8	NL9	NL15	NL17	NL18
	CB6	31	Cash							
48.5		31	Balance c/d		=IF(B21>J21, B21-J21,"")					
=IF(J21>B21, J21-B21,"")					=SUM(I6:I21)					
=SUM(A6:A21)					=A21					
=I21		Jun 1	Balance b/d							

Figure 11 Traditional petty cash book spreadsheet (Figure 10) with the formulae revealed

Note: Some columns that do not contain formulae are hidden in this example because of limitations of space.

NL 3

Nominal ledger

Maintenance and repairs a/c

DR							CR
Date		Details	Amount	Date	Details		Amount
2013							
Jan	5	BL3	50.00				
	9	BL21	75.00				
	22	PCB4	25.50				
	28	BL5	10.50				
			161.00		Balance c/d		161
		Bal b/d	161				161.00
Feb	6	BL3	80.00				
	7	BL5	90.00				
	8	BL7	120.50				
	9	PCB6	10.50				
			462.00		Balance c/d		462
		Balance b/d	462				462.00

Figure 12 Example of a traditional nominal ledger page written up on a spreadsheet

NL 3 **Nominal ledger**
Maintenance and repairs a/c

DR				CR		
Date	Details	Amount	Date	Details	Amount	
2013						
Jan 5	BL3	50				
9	BL21	75				
22	PCB4	25.5				
28	BL5	10.5				
	=IF(D10>0, "Bal c/d",")	=IF(J10>F10, J10-F10,"")	=SUM (E6:E9)		=IF(I10>0,"Balance c/d","")	=IF(F10>J10,F10-J10,"")	=SUM(I6:I9)
		=SUM(E6:E10)			=SUM(I6:I10)	
	=IF(D10>0, "Bal c/d",")	=((I10)			=IF(I12>0,"Balance b/d","")	=D10
Feb 6	BL3	80				
7	BL5	90				
8	BL7	120.5				
9	PCB6	10.5				
	=IF(J17>F17, J17-F17,"")	=SUM (E12:E16)		=IF(I17>0,"Balance c/d","")	=IF(F17>J17,F17-J17,"")	=SUM(I12:I16)
	=SUM(E12:E17)			=SUM(I12:I17)	
	=IF(D17>0,"Bal c/d",")	=((I17)			=IF(I19>0,"Balance b/d","")	=D17

Figure 13 Traditional nominal ledger page spreadsheet (Figure 12) with the formulae revealed
Note: Some columns that do not contain formulae are hidden in this example because of limitations of space.

JOURNAL

Date		Particulars		Details	Fo.	Dr	Cr
2011							
Nov	30	Invoice for cleaning paid by proprietor on personal credit card	Debit	Ace Cleaning Services	BL24	30.00	
			Credit	J. Dobbs	BL25		30.00
Dec	10	Office rent paid on behalf of company by Proprietor	Debit	Office rent	NL21	300	
			Credit	J. Dobbs	BL25		300
	28	Paid standing order to Insurance company without an invoice so to complete the postings that would have been made from an invoice	Debit	Insurance	NL7	60	
			Credit	Bank	CB10		60
	28	Sundries:					
		Motor Van 2			NL39	8000.00	
		Edwards Garage			BL16		8000.00
		Asset disposal A/C			NL40	3350.00	
		Motor van 1			NL10		3350.00
		Edwards Garage			NL16	2000.00	
		Asset disposal A/C			NL40		2000.00
		Profit and Loss A/C			NL41	1350.00	
		Asset disposal A/C			NL40		1350.00
		Edwards Garage			BL16	6000.00	
		Bank			CB18		6000.00
		To record the details of the purchase, by cheque, of a motor van with part exchange on old motor van.					

Figure 14 Spreadsheet configured for journal

You can even shortcut this process by simply clicking into the cell that is to hold the sum and then clicking on the sigma icon, close to the right-hand side of the ribbon. That will place the '=SUM( )' part of the formula into the cell. Then you just click into the first cell, press the shift key (if the cells to be added are adjacent) or the control 'Ctrl' key (if they are not) and click into the next in the range. Press return and the formula will automatically be placed into the cell.

The triple balance mechanism of *bilancio* (balance c/d), *saldo* (balancing column totals) and *resto* (balance b/d), traditionally employed in the ledger divisions, requires a balance carried down to be calculated, so the debit and credit columns need to be summed without showing the lesser total in the final sheet. Therefore an extra column needs to be inserted to the right of the debit and credit columns to hold this intermediate figure. These columns can subsequently be hidden as they are only for calculating purposes and will serve no purpose in the final display.

The cells to sum in the debit and credit columns go right down to the saldo boxes but the cells to hold the totals of each column for the purpose of calculating the c/d balance go down one place less.

You need to enter a formula in the penultimate cell of the debit and credit columns to deduct the total of one side from the other and place a balancing figure if necessary to make both sides add up to the same figure in the saldo box.

These formulae make use of the 'If' function and the 'Greater than' symbol. The fully constructed formula tells the system that if the total of the other column is greater than the total of this column deduct the total of this column from the total of that column to see how much must be added to this column to even the two sides up and place it here.

The final thing to which to attend is to place the resto figure in the appropriate cell to show the balance b/d. All you need to do for this is to place, in the cell below the saldo box in the debit column, the reference of the cell above the saldo box in the credit column and vice versa for the credit column.

There is no point in showing zeros in these cells, so if they do appear click on the tools menu and select options. Make sure 'Zero values' is not ticked and then press the key labelled 'OK'.

You don't need to go through the process of inserting these answer boxes and entering the formula each month, you can just cut and paste the three lines that contain the borders and the formulae for balances c/d, balancing totals and balances b/d from month to month and then just check and adjust the formulae as appropriate.

6   Speeding up traditional ledger posting

You can keep all accounts of a single ledger division (e.g. all customer accounts) on the same sheet, one after the other, as the placing of automated summing and balancing instructions will ensure that the accounts do not get mixed up. Each ledger division becomes a different sheet (e.g. sheet 1 = sales daybook, sheet 2 = nominal ledger and sheet 3 = sales ledger). A big advantage of doing this is that you can make posting from daybooks to ledger sheets easy, by putting all the sheets involved on the screen at once. The larger your screen the easier this will be. Then you can simply use copy and paste across the boundaries of the sheets to do your posting.

   For example, to post a transaction from the sales daybook to the relevant ledger sheets, just follow these steps:

1.   Call up all the relevant sheets on the screen at once.
2.   Click on the gross invoice value for each entry on the sales daybook sheet. Hold down 'Ctrl' and press 'C' at the same time.
3.   Scroll down the sales ledger sheet to the personal account of the customer concerned.
4.   Click on the next available space in the debit column. Hold down 'Ctrl' and press 'V' at the same time.
5.   Enter the date in the date column.
6.   When all the entries have been posted to the sales ledger accounts, proceed as follows.
7.   Click on the net total in the sales daybook. Hold down 'Ctrl' and press 'C' at the same time.
8.   Scroll to the next available space in the credit column of the sales account in the nominal ledger.
9.   Hold down 'Ctrl' and press 'V' at the same time.
10. Click on the VAT total in the sales daybook and hold down 'Ctrl' and press 'C' at the same time.
11. Scroll to the next available space in the credit column of the VAT account in the nominal ledger and hold down 'Ctrl' and press 'V' at the same time.

7   Depreciation calculations

Depreciation calculations can be done swiftly and simply, using Excel's built-in functions.

Straight line method

1. In the functions library, which can be accessed from the left-hand side of the ribbon, when the formula tab is open, select the financial option.
2. Click, then, on the SLN option.
    The following dialogue boxes will appear on the screen:

    - Asset value
    - Estimated salvage (scrap) value
    - Estimated useful life

3. Enter the relevant figures and click 'OK' to find the annual depreciation figure.

Diminishing balance method of depreciation

1. Do as above, but click on the DDB option this time. The following five dialogue boxes will appear:

    - Cost
    - Estimated salvage value
    - Estimated useful life
    - Start of the period
    - End of the period

2. Enter the relevant figures and click on 'OK' to find the depreciation for the asset.

Sum of the years (or sum of the digits) method of depreciation

1. Follow the same procedure as for the other two methods, but this time selecting the SYD option. A dialogue box will appear asking you to enter four details:

    - Cost
    - Salvage value
    - Lifetime of the asset in years
    - Period expired in years

2. Enter the relevant figures and click on 'OK' to find the depreciation for the asset.

Part Two

Basic Spreadsheet
Bookkeeping

Double entry accounts are kept in the ledger, but daily details of transactions are not normally entered directly into it; it would become too cluttered and difficult to use. For convenience we first of all enter all the day-to-day details of transactions in other books, called books of prime entry. In modern accounting these books are the:

- Purchase daybook
- Purchase returns daybook
- Sales daybook
- Sales returns daybook
- Journal
- Cash book
- Petty cash book

Daybooks or journals

This group of books can be called either daybooks or journals. We will use the term daybooks here for the four that are identically ruled and most often referred to as daybooks: the purchase daybook, purchase returns daybook, sales daybook and sales returns daybook. The word journal we will keep for the journal proper, because of its individual ruling, and the others we will call books of prime entry. It is the four daybooks as defined here that we will explain in this section.

Source documents for the bookkeeper

The sources of information we need to enter into the daybooks are invoices and credit notes. When a firm receives invoices or credit notes for goods it has purchased, they are known as purchase invoices and credit notes inwards respectively. When it sends them out, they are called sales invoices and credit notes outwards. Whether the documents refer to sales or purchases, their format is basically the same. After all, what is a purchase invoice to one party in the transaction is a sales invoice to the other and similarly for credit notes.

Debit notes

Sales office clerks occasionally make mistakes and undercharge a customer for goods so firms usually print the term E&OE on their invoices, which means 'errors and omissions excepted'. This means the firm reserves the right to ask for more money for the goods if it realizes it has inadvertently undercharged. If this has to be done the document used is known as a debit note.

Bookkeeping and confidentiality

Bookkeeping and accounting technicians have a duty to treat all information to which their job exposes them in strictest confidence, disclosing details only to those who have a professional right to know them. Examples are:

- employers or employees who need the information to carry out their professional role;
- professionals outside the company who work on behalf of the company who need the information to carry out their function;
- any other person to whom their employer or officer senior to themselves instructs them to disclose information, since it must be assumed that the employer or senior officer will also be working within the confines of such confidentially rules.

9 The purchase daybook

The purchase daybook is where we first enter up all our purchases on credit. The book itself is not part of the 'accounts': it is just one of the sources from which the accounts will be written up later on.

How to write up the purchase daybook
What you need:

- the purchase daybook;
- the invoices for the period (day, week, etc.).

First, sort the invoices into date order. Next, write or stamp a purchase invoice number on each one. (This is not the invoice number printed on the document when the firm receives it; that is the sales invoice number of the firm that sent it). The idea is to help the bookkeeper find an invoice easily if they have to look up details of an old transaction.

Many firms keep a list of consecutive numbers for this purpose. Others use a two-part number made up of the month number and a number from a consecutive list for that month.

Setting up the purchase daybook worksheet
1. Open your Excel program by clicking on the Excel icon.
2. Left-click on the second worksheet tab on the bottom left of your screen (the first sheet will be the index sheet). A new Excel worksheet will open.
3. Click on rename and type 'Purchase Daybook' and this title will be placed on the tab for easy identification.
4. Click back into the worksheet.
5. Type the following in the cells indicated.

Cell number		Type
C	1	Purchase daybook
A	3	Month
B	3	Day of the month
C	3	Name of supplier
D	3	Invoice number
E	3	Fo.
F	3	Total net
G	3	VAT
H	3	Gross total
I	3	Stationery

6.   In the cells to the right of I3, type appropriate headings for analysis of the purchases, e.g. stationery, office equipment, etc. In all the cash cells in row 4, type and centre '£ : p'.

7.   Click into cell A4. Hold down the shift key and click into B4. This will highlight both cells.

8.   Click on the merge and centre arrow at the right of the icon in the alignment group on the ribbon bar (the square with a little 'a' in it).

9.   Type into that space the current year (e.g. 2014).

10. Click on the format option in the format group at the right-hand side of the ribbon. Select the column width option and then alter it to a width of just five characters. Leave enough lines to allow for roughly the amount of entries you expect to make in the current month, and then place the cursor in the Net invoice total column, hold down the shift key and press the right direction arrow twice to highlight the three adjacent cells in the columns for net invoice value, VAT and gross total.

11. Click on the arrow at the right of the answer box icon, which is situated about a quarter of the way across the ribbon bar. This will reveal a menu of answer box styles. Select the one that has a single top line and a double bottom line and press the return key.

12. Move the cursor one place to the right. Hold down the shift key and click the right direction arrow as many times as necessary to highlight the line of cells in all of the remaining columns.

13. Click on the answer box icon again, and this time select the one that has a single top line only and no bottom line. Press return.

14. Click the cursor into the answer box in column F.

15. Click on the sigma icon and highlight all the cells above the answer box, up to the heading. Press return.

16. Hold down the shift key and scroll diagonally to the answer box at the far right for all columns used.

17. Click on the sigma icon, which is found near the right of the ribbon bar. This will place a summation formula into each of the answer boxes.

18. Click the cursor into cell A1. Hold down the shift key and scroll to the cell that contains the last heading you typed on line 4.

19. Click on the format cells button.

20. Click on format cells option at the bottom of the drop-down menu.

21. Click on protection tab. Ensure the locked option is un-ticked.

22. Return to the worksheet and un-highlight cells.

23. Click on the review tab at the top of your screen.

24. Select the protect worksheet option. You will be asked for a password, which you must create for yourself. Click return, and it will ask you to repeat your

password. Enter it again and click return. Your headings will now be protected against accidental erasure or modification.

You are now ready to enter data.

Entering the data from the invoices, step by step

Enter the month in cell A5. Enter the day of the month in cell B5. You only need to enter the month once and the day of the month only when it changes from that of the previous entry.

1.   Enter the supplier's name, e.g. Morgan and Baldwyn. (If the name extends beyond the column boundary highlight the column by clicking into the 'C' at the top. Click into the format option in the cells group at the right of the ribbon and select the autofit column width option. This will widen the column appropriately. You will have to unprotect the worksheet first, however, and protect it again once you have followed the above procedure.)

2.   Enter your own purchase invoice number in the appropriate column, e.g. 4/1. You will need to change the format by clicking into the format option in the cells group at the right of the ribbon and selecting format cells at the bottom of the drop down menu. Select number and then text

3.   Enter net invoice total in the appropriate column, e.g. £80.00 (net means after deduction of any trade discounts and not including VAT).

4.   Enter the VAT in the appropriate column, e.g. £16.00

5.   Enter the gross invoice total into column H. You could insert a formula here to add the net and VAT totals, e.g. '=Sum(F5:G5)'.

6.   Copy this formula all the way down. If you are feeling confident you could speed this up by highlighting the cells and using the sigma key.

7.   If analysis columns are in use, also enter the net amount of each invoice under the correct heading, e.g. 'Stationery', 'Office equipment', etc.

       The columns will add themselves as you go, ready for you to post (transfer) the totals to the ledger at the end of the month.

Returning unwanted goods

When a firm buys goods or services on credit, it records the details in the daybook, as we saw on the previous pages. Sometimes, however, it has to return what it has bought to the supplier. For example, the goods may be faulty or have arrived damaged. In this case, the firm obtains a credit note from the supplier and the value of the credit note is then entered up in the purchase returns daybook.

All the points that apply to the purchase daybook also apply to the returns daybook. Even the ruling is identical, though of course the details may be different. So once you have become familiar with the ruling of a typical purchase daybook, you will also have a picture of the returns daybook in your mind.

Example

Let's suppose we purchased a quantity of desk diaries from S. Jones (Wholesale Stationery Supplies Ltd) and unfortunately found that some of them were faulty. We told them about the problem and they agreed that we could return them. S. Jones then issued us with a credit note for the value of the faulty goods, plus VAT, a total of £235.00. The credit note is dated 10 February. We now enter the details of this credit note in our purchase returns daybook as follows but first we have some sheet configuring to do.

Setting up your spreadsheet workbook for purchase returns

1. Open the purchases daybook spreadsheet.
2. Hold down the control key and press the A key on your keyboard. This will highlight everything on the page.
3. Right-click and select copy.
4. Click on the next new worksheet tab at the bottom of the screen. Type 'Purchase Returns' and this title will be placed on the tab for easy identification.
5. Right-click and select paste. This will copy all the formatting, headings and formulae of the purchase daybook on to this page. Most of them are the same. We will now change those that are not.
6. Click on cell C1.
7. Now move to the data bar on the header and click on a point immediately between the words 'Purchase' and 'Daybook'. Type in the word 'Returns'.
8. Click into cell D3 and overtype with the abbreviation 'CNN' (which stands for Credit Note Number).
9. Click the cursor into cell A1. Hold down the shift key and scroll to the cell that contains the last heading you typed on line 4.
10. Click on the format cells button.
11. Click on format cells option at bottom of drop-down menu.

12.   Click on protection tab. Ensure the locked option is un-ticked.
13.   Return to worksheet and un-highlight cells.
14.   Click on the review tab at the top of your screen.
15.   Select the protect worksheet option. You will be asked for a password, which you must create for yourself. Click return and it will ask you to repeat your password. Enter it again and click return. Your headings will now be protected against accidental erasure or modification.

   You are now ready to enter your data for the month.

Step by step

1.   On the far left we enter the date, followed by the name of the supplier.
2.   Enter the supplier's name, e.g. S. Jones Wholesale Stationery Supplies Ltd. Widen the column as necessary following instructions given in Chapter 9: 'Entering the data from the invoices, step by step'.
3.   Enter your own credit note number in the appropriate column, e.g. 4/1.
4.   Enter net credit note total in the appropriate column, e.g. £195.83 (reminder: net means after deduction of any trade discounts and not including VAT; we will come to these later).
5.   Enter the VAT in the appropriate column, e.g. £39.16.
6.   If analysis columns are in use, also enter the net amount of each credit note under the correct heading, e.g. 'stationery'.

   The columns will add themselves as you go, ready for you to post (transfer) the totals to the ledger at the end of the month.

A. Frazer records his sales

Let us suppose that A. Frazer is a business stationery supplier. He makes the following sales on monthly credit account during the month of June 2013:

2013
June	1	Edward's Garage	150 white A4 envelopes	= £4.00
			150 small manila envelopes	= £4.00
	6	A. K. Insurance		
		Services	150 large envelopes	= £10.00
	8	J.B.C. Roofing	4 calculators @ £12.50 ea.	
	30	Evans	20 notepads	= £21.60

Let's suppose that, like many firms, A. Frazer has his sales invoices pre-printed with numbers in a chronological sequence and that the above sales were billed on invoice numbers 961/2/3 and 4. He would enter the invoice dates followed by the name of the customers in the first two columns of his sales daybook.

In the next column he would enter the net invoice values (i.e. excluding VAT) and in the next the amounts of VAT charged on each invoice.

Further to the right, he would then 'analyse' the net amounts into handy reference columns. (This analysis will be useful to him later, as he will be able to tell quickly what value of his sales were for stationery, what for calculators and what for any other categories for which he may decide to have analysis columns.)

Date		Supplier	Inv. no.	Net inv. value	VAT 20%	Statnry	Calcs.
2013							
Jun	1	Edward's Garage	961	8.00	1.60	8.00	
	6	A.K. Ins. Services	2	10.00	2.00	10.00	
	8	J.B.C. Roofing	3	50.00	10.00		50.00
	30	F. Evans	4	21.60	4.32	21.60	
				89.60	17.92	39.60	50.00

Figure 15 Extract from A. Frazer's sales daybook

Setting up your spreadsheet workbook for sales

1. Open the Purchases Daybook spreadsheet.
2. Hold down the control key and press the A key on your keyboard. This will highlight everything on the page.
3. Right-click and select copy.
4. Click on the next new worksheet tab at the bottom of the screen.
5. Type 'Sales Daybook' and this title will be placed on the tag for easy identification.

6.   Right-click and select paste. This will copy all the formatting, headings and formulae of the purchase daybook on to this page. Most of them are the same. We will now change those that are not.

7.   Click on cell C1.

8.   Now move to the data bar on the header and change the word from 'Purchase' to 'Sales'.

9.   Click into cell D3 and overtype with the abbreviation 'Inv.' (which stands for Invoice).

10. Click the cursor into cell A1. Hold down the shift key and scroll to the cell that contains the last heading you typed on line 4.

11. Click on the format cells button.

12. Click on the format cells option at the bottom of the drop-down menu.

13. Click on protection tab. Ensure the locked option is un-ticked.

14. Return to the worksheet and un-highlight cells.

15. Click on the review tab at the top of your screen.

16. Select the protect worksheet option. You will be asked for a password, which you must create for yourself. Click return and it will ask you to repeat your password. Enter it again and click return. Your headings will now be protected against accidental erasure or modification.

You are now ready to enter your data for the months from the credit notes.

Step by step

1.   On the far left we enter the date, followed by the name of the supplier.

2.   Enter the customer's name, e.g. Morgan and Baldwyn.

3.   Enter the sales invoice number in the appropriate column, e.g. 4/1.

4.   Enter net sales invoice value in the appropriate column, e.g. £80.00 (reminder: net means after deduction of any trade discounts and not including VAT).

5.   Enter the VAT in the appropriate column, e.g. £16.00.

6.   If analysis columns are in use, also enter the net amount of each sales invoice under the correct heading, e.g. 'stationery'.

The columns will add themselves as you go, ready for you to post (transfer) the totals to the ledger at the end of the month.

Invoice

D. Davidson (Builder)   Delivered to:
1 Main Road   Broad Street
Anytown   Anytown
Lancs   Lancs

P356 20/12/2013   £ p
20 bags of cement at £10.00 per bag   200.00
15 5 litre tins of white emulsion @ £1.00 per tin   15.00
32 bags of sand @ £5.00 per bag   160.00
40 metres of 100mm x 50mm pinewood @ £1.00 per metre   40.00
                                                                 415.00
VAT @ 20%   83.00
                                                                 498.00
E&OE

Figure 16 Example of an invoice

Credit Note

D. Davidson (Builder)   Delivered to:
1 Main Road   Broad Street
Anytown   Anytown
Lancs   Lancs
CN 3756 20/01/2013

                                                                    £ p
5 x 10 Litre cans of white gloss paint @ £5.00 each, returned as faulty   50.00
VAT 20%   10.00
E&OE   60.00

Figure 17 Example of a credit note
Note: E&OE stands for errors and omissions excepted.

When a customer asks for a credit

When a firm sells goods or services on credit, it records the details in the sales daybook as we saw on the previous pages. Sometimes, however, the customer has to return what they have bought. For example, the goods may be faulty or have arrived damaged. In this case, the firm sends a credit note to the customer, and the value of the credit note is then entered up in the sales returns daybook.

All the points that apply to the sales daybook also apply to the sales returns daybook; even the ruling is identical, though of course the transaction details may be different. So once you have become familiar with the ruling of a typical daybook, you will also have a picture of the sales returns daybook in your mind.

Example

Look at the example given in Figure 17. We sold 50 litres of white gloss paint to D. Davidson (Builders) who unfortunately found it to be faulty. They returned the goods to us and we issued them with a credit note for the value plus VAT, a total of £58.75. The credit note is dated 8 March 2013. We now enter the details of this credit note in our sales returns daybook.

Setting up your spreadsheet workbook for sales returns

1. Open the sales daybook spreadsheet.
2. Hold down the control key and press the A key on your keyboard. This will highlight everything on the page.
3. Right-click and select copy.
4. Click on the next new worksheet tab at the bottom of the screen.
5. Type 'Sales Returns Daybook' and this title will be placed on the tab for easy identification.
6. Right-click and select paste. This will copy all the formatting, headings and formulae of the sales daybook on to this page. Most of them are the same. We will now change those that are not.
7. Click on cell C1.
8. Now move to the data bar on the header and click on a point immediately between the words 'Sales' and 'Daybook'. Type in the word 'Returns'.
9. Click into cell D3 and overtype with the abbreviation 'CNN' (which stands for Credit Note Number).
10. Click the cursor into cell A1. Hold down the shift key and scroll to the cell that contains the last heading you typed on line 4.
11. Click on the format cells button.
12. Click on the format cells option at bottom of the drop-down menu.
13. Click on the protection tab. Ensure the locked option is un-ticked.
14. Return to the worksheet and un-highlight cells.

15. Click on the review tab at the top of your screen.
16. Select the protect worksheet option. You will be asked for a password, which you must create for yourself. Click return and it will ask you to repeat your password. Enter it again and click return. Your headings will now be protected against accidental erasure or modification.

You are now ready to enter your data for the months from the credit notes.

Step by step

1. On the far left we enter the date.
2. Enter the customer's name, e.g. D. Davidson (Builders).
3. Enter the credit note number in the appropriate column, e.g. 4/1.
4. Enter net credit note value in the appropriate column, e.g. £48.99 (reminder: net means after deduction of any trade discounts and not including VAT).
5. Enter the VAT in the appropriate column, e.g. £9.79.
6. If analysis columns are in use, also enter the net amount of each credit note under the correct heading, e.g. 'stationery'.

The columns will add themselves as you go, ready for you to post (transfer) the totals to the ledger at the end of the month.

What is the cash book?

The cash book is where we record the firm's cash and cheque transactions. In it we record all the payments coming in and all the payments going out. Like the four daybooks, it is a book of prime entry, the first place we record a transaction. However, unlike the daybooks, it is also a book of account, i.e. part of the ledger. The cash book and petty cash book are the only ones with this dual status.

The cashier is responsible for writing cheques to pay bills, banking money received and drawing funds for petty cash. Most people are familiar with the process of writing cheques, banking funds and drawing cash from banks so no treatment of this will be given here. Similarly most people understand what payments by standing order and direct debit mean.

What they may not be familiar with, however, is receiving and making payments by electronic means, e.g. *BACS* and *CHAPS* transfers. Both are electronic forms of funds transfer for which a form has to be completed at the bank branch or online. BACS takes around three to four working days to reach the recipient, but CHAPS payments are usually received the same day.

The advantages of making payments by BACS or CHAPS include:

- There is no need to write individual cheques.
- The payments are more secure, as they are not physically handled in any form.

The advantages of receiving payments in this way include:

- The funds are available as soon as the instruction is received by the recipient's bank branch, as no clearance time is needed.
- They are less time-consuming as the need to visit the bank to pay in a cheque is eliminated.
- No bank paying-in slip has to be filled in.
- The payments are more secure as the funds are not physically handled.

Recording cash and bank transactions

The cash book is where we first record the details of cash and banking. This includes all cash or cheques received from such customers or, indeed, from anyone else and all cash or cheques paid out to suppliers or to anyone else (disbursements). Banks debit firms directly for their services – they don't send out invoices for payment of interest and bank charges. The firm must record details of these amounts in the cash book as soon as it knows about them from the bank statement.

Source documents

To write up the cash book we need:

- Cheque book stubs (counterfoils) and paying-in book stubs (counterfoils) for all transactions that involve the bank account.
- Details of payments and receipts through internet banking.

- Any bank advice slips, bank statements or other information received from the bank from time to time. This might include, for example, a letter advising that a customer's cheque has been returned unpaid by their bank owing to lack of funds, or information on standing orders, direct debits or bank charges and so on: anything that tells us about any payments going out from, or receipts coming into, the firm's account.
- Cash purchases invoices, receipts for cash paid out and copies of receipts given for cash paid in. Any payment advice slips that arrived with cheques or cash received; these will show, for example, whether early settlement discount has been claimed.

Entering debits and credits

All the cash and cheques we receive are entered on the left-hand side of the cash book (debits). All the cheques we write and cash we pay are entered on the right-hand side (credits).

14 Setting up your spreadsheet for recording money paid in

A mirror-image style cash book has ten columns – identical sets of five, with one set for money out and the other set for money in. They differ only insofar as the set on the left has a label 'Dr.' at the top left (standing for debit) and the set on the right has the label 'Cr.' (standing for credit) at the top right.

Each set of five columns is headed Date, Particulars, Fo., Cash and Bank, in that order.

An alternative style, also popular, has the Date, Particulars and Fo. columns once and only the Cash and Bank columns are duplicated. In this style the labels Dr. and Cr. are placed at the top of the money columns, between the Cash and the Bank columns. You therefore have only seven columns with this style: the Date, Particulars and the Fo. columns appearing once only, and Cash and Bank appearing twice. In this book we will use the former, mirror-image style (see Figure 8).

Setting up the automatic ledger balancing mechanism

1.   Open a new worksheet and re-name it 'Cash Book'.
2.   Merge and centre cells A3 and B3 as before and cells J3 and K3.
3.   Format the resulting cells to a width of 5.
4.   Format columns D and N to a width of 4.
5.   Now set up headings in row 3 as follows:

   - A/B 3 Date
   - C3 Particulars
   - D3 Fo
   - E3 Discount
   - F3 Cash
   - G3 Bank

6.   Next, you need to set up your balances. There are three kinds of balances involved here. They used to be called *bilancio*, *saldo* and *resto* in times of antiquity, for anyone who is interested in gems of wisdom, but for most people it is sufficient to remember that these three balances are of different kinds. Saldo is simply the totals of the columns. You might jump to the conclusion that the two sides, income and outgoing, will not necessarily balance, but they will do when we include the bilancio. You'll see. The bilancio is the difference between one column total and the other and this is placed on the last line of the smaller value column. The column totals will then be equal.

7.   However, we have put a fictitious value in the column to make it do so and the data is, as a result, inaccurate by that amount. The way we rectify this is to enter the same value on the other side, on the line immediately below the column total. That is the resto. In the modern day we call it the balance brought down and the bilancio is called the balance carried down.

8. We can enter some code to make the page calculate these values automatically. This is how we do it.

9. Click into G8, click on the sigma icon then highlight cells F4–F6.

10. Copy and paste this formula into cell I7. The software will alter the cell references in the form appropriately.

11. Click into F7 and insert the following formula: =if(I7.G7,I7-G7,"")

12. Copy and paste this formula into H7 and amend as follows:

13. Change the K to G in both parts of the formula.

14. Click into F9 and insert the following formula: =H7.

15. Click into H9 and insert the following formula: =F7.

16. Click into cell E8 and insert a top border, and click into F8, hold down control and click into H8 to highlight the two cells.

17. Now you can test it out with some values. Enter your transactions for the month, including the date, the payee and the amount of each bank lodgement on the debit side, and likewise for each cheque or other form of payment on the credit side. The change in the bank balance should appear as you enter each one, and when you have entered them all the balance should equal the balance as per your bank statement.

18. Figure 9 shows what your page will look like when the formulae are revealed.

19. Now click into cell A3, hold down the shift key and click into I9.

20. Right-click, select copy, left-click into J3, right-click and select paste.

    This will produce a mirror image for the credit side.

15 The cash book: recording money paid in, step by step

1. Turn to your first receipt counterfoil for the period you are handling (day, week, month). Record in the first column of the cash book, on the far left, the date of the transaction. To help keep the page neat and uncluttered, just enter the year once at the top of all the entries for that year. Do the same for the start of each new month.
2. Type the payer's name in the second column.
3. The third column is for the folio reference you will enter later. Leave it blank at this stage.
4. In the fourth column (not used in Figures 8 and 9) enter the amount of any early settlement discount.
5. In the fifth column (cash) enter the amount of cash received (£81.00 in the example).
6. Now turn to your paying-in book counterfoils and do exactly the same – except for one small difference: enter the amounts in the sixth (bank) column this time. Enter in the first (date) column the date of the bank lodgement as shown on the front of the counterfoil. The date written in ink by the payer-in (the cashier) might be different from the bank branch stamp on the counterfoil; the paying-in book might have been written up the day before the lodgement and lodged in a nightsafe at the bank after the close of business, to be paid in properly the next day. Where there is a difference, you should use the date shown on the bank's stamp.
7. Turn over the counterfoil for the period and look on its reverse side. Each counterfoil represents a payment into the bank of a sum of money in cash and/or cheques; it should bear the names of people from whom the cheques have been received (the drawers). Enter in the second column of the cash book (name column) the first name from this list.
8. Again, the third column is for the folio reference, which you will enter later. Leave it blank for now.
9. Enter in the fourth column (discounts) the details of any discount allowed.
10. Enter in the sixth column the actual amount of the cheque.
11. Repeat steps 6 to 10 for all the cheques in the list.
12. Now enter the cash paid into the bank, if any.
13. Type the word 'cash' in the second column (since it is the cashier who is paying it in).
14. Enter the amount in the sixth column (bank column).

     The debit and credit columns for both cash and bank will total and balance themselves automatically, and the balance brought down will be shown, because of the code that has been embedded in them.

16 The cash book: recording money paid out, step by step

Posting to the credit page

We need to do our first piece of double entry bookkeeping. Since the bank has been debited with the money the cashier paid in, the cashier must be credited with the same amount. Otherwise, the cashier will appear to remain indebted for a sum they no longer have.

Step by step

1. Enter the date of the paying-in slip in the date column of the right hand (credit page) of the cash book.

2. In the second (name) column, enter the word 'bank', since it is the bank that is taking the money from the cashier.

3. In the fifth (cash) column, enter the amount of the payment. You have now given the cashier credit for that amount – and so you should! They no longer have it: they have given it to the bank.

4. Now let's do the other credit-side entries. Take the first of the receipt vouchers for cash paid out for the period (day, week, month). Enter the date (taken from the receipt voucher) in the appropriate column of the right-hand page (see step 1 on the previous chapter).

5. In the second column enter the name of the person to whom the cash was paid.

6. Discount details probably won't be relevant here; such discounts arise from early settlement of credit accounts, usually by cheque rather than by cash. If any such account was settled in cash, the cashier would know about it: they would have been the one to arrange payment. In such cases enter the details in the fourth (discount) column.

7. In the fifth column enter the amount of cash paid out.

8. Turn to the first cheque book counterfoil for the period. In the first column of the right-hand (credit) page, enter the cheque date.

9. In the second column enter the name of the payee (the person to whom the cheque is payable).

10. In the fourth column enter details of any discount received. You will find this on the copy of the payment advice slip outwards.

11. In the sixth (bank) column, enter the amount of the cheque.

    The debit and credit columns for both cash and bank will total and balance themselves automatically, and the balance brought down will be shown, because of the code that has been embedded in them.

17 Disagreeing with the bank

Cash book versus bank statement

Every cashier tries to keep the cash book as accurate and up to date as possible. Many receipts and payments may have to be entered up each day. Then, at regular intervals, the firm receives bank statements from the bank: weekly, monthly or quarterly. Unfortunately, the balance shown on the cash book hardly ever agrees with the one shown on the bank statement. There can be various reasons for this.

Noting unpresented cheques

When you get the bank statement and compare the balance with that shown in the cash book, you will see that some cheques you drew have not yet been presented to the bank for payment: they simply don't appear on the bank statement at all, as yet. The cashier enters cheque transactions within a day or two of handling the cheques; but it could be days or even weeks before the payee presents them to your bank for payment.

Noting bank lodgements

Payments into the bank will have been recorded in the cash book, but if they haven't yet been recorded by the bank they won't appear on the bank statement. This could happen, for example, if a bank statement was sent out between the time the cashier lodged the bankings in the nightsafe and the time they actually paid them in over the counter.

Automatic payments

Payments by direct debit or standing order may have been omitted by the cashier, but they will still appear on the bank statement.

Bank charges and interest

A cashier may know nothing about these until the bank statement, containing the details, arrives.

Returned cheques

A customer's cheque may have been returned unpaid – 'bounced' in popular jargon. The cash book will show the money having been received, but the bank won't have received funds for the cheque; so the statement will show a contra entry.

Errors

The cashier could simply have made an error. Bank errors can happen but they are rare.

18   The bank reconciliation

If a discrepancy arose from just one source it would be easy enough to deal with, but usually there are several discrepancies, some distorting the credit side and some distorting the debit side, and liable to cause confusion.

To remove this confusion and explain the discrepancies, the cashier draws up a bank reconciliation statement. The cashier, after all, is responsible for the firm's money, so if the bank statement disagrees with the cash book balance they must clearly show the reason why.

There are three ways of reconciling the two accounts:

1. Reconcile the cash book to the bank statement: start with the closing cash book and check through, step by step, towards the bank balance, explaining the discrepancies as you go.
2. Reconcile the bank statement to the cash book.
3. Correct all the errors and omissions on both the cashier's part and the bank's part, showing how we did it, until we end up with the same balance from both viewpoints (see Figure 18).

The third way is usually the best since it is easier to understand. We'll see how to do a bank reconciliation statement, step by step, on the following pages.

What you need:

*   The cash book worksheet
*   The bank statements for the period (week, month, quarter).

Remember, a page of figures can be bewildering to your reader, who may not understand bookkeeping as well as you or have the time or patience to make sense of muddled words and figures. Simplicity and clarity should be your goal. Head all your cash columns £ and p to avoid having to write these symbols against every single entry. Likewise, when writing dates record the month once only, followed by the individual days. Put a clear heading against the left of each line of your figures. You will probably need two cash columns, one for sub-totalling particular types of transactions. For example, if there are three unpresented cheques you would add their values in a left-hand column and place the sub-total in a main right-hand column.

BANK RECONCILIATION AS AT [date]

	£ : p	
Balance as per cash book	320.00	(in favour)
Add customer's account		
paid by telephone banking (M. Bandura)	40.00	
	360.00	(in favour)
Deduct dishonoured cheque (D. Davidson)	10.00	
	350. 00	(in favour)
Deduct bank charges	50.00	
Updated balance as per cash book	300.00	(in favour)
Balance as per bank statement	500.00	(in favour)
Deduct cheque drawn but not yet		
presented for payments: S. Jones	200.00	
Updated balance as per bank statement	300.00	(in favour)

Figure 18 Example of a bank reconciliation by updating both cash book and bank statement

Bank reconciliation, step by step

1. Compare the balances of the bank statement and the cash book as at the end of the accounting period you are checking. If they disagree then a bank reconciliation will be needed. Proceed as follows.
2. Can you see on the statement any standing orders (STOs), direct debits (DDRs) or bank charges? These items may not have been recorded in your cash book as yet. Also, are there any returned ('bounced') cheques? If there are, they will appear as consecutive entries or at least close together, identical but appearing on opposite sides (Dr and Cr) and will be annotated ₵, 'Contra Entry', or 'Returned Cheque'.
3. Create a new spreadsheet page by clicking on the new worksheet tab at the bottom of your screen.
4. Rename the tag 'Bank Reconciliation as at' plus the date of reconciliation.
5. Type in cell A4 'Bank Reconciliation'.
6. Type in cell A3: 'Balance as per cash book'.
7. Place the actual balance as per the cash book in cell B4.
8. In cell B4, state whether it is in favour or overdrawn.
9. It is important to use a term such as 'in favour' rather than 'in credit', since 'in credit' is ambiguous here. An 'in credit' bank balance means you are 'in the black', but an 'in credit' balance in the cash book means you are 'in the red'. The terms 'in favour' and 'overdrawn' overcome this ambiguity, since they mean the same from both the firm's and the bank's viewpoints.

10. List all the omissions on the cashier's part, in groups, e.g. listing STOs first, then DDRs, then bank charges, etc.

11. Do your additions and deductions as you go to show what difference it would have made to the bank statement if such errors or omissions had not occurred. Insert a bottom line after each new data entry. To insert a bottom line click on the arrow on the right-hand side of the answer box icon on the header bar as before and, this time, select a bottom line only. If you are going to add the previous two values then simply click on the first of them to highlight it, hold down the shift key and scroll to cover the second one and also the blank space below the line for the summation. Then click on the sigma icon on the top right-hand side of the ribbon bar to do the summation. If you are deducting one from the other, then you will have to enter the formula in the blank space for the difference as there is no shortcut icon for this function. The formula is: =SUM (the first cell reference, minus the second cell reference), e.g. '=SUM(D3-D4)'. If you arrive at a figure that is equal to the bank statement balance then the job of reconciliation is done. Type in the adjacent cell, 'Corrected balance as per cash book'. If this does not happen then proceed to reconcile the bank statement to the cash book as follows.

12. Check off each payment listed in the cash book worksheet against the bank statement. Mark each one with an x in column D of the cash book worksheet and with a pencil tick on the bank statement as you go. As you will see, items on the credit side of your cash book appear on the debit side of the bank statement and vice versa. This is because the same account is seen from two opposite viewpoints: the cash book from the firm's viewpoint and the bank statement from the bank's viewpoint.

13. Record next, in column A of your worksheet, the words 'Balance as per bank statement' ('in favour' or 'overdrawn', as appropriate) and place the actual figure next to it. Then list all the errors and omissions on the bank's part, in groups, e.g. listing unpresented cheques first, and then any unshown lodgements. Type your additions and deductions as you go, as before, to show what difference it would have made to the bank statement if such errors or omissions had not occurred.

14. When you have listed all the errors and omissions, if you have done it correctly, the two balances should now match. If so, type in column A, against your latest figure, 'Balance as per cash book' ('in favour' or 'overdrawn' as appropriate).

Updating the cash book

The items in the first part of the reconciliation statement, i.e. the one that starts with balance as per cash book, represent items that the cashier had not previously known about. Now that they are known, the cashier can update the cash book by making the necessary entries.

Take the worked example in Figure 18. The balance as per cash book shows £320 in favour, while the balance as per bank statement shows £500 in favour. The reconciliation statement explains the differences. We can update the cash book by making the entries listed in the second part of the reconciliation, as this shows the entries that belong in, but have not yet been made, in the cash book.

So much for updating the accounts in accordance with the first part of the reconciliation statement, but what about the second part, the one that starts with the balance as per bank statement? Don't worry about that part. It would only update the bank statement and that is merely a copy from an account that is not ours to update. It is the bank's. We don't include the bank statement balance at all in the accounts. Even in the balance sheet the cash figure comes from the balance as per the cash book. In any case, by the time the next statement arrives the figures missing from the current one will have been included.

The petty cash float

The petty cashier looks after a small float such as £50 or £100 in notes and coins. It is used to pay for miscellaneous small office expenses such as staff travel and hotel accommodation, window cleaning and small office items needed quickly. The petty cashier keeps account of all such transactions in the petty cash book.

Using the imprest system

From time to time, the cashier will reimburse the petty cashier for the amount they have spent on the firm's behalf; the float is replenished to the original amount. This is called an imprest system and the original amount of the float, e.g. £50, is called the imprest amount.

Without a petty cash book, cash expenditure on lots of very small items would mean making entries in the ledger for each item of expense, but by using the petty cash book, such items can be analysed into useful columns that can be totalled up immediately with just the final, monthly cash payments posted to the ledger.

Keeping the petty cash secure

The petty cashier is personally responsible for the petty cash, so they should:

- keep it locked away;
- limit the number of people who have access, preferably to one person;
- reconcile cash to records regularly (petty cash vouchers + receipts + cash = imprest value).

A helpful analysis

Even if the firm is small, and the cashier keeps the petty cash book themselves, it is still a very useful means of analysing and totalling office expenditure. Otherwise, all such expenditure would have to be entered in the cash book and later posted individually to the ledger.

Dual status of the petty cash book

The petty cash book, like the cash book, usually has a dual status: it is both a book of prime entry and part of the ledger. However, some firms treat it purely as a book of prime entry to record transactions involving notes and coins. They then write up a 'Petty cash account' in their general ledger. Here, however, we will treat it as part of the ledger. Unless told otherwise, you should do the same. Like the other books of prime entry, such as the daybooks, the petty cash book usually has a few helpful analysis columns but, since it is also part of the ledger, it needs to have both debit and credit columns.

What you need:

- the petty cash book;
- all the cash purchase invoices for the period.

Preparation: numbering and dating

Sort all your cash purchase invoices (receipts) into date order and number them. The numbers already printed on them won't do: they are the cash sales invoice numbers of the firms that issued them and no uniformity between them can be expected). You need to give them consecutive numbers from your own numbering system so that you can file them chronologically for each period. Many firms keep a list of such numbers for this purpose. Others give the cash purchase invoices a two-part number made up of the month number (e.g. 3 for March) and a number from a consecutive list for that month.

Value Added Tax (VAT)

The VAT may not be shown as a separate item on cash purchase invoices for small amounts. If not, the petty cashier will need to calculate the VAT content, if any, of each invoice total. Her Majesty's Revenue and Customs (HMRC) publishes details of current VAT applications and rates, but a little experience will save the cashier having to check this every time. Briefly, if the current VAT rate is 20 per cent, the VAT content of such an invoice is worked out like this:

Divide the VAT percentage rate by itself + 100 and then multiply the quotient by the VAT inclusive invoice figure.

If you don't have a calculator handy then as long as you learned your multiplication tables at school you can easily work it out in your head as follows. Take 20 per cent of the VAT inclusive figure and divide it by 1.20 (which represents 100 per cent + 20 per cent). Taking 20 per cent of a figure is easy; you just move the decimal place one place to the left to get 10 per cent and then double the figure. Dividing by 1.2 is also easy; you just divide by twelve and then move the decimal place one place to the right.

Setting up the petty cash book, step by step

1. Open the purchase daybook spreadsheet.
2. Right-click and choose the select all option to highlight everything on the page.
3. Right-click again and select the copy option.
4. Create a new worksheet by clicking on the appropriate icon at the bottom of the page as before.
5. Overtype a new title on the tab, naming it 'Petty Cash Book'.
6. Click into cell A1, then right-click and select paste.

7. This will copy all of your headings, columns and formatting from the purchase daybook on to this page. Some of them will not be necessary or relevant, and we will remove those that fall into the former category and change those that fall into the latter. Many of the columns, headings and formulae will, however, be just as appropriate to this page as they are to the page from which they were copied.

8. The first thing to do is to change the title of the sheet. So click into cell C3 and type the words 'Petty Cash Book'.

9. Insert two new columns on the far left-hand side of the page. Do this by clicking on any cell in the far left-hand column, holding down the shift key and clicking the right arrow to extend into the column adjacent to it on the right. The two columns will now be highlighted if that has been done correctly. Now click on the format tab, which will appear if the home tab has been selected. The format menu will then appear. Click on the insert option and it will insert two new columns where you have highlighted.

10. Insert two new rows after the title in a similar way. Click on any cell in the first row, after the title, hold down the shift key and extend the highlighting into the next row down by means of the down arrow key. If you have done this right, the two rows will now be highlighted. Again, go to the format menu and select insert row. Press the return key and two rows will be added between the title and the headings.

11. In cell B2 type 'Dr.' (without the quotes) and in cell G2 enter 'Cr.' (without the quotes). They stand for debit and credit. Centre both of these headings by highlighting each cell and clicking on the centre text icon on the ribbon bar.

12. Immediately under the Dr. heading, type 'Receipts' and in the adjacent cell type 'Fo.' This stands for folio reference.

13. Change the heading 'Supplier' to 'Details'.

14. Change the heading 'Inv. No.' to 'Rec. No.'

15. Change the heading 'Net invoice value' to 'Total'.

16. The rest of the headings may or may not be relevant, depending on whether you will have data to be placed in them. If they refer to items on which you would not expect to pay petty cash then remove the columns altogether by clicking on the column, then clicking on the format group on the right of the ribbon bar, selecting the delete option and pressing the return key.

17. Now remove all the data from the purchase daybook you copied.

18. You now need to set up the balancing mechanisms in the two ledger columns of the petty cash book. Copy the last three lines from the cash book page (Figure 8) and, leaving a line below the analysis column totals, click into cell A4 and paste the copied code. This should then provide the column totals

boxes together with the balance c/d and balance b/d values above and below, in the appropriate places.

19. Now enter your petty cash data from your petty cash vouchers and receipts, inserting lines as necessary and analysing the values into the various analysis columns as you go. The columns will add themselves up and the two main cash columns will balance themselves automatically after every value you enter.

20. When you have finished entering you can check you have not missed anything out by placing your curser on the cell containing the VAT column total and, holding down the shift key, scrolling to the right to highlight all the column totals. On the right-hand side of the foot of the page the sum of all of these column totals will appear. This should correspond with the total of the Cr. cash column, which you can ascertain by placing the cursor on the first value in the column and scrolling down to cover all the values in it (not including the total). If they agree then it would appear that you have not missed anything out.

21. The balance b/d showing should equal the cash in the petty cash tin. If it doesn't something has gone in or out without being documented by a receipt or a voucher. It will need to be investigated and resolved.

22. Figure 11 shows what the formulae will look like and Figure 10 shows what the page would look like when the entries have been made for the month.

Step by step

1. Enter in the third column the date that the fund or float was received.
2. Type in the fourth column ('Particulars') the word 'cash' or 'bank' as appropriate, depending on whether the float came from the cashier by cash or from the bank by cheque.
3. Type the imprest amount in the first column (debit cash). Unless the system is being started from scratch, this stage will have been completed previously. The procedure for all other entries will start from step 4 below.
4. Record from each cash invoice the date, purchase invoice number, purpose of expenditure, gross and net invoice total and VAT, as shown in Figure 10. Enter the net total directly into a suitable analysis column.

Entering the folio references

Enter folio references for the debit side in the folio column, e.g. CB7 (cash book item 7). Enter those relating to the credit side at the foot of their respective column totals: it is only the *totals* that will be posted to the ledger, e.g. travelling expenses, folio reference NL8 (Nominal Ledger account number 8) in Figure 10.

A general purpose record

A book of prime entry, the journal is simply a place for making the first record of any transaction for which no other prime entry book is suitable. It has debit and credit columns, but they are simpler than those of the cash book and petty cash book. The journal itself is not part of the accounts, merely one of the sources from which the accounts are written up later on.

Examples of journal entries

Here are some examples of transactions you would need the journal to record:

- opening figures of a new business (e.g. list of assets);
- bad debts;
- depreciation (e.g. of vehicles or equipment);
- purchase and sales of fixed assets (e.g. vehicles or plant);
- correction of errors;
- goods taken for private use (as against for sale);
- ledger transfer needed if a book debt were sold.

Using miscellaneous source documents

There are no routine source documents for this job, as there are, for example, for the purchase daybook (purchase invoices) or for the cash book (cheque counterfoils, etc). The journal is a miscellany and its sources will be miscellaneous. They may be documented by nothing more than a rough note, if indeed they are documented at all. For example, the sales manager may pass a memo to the journal clerk saying that a customer has gone into liquidation, so that its debt to the firm will have to be written off. Similarly a roughly pencilled note from the accountant, saying what depreciation should apply to an asset, may be your only source document for an entry.

Information needed for an entry

When entering a transaction into the journal, you need to record these aspects of it:

- date;
- accounts affected;
- folio references;
- amounts (debit and credit);
- reason.

Type a brief explanation against each entry. Separate each new entry from the one above by inserting a horizontal line right across the page (see Figure 14).

Sometimes you have to make combination double entries, i.e. where there is more than one debit entry per credit entry or vice versa. This is appropriate when journalizing opening figures, which include various assets and liabilities, together with the capital figure to which they relate. A group of entries is recorded in Figure 14 with the prefix 'Sundries', which all relate to trading in an old motor van for a new one.

Below, we will see how to write up the journal, step by step.

1.   The columns required for the journal spreadsheet are the same as those of the cash book. The easiest way to prepare this page is, therefore, to copy the cash book worksheet. Open the cash book page worksheet by clicking on the appropriate tag at the bottom of the screen.
2.   Press Ctrl + A and then Ctrl + C. Click on a new worksheet tag at the bottom of the screen, rename it 'Journal', then click into cell A1 and press Ctrl + V.
3.   Change the title of the page from 'Cash book' to 'Journal'.
4.   Only one debit and one credit cash column is needed in the journal, so if there are two of each in the page you have copied delete one of each. Delete the rows immediately above and below the answer boxes. This will remove the code that you do not need. You do not need codes to balance these columns because all entries in the journal will contain a combination of values that are self-balancing.

Writing up the journal by spreadsheet, step by step

1.   Enter the year in the first place in the far left-hand column under the date heading. This only needs to be entered once, until the year changes.
2.   Underneath this, in the particulars column, enter the word 'Sundries'. This signifies that a combination of entries will follow.
3.   Underneath this, in column A, enter the first three letters of the day of the month and, in the second column, enter the first three letters of the day of the month. The month only needs to be entered once for each month; the day needs to be entered for every combined entry, but not for every component thereof.
4.   Under the word 'Sundries' list the name of each ledger account affected by the transaction being recorded.
5.   In the folio reference column, against each of the items in the particulars column, enter the ledger account reference (e.g. NL1, BL6, etc.). Type the values relating to each component of the transaction in the fifth or sixth columns, depending on whether they are debit or credit values. The total of debit components will equal the number of credit components if the compound transaction has been written up correctly.
6.   Insert a line right across the page using the line option in the insert group on the ribbon to separate this compound transaction from the next one.

Filing source documents

When the daybooks have been written up, the source documents should be filed. Bank statements are filed chronologically, purchase invoices alphabetically or numerically. If the latter, there is an important caveat. The filing must be on the basis of a number you allocate, rather than the supplier's invoice number. Sales invoices are numbered by one of the following methods:

- they are pre-printed with consecutive numbers;
- the invoice clerk obtains consecutive numbers from a logbook;
- they are given numbers consisting of the year, month and consecutive number of issue in that month, in the form of yy/mm/consecutive number, as and when they are produced.

21 The ledger

The firm's official record

The ledger is the 'official' record of a firm's accounts. We sometimes speak of the general ledger, the bought ledger, the sales ledger and the cash book separately – as if they are separate 'ledgers'. But to an accountant the ledger is a single unit, even if it is made up of physically separate books. The ledger is really a 'system' rather than a book. Whatever form it takes – books or computer disks, etc. – 'the ledger' means the master record of all the firm's financial affairs.

Divisions of the ledger

We have already discovered two parts of the ledger – the cash book and the petty cash book – which also happen to be books of prime entry. The only difference in the ruling between that and the other divisions we will now deal with is that the latter are simpler. The cash book has three cash columns on each side; the other divisions of the ledger have only one. (However, where ledger posting is done on a computer the format involves three columns: a debit and credit column and a running balance column. This is because the running balance can easily be calculated electronically – it doesn't call on the time and effort of the bookkeeper. In manual systems, working out such running balances is considered a waste of time.)

The other ledger divisions are:

- the general ledger (often called the nominal ledger);
- the personal ledger, subdivided into bought ledger (or purchase ledger) and sales ledger (or debtors ledger);
- the private ledger, in which capital items are posted, for example the proprietor's drawings. It is sometimes kept away from staff because the proprietor considers such information confidential.

The nominal and personal ledger

In the nominal ledger the impersonal aspects of transactions are posted, for example purchases, sales figures, wages, stationery and asset purchases. In the personal ledger the personal side of each transaction is posted, i.e. the credit to suppliers' accounts when the firm has purchased something and the debit to customers' accounts when the firm has sold something.

Different accounts within the ledger

Each part of the ledger contains a number of different accounts – one for each expense item, revenue asset or liability, as they will appear in the final accounts. For example, there will be an account for purchases, an account for sales, an account for wages and a separate account for each asset such as Motor car 1 account, Motor car 2 account, Printing machine account and so on.

A variety of forms

Though the ruling of each type of book is reasonably standard, both the ledger and books of prime entry are found in a variety of forms. Indeed, they don't have to be 'books' at all. They can be sheets of analysis paper in a loose-leaf binder, or written into a computer program so that the rulings appear on a VDU (visual display unit) screen. Entries are then made via the keyboard rather than with pen and paper. It is this kind of media we are concerned with here.

Post only from books of prime entry

Nothing should ever be posted into the ledger except from the books of prime entry.

Never, for example, post information into the ledger directly from such things as invoices, bank statements, cheque counterfoils, petty cash receipt slips and so on. These are source documents for the books of prime entry.

Recording each transaction twice

We have already seen how each transaction in double entry bookkeeping has two aspects: a debit and a credit. So each transaction has to be recorded in two separate places, on the debit side and on the credit side. It follows that at any moment in time the total number of debit entries must exactly equal the total of credit entries (unless a mistake has been made). In a small office, one ledger clerk will probably handle all the divisions (except perhaps the cash book). In a large firm there may be a separate bought ledger clerk, sales ledger clerk and so on.

Preparing your spreadsheet as a ledger page

The ledger, in the style that will be dealt with here, has two more or less identical sides. The only difference is that the left-hand side is headed with the label 'Dr.' while the right-hand side is headed with the label 'Cr.'. It is very similar to the cash book format so the easiest way to set it up is to copy and paste a cash book page and then amend it as necessary.

1. Click on the cash book tag at the bottom of the screen.
2. Press Ctrl + A and then Ctrl + C to copy the page.
3. Open a new worksheet by clicking on the new worksheet icon at the bottom of the page.
4. Rename it with the name of the first supplier in your list or an account number for that supplier.
5. Click into cell A1 and press Ctrl + V to paste the cash book format on to the page.
5. Highlight columns L and M and columns E and F, by making the following key steps: Click into column E, press the shift key and click into column F.

Release the shift key. Hold down the control key and click into column L. Release the control key. Hold down the shift key and click into column M. Release the shift key and click on to the delete tab, in the cells group, on the ribbon. This will delete the two columns that you do not need.

6.   Type the supplier's name and the account number in cell A1, preceded by the letters BL, in bold capitals, in the middle of the top line of the page.

7.   Repeat the process for every one of your suppliers so that you have a worksheet for each one.

You are now ready to make postings from your daybooks to the ledger.

Posting to the ledger from the purchase daybook worksheet

Your first job is to post each purchase invoice (gross) value to the credit of the supplier concerned, in their personal ledger account. The personal ledger should have an index of supplier's names, telling you on what page in the ledger you will find their account. If no account exists, you will need to create one and remember to list it in the index. For information on how to create an index for the accounts go to Chapter 65.

1. Click open the purchase daybook worksheet and press Ctrl + A to copy it.
2. Click on the file tab and then on the 'New' option to make a temporary copy.
3. Click into cell A1 and press Ctrl + V. Now click on the view tab on the ribbon and select the 'View side by side' option. This will enable you to see the purchase daybook that you are posting from and the ledger that you are posting to at the same time.
4. Click open the ledger account to which the first daybook entry is to be posted.
5. In the first (date) column, type the date of entry.
6. Type the name of the account to which the other side of the transaction will be posted, in column 2 ('Particulars').
7. In the fourth (cash) column record the gross value, in other words including VAT, of the transaction.
8. Now make the dual aspect of these postings: click open the relevant nominal ledger accounts in turn and post the column totals for the net amount (i.e. net goods value) and VAT. The procedure is the same as for posting the personal side of the transaction, following steps 1 to 4.

Posting to the ledger from the purchase returns daybook

This is the reverse of posting from the purchase daybook. This time you debit personal accounts in the bought ledger and credit the VAT account and a purchase returns account in the nominal ledger.

Posting from the sales daybook

This is just like posting from the purchase daybook, except that you debit personal accounts in the sales ledger and credit the VAT account and a sales account in the nominal ledger.

Posting from the sales returns daybook

This is the reverse of posting from the sales daybook: you credit personal accounts in the sales ledger and debit the VAT account and a sales account in the nominal ledger.

23   Posting to the ledger from the cash book

The cash book entries are, by their very nature, one side of the double entry. All you have to do now is to make the other side of the entry.

Every time you post in the cash book, make an opposite posting to the relevant personal account in the bought or sales ledger as appropriate. Again, you can, if you wish, make a temporary copy of the cash book and view it side by side with each account to which you are posting the other side of the transaction. The narration against each of these postings will be 'cash' (if the payment was in the cash column of the cash book) or 'bank' (if it was in the bank column).

Now you have to post any discounts from the discounts column. Remember, although the cash book is part of the ledger, this column does not have such status; it is a single entry element sitting inside a ledger division, while not exactly being part of it. So the postings from the discounts column must be twofold, just as for any other prime entry source.

Post the discounts to the correct personal accounts in the same manner, making sure they are posted to the opposite sides to the ones on which they appear in the cash book.

Post the column totals to the other side of the 'Discount allowed' or 'Discount received' accounts in the nominal ledger, as applicable, to complete your dual posting. Use the name of the account to which the dual posting has gone for this purpose in all ledger posting.

Posting from the petty cash book

The petty cash book may, or may not, be treated as part of the double entry system. If it is, as with the cash book, its entries will themselves already contain one side of the ledger posting; you have only to make the other. However, this one aspect of the dual entry is itself split into various postings to nominal ledger accounts and this is why analysis columns have been used.

Their individual totals, together with the VAT column total, provide the figures to be posted to the various accounts denoted by their column headings. The net invoice total column is not posted anywhere.

When posting is done by spreadsheets there is no monthly balancing to do. It is done automatically when the entries are made.

Completing the folio columns

We have now posted all our entries to the ledger. The next stage before extracting the trial balance is to complete the folio columns against each posting in the ledger. These columns show the ledger 'address' (ledger division and page number) where the counterpart posting has been made. Let's take as an example the folio column beside a posting in the sales account of the nominal ledger; we might perhaps type 'SL8' for the address of a personal account in the sales ledger, i.e. it is on sales ledger page 8. The name of the account in which the counterpart posting has been made is entered in the particulars column of each ledger account, so you could say that this extra cross-referencing is unnecessary. But if the ledger divisions are large, a note of the exact page number could save time. Also filling in the folio columns will help the detection of errors. If the trial balance fails, errors of omission can be spotted by the absence of a folio column posting because it will mean that no counterpart posting has been made.

Important points to understand

Of all the things students find difficult to grasp in bookkeeping, two in particular stand out:

- The first is knowing whether to debit or credit an account. Which is the debit aspect and which the credit aspect of the transaction? What does it really mean to debit or credit an account?
- The second is knowing to which nominal ledger accounts to post the impersonal side of transactions, i.e. knowing how to classify expenses and revenues to the right account names in the first place.

Taking the first point first:

1.   The word debit comes from the Latin verb *debere*, meaning 'to owe'; debit is the Latin for he or she owes. In business, a person owes to the proprietor that which was loaned or given to him by the proprietor.
2.   The word credit comes from the Latin verb *credere*, meaning 'to trust' or 'to believe'. Our creditors believe in our integrity and trust us to pay them for goods and services they supply; so they are willing to deliver them without asking for immediate payment.

Perhaps this will help a little in personal ledger accounts; but what about the impersonal accounts of the nominal ledger? Whenever an account has a debit balance it means that it 'owes' the proprietor the value of it (and vice versa for credit balances), as if that account were a person.

25 Discounts

Trade discounts

A trade discount is one given by wholesalers to retailers, so that the retailers can make a profit on the price at which they sell goods to the public. Example:

Wholesale price of 5 litre tin of paint:	£4.00
Trade discount:	£2.00
Recommended retail price:	£6.00

In this example, the trade discount is 33⅓ per cent of the recommended retail price. However, trade discounts have no place as such in a firm's accounts. They are deducted before any entry is made in any of the books. As far as the wholesaler is concerned, his price to the retailer is simply £4.00, so £4.00 is the amount the wholesaler enters in his sales daybook and the amount the retailer enters in his purchase daybook.

Early settlement discounts

These are discounts offered to persuade customers to settle their debts to the firm early. Typically, a discount of 2 per cent might be offered for payment within fourteen days. But the details can vary. Example.

Building materials supplied:	£200.00
Less 2% discount for settlement within 7 days:	£4.00
	£196.00

Firms offer such discounts for two reasons: to speed up cash flow and to reduce the chance of debts becoming bad debts (the longer a debt remains outstanding, the more likely it is to become a bad debt).

If you write up your daybooks daily, you will not know whether or not an early settlement discount will be taken. You will know once the actual payment arrives. So you have to enter the figure without any deduction of discount into your sales daybook. When the debt is paid, if a discount has been properly claimed, the credit entry to that customer's account will be 2 per cent less than the account shows. You then need to enter the discount as a credit to their account and a debit to 'discount allowed account' in the nominal ledger. This will make up the shortfall. It has the same effect as cash on the customer's personal account, and so it should: the offer shown on the invoice is like a 'money off voucher' and we would expect to treat that the same as cash.

Discounts and VAT

An early settlement discount is based on the invoice total (including VAT). Whether it is claimed or not will not alter the net sale value or the VAT amount that will be entered in the books.

Prime entry of discounts in the cash book

You make your prime entry of discounts in the cash book worksheet. But the column you use is unlike the other cash columns: it is not a ledger column, just a prime entry 'lodging place'. Entries in the discount column of the cash book, unlike entries in its other (ledger) columns, are not part of a dual posting; the dual posting is made in the 'discount allowed account' in the nominal ledger group of worksheets, for the one part, and the personal customer account in the sales ledger group of worksheets, for the other (or 'discounts received account' and supplier account, as the case may be). The postings to the discount accounts in the nominal ledger group of worksheets are, of course, column totals rather than individual items.

Entering early settlement discounts

Both the cashier and the ledger clerk will be involved in entering early settlement discounts. When the cheques are first received from customers or sent out to suppliers, the cashier will check whether they have been properly claimed by reference to the time limit for early settlement discount and then enter the discounts in the cash book worksheet when they are entering the other payment details. For this step-by-step process please refer to Chapters 15 and 16.

At the end of each month the ledger clerk will make the dual postings to the ledger worksheets for each item in the discount columns of the cash book.

Step by step

The worksheets that will be affected are: cash book, sales ledger, purchase ledger and nominal ledger.

1. Click on the cash book worksheet.
2. Make a temporary copy of it. Call it 'Cash book temp' and save it.
3. Open both the main workbook and the temporary cash book page. This will place access to both the source document for the posting (the cash book) and the destination documents (the personal ledger accounts in the bought and sales ledger group, and the discount accounts in the nominal ledger group) on the screen at the same time.
4. One by one, post each item in the discounts received column to the debit of the named supplier's purchase ledger account worksheets.
5. Post the column total for the month to the credit of discounts received account in the nominal ledger group of worksheets.

6. One by one, post each item in the discounts allowed column to the credit of the named customer's sales ledger accounts worksheets.
7. Post the column totals to the debit of discounts allowed account in the nominal ledger group of worksheets.

Useful summaries

A control account is a sort of trial balance for just one ledger division. You write the account at the back of the ledger division concerned. The main idea of control accounts is to subdivide the task of the main trial balance. They also provide useful summaries of data for more effective financial management. For example, the boss might want an up-to-date figure for total debtors to help monitor credit control in the firm. Control accounts are sometimes called total accounts (for example, total creditors account).

Subdividing the work

In a small firm, where one bookkeeper posts all the ledgers, control accounts might be unnecessary. But the double entry system can be quickly expanded if necessary by using control accounts. Individual specialist bookkeepers, such as the bought ledger clerk or sales ledger clerk, could balance their own ledger division using a control total, i.e. a balancing item equal to the difference between all their own debit and credit balances. A head bookkeeper could then build up an overall trial balance just by taking the control account totals. In large firms today, control accounts are vital to the smooth running of the accounting system. Without them, reaching a trial balance would really be a difficult, time-consuming and messy business.

Control accounts are summaries of ledger balances in a division of the ledger. For example, purchase ledger control accounts contain the sum totals of all VAT inclusive purchases, payments to suppliers and discounts received.

The postings go on the same side as they do in the individual ledger accounts. However, to avoid duplication on one side of the dual posting either the control accounts or the individual ledger accounts must be left out of the double entry system. If the individual ledger accounts are treated as double entry then the control accounts are not, in which case they are known as memorandum accounts. If, however, the control accounts are treated as part of the double entry system then the individual ledger accounts which they summarize are known as subsidiary ledger accounts and are not part of the double entry system.

Though they are most commonly used for the sales and purchase ledger divisions, control accounts can be used for any ledger divisions, e.g. cash or petty cash. Furthermore, the layout is the same and they are administered in the same way, so once you know how they are used for one type of account you know how they are used for others.

Advantages of using control accounts

The principal advantage of using control accounts is to reduce the need to deal with many sales, or purchase ledger balances to single sales, or the purchase ledger balance. This way interim and final accounts can be drawn up more quickly.

27 Preparing control accounts, step by step

The worksheets that will be affected are:
- the ledger worksheets (or those parts of it for which you want to operate control accounts);
- the relevant daybooks worksheets.

Step by step

1. Unless the control account is a new one, your opening balances will already be there. These are merely the closing balances for the previous month. If the control account is created at the start of a year, you can take your opening balances of assets and liabilities from the trial balance. If you are starting a control account from scratch, click on the next unused worksheet at the bottom of the screen. Rename it ' __ Control a/c', substituting the underscore for the relevant name, e.g. 'Bought Ledger', or 'Sales Ledger'.

2. Take each of the four daybook worksheets relating to sales and purchases. Post the monthly gross invoice (or credit note) totals to the sales or purchase ledger control account as the case may be. Post the totals to the same side as the individual postings were made, i.e. debit customers' accounts for sales and so on. Annotate each posting accordingly, for example 'sales', 'sales returns' and so on.

3. Take each of the other books of prime entry and extract from them totals for all the classes of transaction that relate to the ledger divisions concerned. Post each of these in turn to the relevant control accounts. Again, the appropriate side is exactly the same you would use if you were posting the items individually. Annotate each posting accordingly, for example 'cash', 'bank' and so on.

4. Providing the balancing mechanism has been pasted on the page as with the other ledger accounts, then these control accounts will automatically balance themselves. If they don't, you will need to check that the code in the various cells has not been corrupted. This sometimes needs to be updated if changes have been made to the cells above.

A listing of ledger balances

The trial balance is unlike anything we have seen so far, but it is quite simple to understand and quite simple to do. It is just a listing of all the ledger balances at a particular moment in time. You list the balances in two columns: one for the debit balances and one for the credit balances. If all the ledger divisions have been correctly posted your two columns will balance. Remember, for every transaction there have been two postings, a debit and a credit, so the sum of all the debits should equal the sum of all the credits. We always talk of 'extracting' a trial balance or 'constructing' or 'drawing up' a trial balance.

Summary

The trial balance is:

● a way of checking the accuracy of all previous postings;
● a source, in a useful summary form, for putting together the firm's final accounts later on.

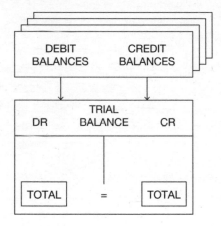

Figure 19 The trial balance is a list of all the ledger balances

The source documents for the trial balance are all the ledger worksheets (except the control accounts), the cash book and the pretty cash book worksheets.

Make sure that all the folio columns have been entered in all of the ledger account worksheets. Enter them now if necessary.

Extracting a trial balance step by step

Click on the next available worksheet tag at the bottom of the screen and rename it 'Trial Balance'.

1.   Head the blank sheet 'Trial balance as at [date]'. Head column 2 and column 3 'debit' and 'credit', respectively.

2.   List the balances of every single ledger account, including the cash book and petty cash book. Put each one in the correct column of your trial balance (debit or credit).

3.   Enter the following code and formatting in the first value column (column 2) below the balances you have listed (substituting for the variable x the number of the last filled row in the column).

```
=SUM(B3:Bx)
```

4.   Copy that cell and paste it into the adjacent cell in column C. The formula will be adjusted to be appropriate for that cell, as this form of coding is relative formula referencing rather than absolute formula referencing. It will now look like this:

```
=SUM(B3:Bx)       =SUM(C3:Cx)
```

5.   Insert a column between each answer box. The cell reference of the second one will be changed accordingly. It will now look like this:

```
=SUM(B3:Bx)       =SUM(D3:Dx)
```

6.   Copy the code from the answer box in the first column and paste it to the cell in column C that lies in the row above the answer box, i.e. the row diagonally above right of the first total box. Change the second term so that it deducts 1 from the row number of that term, e.g. if the x value is 20, then change it here to 19. Example:

```
=SUM(B3:B19)
```

7.   Copy this cell and paste it into the cell diagonally right above the second total box. The formula will change itself to reflect the fact that it is now in column E. If it has not, then make the change yourself.

8.   Your page so far will look like this.

=SUM(B3:B19)   =SUM(D3:D19)
_____   _____
=SUM(B3:B20)   =SUM(D3:D20)
_____   _____

9.   Next you need to enter the following code into the cells above the totals boxes in columns C and E to carry out the balancing process.

10.   =If(E20>C20,E20-C20,"") and =If(C20>E20,C20-E20,"").

11.   Your page will now look like this:

=IF(E19>C19,   =SUM(B3:B19)   =IF(C19>E19,   =SUM(D3:D19)
E19-C19,"")   C19-E19,"")
_____   _____
=SUM(B3:B20)   =SUM(D3:D20)
_____   _____

12.   All that is left to do now is to enter, below each total box, the diagonally opposite column B and D cell references to show the value by which the two columns fail to balance. This will help you in your search for the reason why the columns have not balanced. Your page will look like this if the 'Show formulas' icon is clicked on the ribbon bar:

=IF(E19>C19,   =SUM(B3:B19)   =IF(C19>E19,   =SUM(D3:D19)
E19-C19,"")   C19-E19,"")
_____   _____
=SUM(B3:B20)   =SUM(D3:D20)
_____   _____
=(D20)   =(B20)

You will only need to construct this once. Thereafter, you can just copy and paste it on to each new sheet on which a trial balance is carried out. The page will now either balance or show the amount by which it fails to balance.

13.   If it fails to balance proceed as follows.

14.   Look for an error of complete omission of an account balance in the trial balance or of one side of a posting in the ledger. You should spot this if you look for a figure equal to the error. You can use the find facility for this. Just click on the 'Find and select' icon at the far right of the ribbon, while on the home tab. Enter the error value and then click each of the ledger worksheets. It will reveal any value of that amount.

15.   If this fails, look for an error due to something being entered on the wrong side of the trial balance, or both sides of a transaction being posted to the same side in the ledger. Divide the discrepancy in your trial balance by two, and look for a figure that matches this. Use the 'Find and select' facility in the way already mentioned.

16. If this fails, look for an error of transposition. Is the discrepancy divisible by nine? If so, there could well be such an error. Again, use the 'Find and select' facility to spot any such value in any of the sheets.

17. If these methods all fail, the error could be due to understating or overstating one side of a transaction, or a mixture of errors.

18. Check through the ledger again to look for any folio column omissions.

19. Check off each ledger balance against the trial balance. Have you recorded it on the correct side? Type an x in a spare right-hand column as you go.

20. If this does not solve the problem, check that the values in the posting of both sides of each transaction are equal. Start at the first page of the ledger and work through to the end. Type an x in a spare right-hand column as you go.

If you have carried out all the steps accurately, the trial balance will now balance. Note: a small error need not hold up the preparation of final accounts; you can post the error to a 'suspense account' to save time. When, eventually, the error is tracked down a 'statement of amended profit or loss' can be drawn up.

30   The trial balance: errors

Errors revealed and errors not revealed

The trial balance will immediately show that there is an error if it does not balance. However, it will not guarantee that the posting is error free if it does. In other words, things cannot be right if it does not balance, but can still be wrong if it does! Furthermore, a failure to balance does not tell us where in the posting the error or errors exist. So while the trial balance performs something of an error-checking role, it is not a foolproof one.

Errors not revealed

- Errors of complete omission, where neither debit nor credit has been entered.
- Compensating errors, where errors of equal value cancel each other out.
- Errors of commission – posting to the wrong accounts, though to the correct sides of the correct ledger division.
- Errors of reverse posting: the debit entry of a transaction has been wrongly posted to the credit side, and vice versa.
- Errors of principle, for example the posting of an asset to an expenses account.

Errors which will be revealed by a trial balance

- Errors arising from both parts of the double entry (debit/credit) being posted to the same side (e.g. debit).
- Errors of partial omission, for example, where only one side of a transaction was posted, such as the credit side but not the debit side, or vice versa.
- Errors of transposition, where digits have been accidentally reversed, for example 54 has been written as 45 (sec the previous chapter for how to identify this error).
- Errors due to understating or overstating one side of the transaction.
- Errors of original entry, for example when making a mistake while entering a sales invoice into the sales daybook.

Adjustments to accounts

Accruals and prepayments are adjustments we need to make to the accounts at the end of the year (or another management accounting period).

Accruals are sometimes called accrued expenses, expense creditors or expenses owing. Accruals are a liability for expenses for goods or services already consumed, but not yet billed (invoiced).

Prepayments are an asset of goods or services already paid for, but not yet completely used. Prepayments are, therefore, in a sense the opposite of accruals.

Example of accrued expenses

Suppose we are drawing up accounts for the year ended 31 March. We know there will be an electricity bill for the three months ending 30 April, a month after the end of our financial year. By 31 March, even though we haven't had the bill, we would already have used two months' worth of it, but as things stand the cost of this won't appear in our accounts, because it is too soon to have received a source document (i.e. the invoice) from which to enter it. Still, electricity clearly was an expense during the period, so we have to 'accrue' a sensible proportion. For example:

Electricity account period	1 February to 30 April
Estimated charge	£630.00 (three-month period)
Period falling within our accounts	1 February to 31 March (two months)
Charged accrued for period	£630.00 x 2 months = £420.00

Wages and rent

Other items that often have to be accrued are wages and rent. The firm receives the benefit of work and of premises before it pays out wages and rent (assuming rents are payable in arrears; if rent is payable in advance we would need to treat it as a prepayment).

Example of prepayment

A prepayment arises, for example, where an insurance premium or professional subscription is paid annually in advance, but only one or two month's benefit have been used by the end of the year. We must adjust the figures so that we don't charge the whole amount against profits for the year. Clearly, much of the benefit remains as an asset for use in the next year. Example, again assuming that our accounting period ends on 31 March:

Professional subscription for calendar year:	£100.00
Period falling within our accounts	1 January to 31 March
Period falling into next accounting period:	1 April to 31 December (9 months)
Prepaid for next year	£100.00 x 9 = £75.00

Carrying down accruals and prepayments

When these amounts have been calculated or assessed, you place them in the relevant ledger accounts as 'carried down' balances. In this way you increase or decrease the amount to be transferred to the profit and loss account for the year, depending on which side the posting is made. The resulting 'b/d' balances are listed in the balance sheet just like any other balance remaining on the nominal ledger at the end of the year. If they are credit balances (accruals) they are current liabilities. If they are debit balances (prepayments) they are assets.

The trading account and profit and loss account

The revenue accounts are a pair of ledger accounts called the trading account and the profit and loss account. They are much like any other ledger account except that they are not ongoing (except for limited companies, dealt with later). Also, they are needed by more people outside the firm, for example:

- HM Revenue and Customs to assess tax liability;
- shareholders to see how the business is doing;
- prospective purchasers to value the business;
- prospective lenders to assess the risk of lending to the business and its ability to pay interest.

But we adapt these accounts to a more easy-to-read version. Instead of two main columns we have only one (though we also use subsidiary columns for calculations). The two sides of the accounts are then represented in progressive stages of addition and subtraction. So the revenue accounts forwarded to interested parties don't look like ledger accounts at all.

The trading account

This shows the gross profit, and how it is worked out:

sales − cost of goods sold = gross profit

To work out the cost of goods sold (i.e. cost of sales):

purchases + opening stock + carriage inwards, packaging and warehouse costs − closing stock = cost of sales

When transferring the balances to the trading account, deduct sales returns from sales before posting in the trading account. After all, they are merely 'un-sales', so to speak. The same goes for purchase returns: there is no place for any returns in the trading account.

Contribution to overheads

Gross profit is not the same things as net profit. Gross profit is first and foremost a contribution to overheads. It is only when they are paid for that any net profit may, or may not, be available for shareholders.

The profit and loss account

The profit and loss account sets out the calculation of net profit like this:

gross profit + other income − expenses = net profit

We know that there must be two sides to every ledger posting. As you post each item in the revenue accounts you make an opposite side posting in the original ledger account from where your balance came. Against such postings just type 'Trading account' or 'Profit and loss' account. You are now closing down the revenue and expense ledger accounts, ready for a fresh start in the next accounting period.

Opening and closing stock

Stock is dealt with three times in the revenue accounts and balance sheet: once as opening stock and twice as closing stock. Suppose we started the year with £1,000 worth of stock; we purchased a further £10,000 of stock during the year, but had none left at the end of it. Altogether, it means that we have sold assets of £11,000 during the year. Purchases and opening stock must be the same kind of asset, since they were both finished goods on the shelf; otherwise we could not have sold them both and had nothing left to sell. Clearly, stock and purchases need to be treated in the same way in the final accounts.

This year's opening stock was, in fact, last year's closing stock. Throughout this year it was an asset, appearing on the debit side of the ledger. So this year's closing stock must also be carried forward to the next year as an asset; it too must stay on the ledger, just like all other assets at the end of the year. The only balances we must transfer out permanently to the revenue accounts are those for expenses and revenues (which, of course, are not assets).

Physical stock take

Closing stock will not even be in the ledger until we have done a stock take (a physical counting and valuation of the stock in hand). We must then post to the debit side of the stock account in the nominal ledger group of worksheets the actual asset value of stock remaining and being carried forward into next year.

Why we need a counter-entry for stock

The counter-entry must be posted to the credit of the trading account. Why? Let us go back to our basic example. We posted opening stock as a debit in the trading account because we assumed it had all been sold, along with the purchases for that year. But what if we bought £12,000 worth but still had £2,000 worth left? We will need to make an entry to the opposite side for this. Closing stock is a credit posting in the trading account.

Another way to look at it is this: if we purchased £12,000 worth of stock but only sold £10,000, it would be as if we had purchased only £10,000 worth for sale during the year. The other £2,000 worth would be for sale in the next year. So we are right to deduct closing stock from purchases.

Remember, a credit posting in the final accounts can also be done as a subtraction from the debit column. You have to do this when converting the ledger format to vertical format.

The worksheets involved in the process

- The trial balance;
- the ledger groups of worksheets;
- the journal worksheet.

Also needed:

- details of end of year adjustments to the accounts, such as depreciation, bad debts and closing stock.

Adjustments before you start

You will need to adjust the trial balance for various end of year adjustments. It's best to open a new worksheet tag. Rename it 'Adjusted Trial Balance'. Click on it, hold down the left mouse button and drag it to a position adjacent to the original 'Trial Balance' tag.

Remember to make all your adjustments into the trial balance twice, once on the debit side and once on the credit side. You can achieve the same effect by adding to and subtracting from the same side as, indeed, you would need to with accruals and prepayments. For a prepayment, for example, you would debit 'Prepayments' in the trial balance, and subtract the same amount from the debit balance of the expense account concerned, e.g. 'insurance'. Check that the trial balance still balances after you have adjusted it: there is no point in starting to put together your final accounts until it is correct.

Getting the right balance into the right accounts

It is a good idea to label each balance to show where it will go in your final accounts. For example, against 'sales' type, in column D, 'T' for trading account'. Type 'P & L' beside 'rent & rates' to show that it is going into the profit and loss account. Type 'B' beside each asset account to show that you will be taking it into your balance sheet.

Items on the debit side of the trial balance are expenses or assets; those on the credit side are revenues or liabilities. In the revenue accounts we are only interested in revenues and expenses. How do we recognize them?

A revenue is an income; an expense is an outgoing. Neither has to be in cash. If you have more stock left at the end than you had at the beginning of the accounting period, that is just as much a revenue as a sales figure. Another way of putting it is to say that excesses of expenses over revenues are called losses. Expenses represent an outflow of funds within the period. They include such things as electricity, motor expenses, rents paid or payable and discounts allowed. Items classed as revenues represent incomes within the same period. They include things like commissions, rents receivable and discounts received.

35 Configuring a spreadsheet for revenue accounts, step by step

Once you have labelled each item in the trial balance according to where it will go in the final accounts you can put together your revenue accounts as follows.

1. Head the blank sheet 'Revenue accounts as at [date]'. Head column 2 and column 3 'debit' and 'credit', respectively.
2. Enter the following code and formatting in the first value column (column 2) below the balances you have listed (substituting for the variable x the number of the last filled row in the column):

   =SUM(B3:Bx)

3. Copy that cell and paste it into the adjacent cell in column C. The formula will be adjusted to be appropriate for that cell, as this form of coding is relative formula referencing rather than absolute formula referencing. It will now look like this:

   =SUM(B3:Bx)   =SUM(C3:Cx)

4. Insert a column between each answer box. The cell reference of the second one will be changed accordingly. It will now look like this:

   =SUM(B3:Bx)   =SUM(D3:Dx)

5. Copy the code from the answer box in the first column and paste it to the cell in column C that lies in the row above the answer box, i.e. the row diagonally above right of the first total box. Change the second term so that it deducts 1 from the row number of that term, e.g. if the x value is 20, then change it here to 19. Example:

   =SUM(B3:B19)

6. Copy this cell and paste it into the cell diagonally right above the second total box. The formula will change itself to reflect the fact that it is now in column E. If it has not, then make the change yourself.
7. Your page so far will look like this:

=SUM(B3:B19)		=SUM(D3:D19)
=SUM(B3:B20)		=SUM(D3:D20)

8. Next you need to enter the following code into the cells above the totals boxes in columns C and E to carry out the balancing process.
9. =If(E20>C20,E20-C20,"") and =If(C20>E20,C20-E20,"")

10.   Your page will now look like this:

=IF(E19>C19, E19-C19,"")	=SUM(B3:B19)	=IF(C19>E19, C19-E19,"")	=SUM(D3:D19)
=SUM(B3:B20)		=SUM(D3:D20)	

11.   All that is left to do now is to enter, below each total box, the diagonally opposite column B and D cell references to show the value by which the two columns fail to balance, to help you in your search of the reason why. Your page will look like this if the 'Show formulas' icon is clicked on the ribbon bar.

=IF(E19>C19, E19-C19,"")	=SUM(B3:B19)	=IF(C19>E19, C19-E19,"")	=SUM(D3:D19)
=SUM(B3:B20)		=SUM(D3:D20)	
=(D20)		=(B20)	

You will only need to construct this once. Thereafter, you can just copy and paste it on to each new sheet on which a trial balance is carried out.

12.   The page will now either balance or show the amount by which it fails to balance.

13.   If it fails to balance proceed as follows.

14.   Now copy and paste all that you have already done so that you now have two identical parts to the revenue account worksheet. At the top of the first part, immediately below the main heading, type the sub heading 'Trading a/c'.

15.   At the start of the second part (immediately over the second balancing mechanism, type the sub-heading 'Profit and Loss a/c'.

36 Compiling a spreadsheet for revenue accounts, step by step

1. In the next available space in the 'Particulars' column of the journal, type 'Sales'.
2. Against this, in column C, enter the balance of your sales account.
3. Beneath the last entry in the 'Particulars' column, indenting slightly, type 'Opening Stock'.
4. Against this, in column B, enter the value of opening stock. This can be taken from the closing stock last year or from the opening figures for the current year.
5. Next, in column B, enter the value of the closing stock, taken from the physical stocktake figures.
6. Next, in column B, place the figure that represents the balance of the purchases account and against it in column A type the word 'Purchases' to signify that this is the account from which the value is being transferred to close it down.
7. Remove any excess rows, other than a single blank row above the total box, and type in the latter, in column A, 'Gross profit /loss c/d to profit and loss account'.
8. Type in column A, immediately below the total box, 'Gross profit b/d to trading account'.
9. Now list any other income balances in column A, together with their values in column C, and list all the expense account balances in column A, together with their values in column B.
10. Remove any excess rows, except for a single blank row above the total boxes. Type in column A, in the row immediately above the totals box, 'Net profit c/d to balance sheet' and in the row two immediately below the total box 'Net profit loss b/d to balance sheet'.
11. Now post the counter entries for each of those you have just made in the revenue accounts.

The trading, profit and loss account is, after all, just another ledger account, so when you post to either of the two parts of this you also have to make a counter entry to the opposite side of another ledger account in order to maintain the double entry and keep the total debits equal to the total credits.

The only difference with the format of this ledger account is that it has two parts: the first (trading account) is balanced off and the balance b/d becomes the opening figure for the second part (profit and loss account). Consequently the balancing formatting and code has to be pasted twice on the page – at the ends of both parts of the ledger. This has been explained above.

A financial snapshot

We have already seen standard sorts of statements summarizing particular aspects of the business. The bank reconciliation was an example. The balance sheet is another – but a much more important one. Unlike the trading, profit and loss account, the balance sheet is not an 'account' as such. Rather, it is a useful snapshot of the firm's financial situation at a fixed point in time. It sets out clearly all the firm's assets and liabilities and shows how the resulting net assets are matched by the capital account.

The balance sheet always goes hand-in-hand with the trading, profit and loss account. We need it to show:

- where the net profit has gone (or how the net loss has been paid for);
- how any net profit has been added to the capital account;
- how much has been taken out as 'drawings' and whether any of it has been used to buy new assets (stating what those assets are).

Management data

Accounting ratios can be worked out to help decision-making. For example, the ratio of current assets/current liabilities shows how easily a firm can pay its debts as they become due (a ratio of 2:1 is often seen as acceptable in this respect). More will be said about these ratios later.

Five main components of the balance sheet

The balance sheet tells us about five main categories:

1. Fixed assets. These are assets the business intends to keep for a long time (at least for the year in question). They include things like premises, fixtures and fittings, machinery and motor vehicles. Fixed assets are not for using up in day-to-day production or trading (though a small part of their value is used up in wear and tear and that is treated as an expense –'depreciation'. Property should be valued at net realizable value or cost, whichever is the lower.
2. Current assets. These are assets used up in day-to-day trading or production. They include such things as stock, debtors, cash at bank and cash in hand.
3. Current liabilities. These are amounts the business owes to creditors and which usually have to be paid within the next accounting year. They include trade creditors and bank overdraft.
4. Long-term liabilities. These are liabilities that do not need to be settled within the trading year.
5. Capital. This is the equity of the proprietor or shareholders.

1. Create a new worksheet by clicking on the new worksheet tab at the foot of the screen.

    - Rename the tab 'Balance Sheet'.
    - Make a heading, in the middle of row 1, 'Balance sheet of [firm] as at [date]'.
    - Make a sub-heading on the left, in cell A3, 'Fixed assets'.
    - Beneath this, in column C type the value of any premises. Annotate it, in column A, 'Land and buildings'.

2. In column B, list the balances of other fixed assets, in order of permanence. Annotate each one, in column A. Beneath each one record the provision for depreciation, annotating, in column A, 'Less provision for depreciation'.
3. Insert a bottom line beneath the depreciation by clicking on the borders icon and choosing the bottom borders option.
4. Subtract the depreciation from each asset and place the difference in column C by inserting the formula into the cells where the totals are to go.
5. Insert a bottom line in column C by clicking on the borders icon and choosing the bottom borders option.
6. Total up column C by inserting the formula into the cell where the total is to go.

    - Now make a second sub-heading, 'Current assets'.
    - Beneath this, in the second cash column (column C), type the balances of the short-life assets, in the order of permanence, annotating accordingly.

7. Insert a bottom line in column C by clicking on the borders icon and choosing the bottom borders option.
8. Total up these balances by inserting the formula into the cell where the total is to go.
9. Make a third sub-heading in column A, on the left, 'Less current liabilities'.
10. Below that list, in column B, enter the creditors figure and the bank overdraft figure, if there is one.
11. Insert a bottom line in column C by clicking on the borders icon and choosing the bottom borders option.
12. Total up this column by inserting the formula into the cell where the total is to go. That is, in column B, beneath that for current assets. If there is only one item you can place it directly into the second column.
13. Insert a bottom line in column B, by clicking on the borders icon and choosing the top and bottom borders option.
14. Subtract the latter total from the former by inserting the formula into the cell where the total is to go. That is in column C, below the total for fixed assets, annotating it, in column A, 'Working capital'.

15. Add these two totals by inserting the formula into the cell where the total is to go, which is in the total box with a top and bottom double border, annotating it, in column A, 'Total net assets'.
16. Make a sub-heading below this, 'Represented by'.
17. Enter the opening capital in column C, annotating it, in column A, 'Opening capital'.
18. Enter the drawings balance, in column C, annotating it, in column A, 'Less drawings'.
19. Insert a bottom line in column C by clicking on the borders icon and choosing the bottom borders option.
20. Subtract the drawings from the opening capital by inserting the formula into the cell where the total is to go.
21. Next, enter the profit in column C, annotating it, in column A, 'Add profit'.

    - Insert a top and bottom border by clicking on the borders icon and choosing the top and bottom borders option.
    - Insert the formula into the cell where the total is to go, which is within the cell which has a top and bottom border.
    - Sum the last two values and annotate the sum 'Closing capital'.

Horizontal and vertical formats

A balance sheet may be shown in horizontal or vertical formats. Unless told otherwise, use the vertical format in exams and in practice.

We need to show two important cost figures in the manufacturing account:
Prime cost: the sum of the costs of direct labour, direct materials and direct expenses;
Overheads: the sum of all costs which cannot be directly related to output (e.g. factory rent).

Three stages of the production process are shown in a manufacturing account:

- raw materials consumed;
- adjustment for stocks of partly finished goods (work in progress);
- finished goods transferred to trading account.

The cost of raw materials consumed is arrived at like this:

Opening stocks	600
Add purchases	200
	800
Less closing stocks	150
Cost of raw material consumed	650

The prime cost is found by adding the direct wages and direct expenses to the cost of raw materials consumed.

Work in progress is calculated similarly:

Opening stocks	600
Less closing stocks	150
Work in progress adjustment	450

Purchases do not come into this equation. The end product of the manufacturing account is the value of the stock of finished goods (just as the gross profit is the end product of the trading account). This value is then transferred to the trading account, just as the trading account transfers its gross profit to the profit and loss account.

40 Compiling a manufacturing account, step by step

1. Calculate the cost of raw materials consumed and insert the value in column C. Type, in column A, the correct heading against each line of your calculation.
2. Insert, in column B, the figures for direct wages and direct expenses, annotating accordingly, in column A.
3. Insert a bottom border under the last of these values.
4. Sum them by inserting the formula into the cell where the total is to go, which is in column C.
5. Annotate each, in column A, the total 'Prime cost'.
6. Itemize the various overhead expenses. Note: it may be that only part (e.g. half) of a cost (e.g. rent) can be fairly attributed to the manufacturing process, the other part being more fairly attributed, for example, to sales. In such a case, only the first part should be itemised. Just mark it like this: 'Rent (1/2)'.
7. Total up this column by inserting the formula into the cell where the total is to go, which is in column C.
8. Enter your work-in-progress adjustment.
9. Type, in column A, the correct heading against each line of your calculation.
10. Place the resultant figure in your main cash column and add or deduct it from your subtotal by inserting the formula into the cell where the total is to go.
11. Type, in column A, against the difference: 'Cost of finished goods transferred to trading account'.

When assets drop in value

So far we have recorded figures, analysed them, summed and balanced them, and learned the standard ways of doing so. Now, with depreciation, we will also need to make calculations involving percentages.

Depreciation is the drop in value of an asset due to age, wear and tear. This drop in value is a drain on the firm's resources and so we must put it in the accounts as an expense. We will need to write down the value of the asset in the book to reflect its value more realistically. A company car, for example, loses value over time. So do plant, equipment and other assets. All have to be written down each year.

Methods of calculating depreciation

- Straight line method
- Diminishing (or reducing) balance method
- Sum of the digits method
- Machine hours method
- Revaluation method
- Depletion method
- Sinking fund method
- Sinking fund with endowment method

Even this list is not exhaustive, but the first two are the most common.

Straight line method

This involves deducting a fixed percentage of the asset's initial book value, minus the estimated residual value, each year. The estimated residual value means the value at the end of its useful life within the business (which may be scrap value). The percentage deducted each year is usually 20 per cent or 33.33 per cent and reflects the estimated annual fall in the asset's value. Suppose the firm buys a motor van for £12,100 and expects it to get very heavy use during the first three years, after which it would only be worth £100 for scrap. Each year we would write it down by one-third of its initial value minus the estimated residual value, i.e. £4,000 per year. On the other hand, suppose we buy a company car for £12,300 and we expect it to get only average use and to be regularly serviced. We expect to sell it after five years for £4,800. In that case we would write down the difference of £7,500 by one-fifth (20 per cent) each year, i.e. £1,500 per year.

This method is useful where value falls more or less uniformly over the years of the asset's lifetime.

42 Depreciation: the diminishing balance method

The diminishing balance method (or reducing balance method) also applies a fixed percentage, but it applies it to the diminishing value of the asset each year – not to the initial value. It is used for assets that have a long life within the firm and where the biggest drop in value comes in the early years, getting less as time goes on.

Suppose a lathe in an engineering workshop cost £40,000 to buy. In the first year it will fall in value much more than it ever will in later years. The guarantee may expire at the end of the first year. The bright smooth paint on the surface will be scratched and scarred; the difference between its appearance when new and its appearance a year later will be quite obvious. But the next year the change will seem less; who will notice a few more scratches on an already scarred surface? Nor will there be a great drop due to the guarantee expiring, for it will not have started out with one at the beginning of the second year. And so it will go on; the value of the asset will depreciate by smaller and smaller amounts throughout its life. Most people would agree that a three-year-old machine has less value than an otherwise identical two-year-old one, but who could say that a sixteen-year-old machine really has any less value than a fifteen-year-old one? Since the value of these assets erodes in smaller and smaller amounts as the years go by, we use the diminishing balance method of calculation.

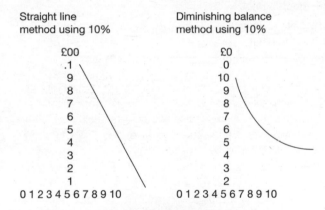

Figure 20 Common methods of depreciation
Note: The figure of 10 per cent is used in both cases to illustrate the comparison (it is not necessarily the most common percentage to be used).

43 Depreciation, step by step

1. Open the journal by clicking on the journal tab in the daybook range of worksheets.
2. In the next available row, type the date in the date column and 'Profit and loss' in the 'Particulars' column. Remember, never post directly to the ledger – only via a book of prime entry (in this case the journal, a useful book for miscellaneous recordings like depreciation).
3. Move the cursor to the debit (left-hand) cash column and click on the financial option in the formulas range of icons on the ribbon bar.
4. Select the option for the method of depreciation you have decided is most appropriate, e.g. SLD for straight line method, DB for the diminishing balance method or SOY for the sum of the years method. The formula will be placed invisibly in the cell and the actual value of depreciation will be shown.
5. Underneath the last entry in the 'Particulars' column, indenting slightly, type: 'Provision for depreciation on [name of asset]'.
6. Repeat for any other assets you need to depreciate in the accounts.
7. Enter the same value in the credit cash column.
8. Open a 'Provision for depreciation' account for each asset concerned. Record the page numbers in the index.
9. Make postings to each of these ledger accounts, following the instructions you have just written in the journal.

   Note: A Statement of Standard Accounting Practice (SSAP) was issued in December 1977 and revised in 1981 for the treatment of depreciation in accounts (SSAP12). The student can refer to this for further information if desired.

Not every credit customer (or other debtor) will pay what they owe. They may dispute the amounts; some may disappear or go out of business. The debts they owe to the business may be bad or of doubtful value. If so, our accounts must reflect the fact.

Accounting for bad and doubtful debts, like depreciation, means estimating an erosion of value. But it differs from depreciation because there it is time that erodes the value. Here it is more a product of fate. We can predict what effect age will have on physical assets like motor cars, but we cannot very easily predict which, and how many, debtors won't pay their bills. If we could, we should never have given them credit in the first place! There are no special calculation techniques for bad and doubtful debts as there are in depreciation. You just need to choose a suitable overall percentage and make specific adjustments from time to time in the light of experience.

When a company becomes aware that a debt is uncollectable because, for example, the customer has been declared bankrupt or the company has gone into liquidation, the debt is written off by crediting the relevant sales ledger account and debiting the bad debts account.

Postings

We may know a debt has become worthless because the individual has gone bankrupt or a company has gone into liquidation. Such a debt must then be posted to a 'Bad debts account'. This is an account for specific debts we know to be bad. This is quite aside from our provision for a percentage of debtors-going-bad control account. If bad debts are recovered later on, we will treat them as credits to bad debts account and a debit to cash account. We do not need to reopen the individual debtor account, since the posting would result in its immediate closure anyway.

Only if a firm is in liquidation, or if an individual has too few assets to be worth suing, do we need to write off the debt to a bad debts account. If the non-payer does have sufficient funds, the firm may be able to sue them successfully for the debt.

Saving tax and being realistic

The reason we need to write down bad or doubtful debts is twofold. Firstly, the firm will be charged income tax on its profits. If the profit figure is shown without allowing for the cost of bad and doubtful debts it will be higher than it should rightly be and the firm will end up paying more tax than it should.

Secondly, the balance sheet should show as realistically as possible the value of the assets of the business. After all, interested parties such as bankers, investors and suppliers will rely on it when making decisions about the firm. Failure to write off bad debts, and too little provision for doubtful debts, will mean an unrealistically high current asset of debtors being shown. Accountants are guided by the principle of *prudence*. This provides that (a) losses should be provided for as soon as anticipated and (b) it is preferable to understate profit than overstate it.

45 Accounting for bad and doubtful debts, step by step

Posting to the 'Provision for doubtful debts account' and 'Bad debts account'

You will need:

- the journal worksheet;
- the nominal ledger worksheet;
- the sales ledger worksheet.

Step by step

1. Decide the percentage figure and from that the actual amount you will use as a provision for doubtful debts (e.g. 1 per cent or 2 per cent).
2. Type, in the next available space in the journal, the date (in the date column) and the words 'Profit and loss account' in the 'Particulars' column.
3. Enter the value of your provision in the debit cash column.
4. Beneath the last entry in the 'Particulars' column, indenting slightly, write: 'Provision for doubtful debts'.
5. Enter the same value in the credit cash column.
6. Insert a line to rule off this pair of instructions.
7. Repeat the process when writing off any actual bad debts, but in this case you need to debit the bad debts account and credit the individual debtor accounts.
8. Now post to the nominal and sales ledger, exactly following the instructions you have just written in the journal.

The appropriation account is just an extension of the trading, profit and loss account. In it, we post the appropriation (i.e. sharing out) of net profit between the partners. We do not need an appropriation account in the accounts of a sole proprietor because all the net profit goes to the proprietor's capital account. In a partnership or limited company, things are a little more complicated.

- In a partnership some of the profit may be owed to the partners for interest on capitals they have invested.
- If a partner has drawn money from the business (other than salary) they may have to pay interest on it, according to arrangements between the parties. Any such interest payment will have to be deducted from any interest due to them on their capital. We show such transactions in the appropriation account.
- If a partner has lent money to the partnership, however, that is a very different thing. Any interest payable to that partner would be an expense to the business, not an appropriation of profit. Its proper place would be in the profit and loss account.

After deducting these items from the net profit (brought down from the profit and loss account) we have to show how the rest of the profit will be shared out. We will show an equal split, or an unequal one, depending on the profit-sharing arrangements between the partners.

What you need:

- the ledger worksheet;
- details of interest rate on capital due to partners;
- details of interest rate payable by partners on drawings;
- details of partners' capitals;
- details of partners' drawings;
- details of partners' salaries and/or fees;
- details of profit-sharing arrangements.

Preparation

Work out the interest on capital due to each partner. Remember to apply the correct percentage interest rate. Work out the interest payable by each partner on their drawings, again applying the correct percentage interest rate.

Step by step

1. Change the annotation of the net profit b/d in the Revenue accounts, so that instead of it saying 'Net profit b/d to balance sheet', it says 'Net profit b/d to profit and loss appropriation account'.
2. In column C, record the interest payable on drawings for each partner, annotating it, in column A, accordingly.
3. Insert a bottom border in the cell which holds this value.
4. Add the last two figures in this column by placing the summation formula in the cell below.
5. Next, in column C, enter the interest on capital for each partner, annotating each entry, in column A, accordingly.
6. Next, in column B, record the value of individual partner's salaries, annotating each one in column A, accordingly.
7. Next, in column B, record the individual profit shares of each partner, annotating each one accordingly. Show the proportion, e.g. ½ or a percentage such as 50 per cent.
8. Place a top and double bottom border in the next cell in column C.
9. Sum the last three values by placing the appropriate formula in the cell where the total is to go (the balance c/d will be zero).

Converting final accounts into vertical format

Figure 21 shows a horizontal layout, but vertical formats are much more popular in Britain and you should use them in exams and in business unless told otherwise. You can now rewrite your final accounts in a more useful vertical format. If you do, change the appropriation account in the same way. Figure 22 shows how this is done.

A. FRAZER
Trading, profit and loss account
for year ended 31 March 2013

Stock as at 1 April 2012	10,000	Sales	100,000
Purchases	60,000	Stock as at	
Carriage inwards	3,000	31 March 2013	9,000.00
Gross profit C/D	36,000		
	109,000		109,000
		Gross profit b/d	36,000

Profit and loss account

Wages	6,000		
Motor expenses	2,000		
Heat and light	450		
Cleaning	1,500		
Depreciation	2,550		
Net profit c/d	23,500		
	36,000		36,000
		Net profit b/d	
		capital account	23,500

Figure 21 Trading profit and loss account in horizontal format

A. FRAZER
Trading, profit and loss account
for year ended 31 March 2013

Sales			100,000
Less purchases		60,000	
Carriage inwards		3,000	
Opening stock	10,000		
Less closing stock	9,000	1,000	64,000
Gross profit b/d			36,000
Less expenses			
Wages	6,000		
Motor expenses	2,000		
Heat and light	450		
Cleaning	1,500		
Depreciation	2,550		12,500
Net profit b/d to capital account			23,500

Figure 22 Trading profit and loss account in vertical format

Example: Frazer and Baines

Frazer and Baines are partners. Frazer initially invested £20,000 in the business and Baines £50,000. Frazer took drawings of £2,000 during the year and Baines £2,500. It had been agreed at the onset that 10 per cent interest would be paid on capital, interest of 12 per cent would be payable on drawings and that Frazer, because he alone would be working full-time in the business, would receive a salary of £8,000. Suppose, also, that the net profit shown in the profit and loss account at the end of the current year is £21,000. Following the step-by-step instruction given here, Figure 23 shows what the appropriation account might look like.

Horizontal format

FRAZER AND BAINES
Profit and loss appropriation account
for year ended 31 March 2013

Net profit b/d					21,000
Interest on capital (10%)			Interest		
			on drawings (12%)		
Frazer	2,000		Frazer	240	
Baines	5,000		Baines	300	540
Salary: Frazer	8,000	15,000			
Share of					
residual profits					
Frazer (67%)		2,180			
Baines (33%)		4,360			
depreciation		21,540			21,540

Vertical format

FRAZER AND BAINES
Profit and loss appropriation account
for year ended 31 March 2013

Net profit b/d			21,000
Frazer			
Interest on capital (10%)	2,000		
Less interest on drawings (12%)	240		
	1,760		
Salary: Frazer	8,000	9,760	
Baines			
Interest on capital (10%)	5,000		
Less interest on drawings (12%)	300	4,700	
Share of profits in ratio 2:1			
Frazer	2,180		
Baines	4,360	6,540	21,000
			0

Figure 23 Alternative formats for appropriation accounts

Consolidation

Now we come to a new accounting technique: consolidation. The idea is to consolidate or amalgamate the accounts of two separate businesses into those of a single partnership. The method is very simple. We just add each of the individual balance sheet items together, after making adjustments in each for any changes in asset values agreed by the parties.

Making the adjustments

Such adjustments may arise, for example, because A thinks their 'provision for bad debts' of 5 per cent is reasonable, while B feels it should be 7.5 per cent; or B might feel that one of A's machines is not worth what A's balance sheet says it is; and so on. If the amalgamation is to go ahead, the parties will have to settle all such disagreements first.

When we make such adjustments, it is bound to affect the capital figure. So we also need to make the adjustment to the capital accounts, before consolidating the balance sheets by adding all their components together. Indeed, if we didn't adjust the capital accounts, the individual balance sheets would cease to balance and then the consolidated one would not balance either.

The 'goodwill' value of each business

The parties may agree that different values of goodwill existed in their businesses before amalgamation. Perhaps one business was long-established, while the other one was rather new and had not yet built such a good reputation. In such a case, each business would write an agreed figure for goodwill into its balance sheet before amalgamation. It would post the other side of the dual posting to the credit of its capital account. On amalgamation we then add the two goodwill amounts together, just like all the other assets.

Writing off goodwill after amalgamation

If it is decided later on to write it off, the one aggregated goodwill figure in the post-amalgamation accounts will be credited to the goodwill account; the debit entry to complete the dual posting will be posted to the partners' current accounts, in proportion to their profit-sharing arrangements (unless a different agreement exists between them).

Consolidating two balance sheets is quite a simple procedure. The sources you need are:

- the two balance sheets;
- details of any changes (adjustments) to the item values, as agreed between the owners of the two businesses.

Step by step

1. Adjust any item values as appropriate; in other words correct the amounts from their original values to the new agreed values.
2. Take care to amend the capital values, too, so that the individual balance sheets do, in fact, still 'balance'.
3. Add together the values of each item (other than depreciation). Then prepare a consolidated balance sheet for the new partnership.

Note on depreciation

Provision for depreciation is not carried over into the new partnership because the business unit has in effect purchased the assets at their already written-down value.

Example

In Figure 24 we can see the consolidated balance sheet of the businesses of Frazer and Baines (their separate balance sheets are shown in Figure 25. Notice how the newly amalgamated partnership treats the machinery, motor van and motor lorry. The consolidated value of the machinery is £6,650, representing £3,800 (its written-down value is in Frazer's balance sheet) plus £2,850 (its written down value is in Baines's balance sheet).

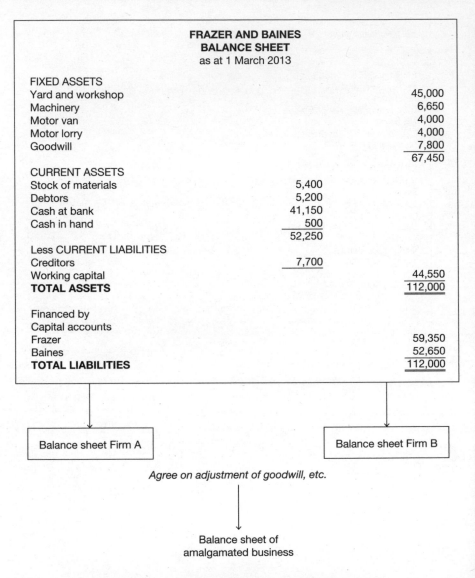

FRAZER AND BAINES
BALANCE SHEET
as at 1 March 2013

FIXED ASSETS
Yard and workshop   45,000
Machinery   6,650
Motor van   4,000
Motor lorry   4,000
Goodwill   7,800
                                                             67,450

CURRENT ASSETS
Stock of materials   5,400
Debtors   5,200
Cash at bank   41,150
Cash in hand   500
                                         52,250
Less CURRENT LIABILITIES
Creditors   7,700
Working capital   44,550
TOTAL ASSETS   112,000

Financed by
Capital accounts
Frazer   59,350
Baines   52,650
TOTAL LIABILITIES   112,000

Balance sheet Firm A   Balance sheet Firm B

Agree on adjustment of goodwill, etc.

Balance sheet of
amalgamated business

Figure 24 Opening (consolidated) balance sheet of a new partnership

Before amalgamation

A. FRAZER
BALANCE SHEET
as at 28 February 2013

FIXED ASSETS			
Workshop and yard	4,000		45,000
Machinery	200	3,800	
Less provision for depreciation	6,000		
Motor van	2,000	4,000	7,800
Less provision for depreciation			5,800
Goodwill			58,600
CURRENT ASSETS			
Stock of materials	4,500		
Debtors	1,200		
Cash at bank	150		
	5,850		
Less CURRENT LIABILITIES			
Creditors	5,100		
Working capital			750
TOTAL ASSETS			59,350
Financed by			
CAPITAL as at 1 March 2013			57,050
Add profit			11,300
			63,350
Less drawings			9,000
TOTAL LIABILITIES			59,350

Before amalgamation

E. BAINES
BALANCE SHEET
as at 28 February 2013

FIXED ASSETS		
Machinery	3,000	
Less provision for depreciation	150	2,850
Motor lorry	5,000	
Less provision for depreciation	1,000	4,000
Goodwill		2,000
		8,850
CURRENT ASSETS		
Stock of materials	900	
Debtors	4,000	
Cash at bank	41,000	
Cash in hand	500	
	46,400	
Less CURRENT LIABILITIES		
Creditors	2,600	
Working capital		43,800
TOTAL ASSETS		52,650
Financed by		
CAPITAL as at 1 March 2013		42,450
Add profit		10,200
TOTAL LIABILITIES		52,650

Figure 25 Separate balance sheets of two partners prior to amalgamation

New partner joining

When a new partner is admitted to a partnership their acquisition of a share in the existing value of goodwill means that other partners will lose. Those partners who gain should be charged the amount of their gain and those who lose should be compensated for their loss. Figure 26 shows the four stages in the process.

| | *Stage 1* | | *Stage 2* | | *Stage 3* | *Stage 4* | |
Partners	Old profit-sharing ratios	Share of goodwill	New profit-sharing ratios	Share of goodwill	Gain/loss	Adjustment required	
	%		%				
Able	33	15,000	25	11,250	3,750.00	Loss	Pay Able, or credit his/her capital account
Bryce	33	15,000	25	11,250	3,750.00	Loss	Pay Bryce, or credit his/her capital account
Collins	33	15,000	25	11,250	3,750.00	Loss	Pay Collins, or credit his/her capital account
			25	11,250	3,750.00	Gain	Charge Dean, or debit his/her capital account

Goodwill

Able	Capital	15,000	Balance c/d	45,000
Bryce	Capital	15,000		
Collins	Capital	15,000		
		45,000		45,000

Figure 26 The four stages of adjustment of the profit-sharing ratios and shares of goodwill, together with the recording of capital changes on the admission of a new partner

Paying for the goodwill acquired

The new partner can pay for their share of goodwill in one of four ways. They can pay each partner for the amount of goodwill they have lost in allowing them to take a proportion of the total (see Figure 26). Able, Bryce and Collins each gave up £3,750 of goodwill to the new partner, so a simple way would be for Dean to pay each of them a cheque for £3,750 which they can bank in their private accounts and no goodwill account needs to be opened.

Alternatively, a sum equal to the combined loss of goodwill (£11,250) can be paid into the partnership's account and this sum credited proportionally to the capital accounts of Able, Bryce and Collins, i.e. £3,750 to each. Again, there would be no need to open a goodwill account in this case.

A third method would be to debit the new partner's capital account with the goodwill share they have acquired and credit the same to the capital accounts of the existing partners in accordance with their profit-sharing ratios. Again, there would be no need to open a goodwill account in this case.

A fourth method is to open a goodwill account and capitalize the existing goodwill shares, i.e. debit the goodwill account with the total value of the goodwill and post the equivalent value to the credit of the existing partners' capital accounts in the proportions of their profit-sharing ratios.

Example

Suppose Dean joins the partnership of Able, Bryce and Collins. Goodwill is valued at £45,000 and the partners will share profits equally as has always been the case in the past. Their capitals are different, as you will see, but this does not affect the profit-sharing ratios as their capitals are remunerated by interest paid on them. Figure 27 shows the entries that will be made in the ledger to record the changes.

Capital accounts

	Able	Bryce	Collins	Dean			Able	Bryce	Collins	Dean
Balances c/d	65,000	45,000	35,000	50,000	Balances c/d		50,000	30,000	20,000	50,000
					Cash for capital					
					Goodwill		15,000	15,000	15,000	
	65,000	45,000	35,000	50,000			65,000	45,000	35,000	50,000

Goodwill

Balance b/d	45,000	Able	Capital	11,250
		Bryce	Capital	11,250
		Collins	Capital	11,250
		Dean	Capital	11,250
	45,000			45,000

Figure 27 Illustration of the ledger entries, including the writing off of goodwill after the admission of a new partner

Writing off the goodwill

After the adjustment has been made the goodwill can be written off by crediting the goodwill account with the full amount to close it down and debiting the partners' capital accounts in the proportions of their new profit-sharing ratios.

Changes in profit-sharing ratios for other reasons

The admission of a new partner is not the only circumstance in which profit-sharing ratios may change. They may change because a partner ceases to work full-time or their skills cease to be as important as those of the other partners. If a partner agrees to take a smaller percentage of profits they deserve to be compensated for what they have given up. The financial adjustments can be made by the same methods as for changes in profit sharing as a result of a new partner joining (see Figure 26).

Death or retirement of a partner

If a partner dies or retires from the partnership, goodwill has to be accounted for so that the retiring partner, or their estate if deceased, can be paid a fair value for their share in the business. The process is essentially the same as for a joining partner and once the adjustments to the capitals have been made the goodwill can be written off if desired and the account closed down.

Example
Suppose Bryce is retiring from the partnership of Able, Bryce, Collins and Dean. The value of goodwill has been agreed as £48,000. Their capitals are £50,000, £30,000, £20,000 and £50,000 respectively, but they share profits equally. Figure 28 shows how this would be dealt with in the accounts.

Capital accounts

	Able	Bryce	Collins	Dean
Balances c/d	50,000	30,000	20,000	50,000
Shares of goodwill	12,000	12,000	12,000	12,000
	62,000	42,000	32,000	62,000

	Able	Bryce	Collins	Dean
Balances c/d	62,000	42,000	32,000	62,000
	62,000	42,000	32,000	62,000

Figure 28 Illustration of using the goodwill account to adjust the capital accounts on the retirement of a partner

Bryce's capital account stands at £42,000 now that his share of goodwill has been capitalized, so on retiring from the partnership he will receive this amount.

If a goodwill account had already existed it may have needed updating. It may have been undervalued or overvalued. If a goodwill account is undervalued debit it with the amount by which it should be increased and credit the partners' capital accounts in the proportions of their profit-sharing ratios. If goodwill is overvalued in the accounts then do the exact opposite.

Again, once the adjustments have been made the goodwill can be written off by crediting the account with the full value of goodwill and debiting the partners' capital accounts in the proportions of their post-adjustment, profit-sharing ratios.

50 Limited companies

Public and private companies

The form and extent of the accounts of limited companies are governed by the Companies Act 1985.

There are two main types of limited company:

- **public** limited companies, which have 'plc' after their name;
- **private** limited companies, which have 'Ltd' after their name. Public companies have to disclose more information than private companies.

The company as a 'person'

The main difference between the company and other business entities is that it is a legal entity or 'person' quite separate from the shareholders. The partnership and the sole proprietorship, on the other hand, are inseparable from the people involved: if these two businesses cannot pay their debts then the partners or proprietors may be called upon to settle them personally because 'the business's debts' are in reality 'their debts'. In contrast, a company's debts are its debts alone. The shareholders cannot be called upon to settle the company's debts: their liability is limited to the original value of their shares. In law, a company is a separate legal 'person' (though obviously not a human one), and so has its own rights and obligations under the law.

Share capital

The capital account has its own special treatment in limited company accounts. The capital of limited companies is divided into shares, which people can buy and sell. A share in the capital of the company entitles the shareholder to a share of the profits of the company – just as a partner owning capital in a firm is entitled to profits.

Authorized share capital

Authorized share capital is just a statement of the share capital a company is authorized to issue, not what it has issued. The issued share capital is the amount of that limit that it actually has issued, i.e. the shares it has sold. It is only this latter amount that actually represents the company's capital.

The authorized share capital shows the nominal value of the company's shares. That is a rather arbitrarily chosen rounded-figure value at the incorporation of the business selected for the purpose of making it easy to divide up the equity of the firm. Suppose a sole proprietor, whose total net assets are £360,000, is incorporating their business in order to take in two other investors, but wishes to retain the controlling share of 51 per cent. Allocation of shares representing the net assets would be a messy business unless an easily divisible figure was used to represent the £360,000 net asset value. A figure of £100,000 can be registered as its authorized share capital, divided into 100,000 ordinary shares of £1, each of which represents £3.60 of the actual share capital.

106

Even if the authorized share capital did reflect exactly the net assets of the business, as might be the case where a new business is incorporated from scratch, five years later the company may be worth twice as much as when it started because of reinvested profits. Therefore any shares still to be issued will be worth probably twice as much as they were when the company started even though their nominal value will still be listed as the same figure as when the company was formed. It is necessary to keep them listed at their nominal value because that reflects the nominal proportion of the share capital that they represent. The difference between the nominal value and the market value is known as the *share premium*. The excess over nominal value that is charged for the shares is posted to the 'Share premium account' and shows up in the balance sheet as such.

Ordinary and preference shares

Limited companies can have different kinds of shares with different kinds of entitlements attached to them, e.g. *ordinary shares* and *preference shares*.

- Preference shares receive a fixed rate of dividend (profit share), provided sufficient profit has been made. For example, it might be 10 per cent of the original value of the preference shares.
- Ordinary shares have no such limit on their dividend, which can be as high as the profits allow. However, they come second in the queue, so to speak, if the profit is too little to pay dividends to both the preference and ordinary shareholders.

Furthermore, a company is allowed to retain part of the profits to finance growth. How much is up to the directors.

Unless otherwise stated in the company's memorandum of association, preference shares are cumulative, in other words any arrears of dividend can be carried forward to future years, until profits are available to pay them. Since the Companies Act 1985, a company is allowed to issue redeemable shares, both preference and ordinary. These are shares that the company can redeem (buy back) from the shareholder at their request.

Debentures

Some of the net assets of a company may be financed by debentures. These are loans and interest has to be paid on them. Since debentures have to be repaid, we have to show them as liabilities in the balance sheet.

Directors' duties regarding accounts

The directors and auditors of companies are responsible by law for compiling an annual report in a form governed by law. This is for shareholders, the public and HMRC.

The annual report must include a trading, profit and loss account and balance sheet, showing fixed and current assets, all costs of current and long-term liabilities, share capital and reserves, provision for taxation and loan repayments. The report must also include any unusual financial facts, e.g. effects of any changes in accounting procedures. It must also disclose things like values of exports, donations to political parties and directors' salaries, where they exceed £60,000 per annum.

- The auditors' report must also state the methods of depreciation used.
- The combined document must give a *true and fair view* of the financial affairs of the company.

The reasons companies must publish their accounts are:

- to provide information to enable shareholders to make informed decisions on whether to invest;
- to help prevent fraud and corruption.

The Companies Act 1985 gives four alternative layouts for the profit and loss account (two horizontal and two vertical) and two for the balance sheet (one horizontal and one vertical). The choice is up to the directors, but must not then be changed without good and stated reasons. Vertical layouts are the most popular in the UK, so it is those we will deal with here. Remember, though, that the trading, profit and loss account is first of all a ledger account, so it inevitably starts out in horizontal format. When we are ready to distribute it, inside or outside the firm, we can rewrite it in the more popular vertical format. The two alternative vertical formats laid down by the Companies Act 1985 are shown in Figure 29.

Format 1

1. Turnover
2. Cost of sales
3. Gross profit or loss
4. Distribution costs
5. Administrative expenses
6. Other operating income
7. Income from shares in group companies
8. Income from shares in related companies
9. Income from other fixed asset investments
10. Other interest receivable and similar income
11. Amounts written off investments
12. Interest payable and similar charges
13. Tax on profit or loss on ordinary activities
14. Profit or loss on ordinary activities after taxation
15. Extraordinary income
16. Extraordinary charges
17. Extraordinary profit or loss
18. Tax on extraordinary profit or loss
19. Other taxes not shown under the above items
20. Profit or loss for the financial year

Format 2

1. Turnover
2. Change in stocks of finished goods and in work in progress
3. Own work capitalised
4. Other operating income
5. (a) Raw materials and consumables
   (b) Other external charges
6. Staff costs:
   (a) wages and salaries
   (b) social security costs
   (c) other pension costs
7. (a) Depreciation and other amounts written off tangible and intangible fixed assets
   (b) Exceptional amounts written off current assets
8. Other operating charges
9. Income from shares in group companies
10. Income from shares in related companies
11. Income from other fixed asset investments
12. Other interest receivable and similar income
13. Amounts written off investments
14. Interest payable and similar charges
15. Tax on profit or loss on ordinary activities
16. Profit or loss on ordinary activities after taxation
17. Extraordinary income
18. Extraordinary charges
19. Extraordinary profit or loss
20. Tax on extraordinary profit or loss
21. Other taxes not shown under the above Items
22. Profit or loss for the financial year

Figure 29 Alternative vertical formats laid down by the Companies Act 1985

Turnover and cost of sales

Turnover means sales. Cost of sales is found by adding purchases and opening stock, plus carriage inwards costs, and deducting the value of closing stock.

Distribution costs

These include costs directly incurred in delivering the goods to customers.

Administration expenses

These include such things as wages, directors' remuneration, motor expenses (other than those included in distribution costs), auditors' fees and so on.

Other operating income

This means all income other than from the firm's trading activities, e.g. income from rents on property or interest on loans.

Directors' report

A directors' report must accompany all published accounts. 'Small' companies, however, are exempt from filing one with the Registrar of Companies. They also only have to file a modified version of their balance sheet and do not have to file a profit and loss account at all. Medium-sized companies also have some concessions, in that a modified form of profit and loss account and accompanying notes is allowed.

Limitations of published accounts

• Creative accounting can hide negative information.
• Not all the relevant facts have to be disclosed.

Internal accounts

Internal accounts or management accounts are those prepared only for use within the company. Unlike published accounts, they are not required by law to be set out in a certain way. However, it pays to keep them as consistent as possible with the published accounts, so that the latter can be drawn up just by adapting the internal accounts slightly.

Part Three

Advanced Spreadsheet Bookkeeping

So far, this book has showed you basic spreadsheet use as an alternative to paper books in the conventional bookkeeping system. Now you will how you can completely automate the process, thereby cutting out a lot of the manual bookkeeping steps and saving a great deal of time.

This will require us to replace the daybooks and general ledger with a combined analysis sheets. The double entry process, however, will be preserved.

The system we create will involve twenty spreadsheets. It will have the advantage of being able to expose errors in the double entry as and when they arise, rather than having to wait until the trial balance. It will automatically compute the figures for the VAT returns and even complete the forms. The trial balance and profit and loss account balance sheets will be a continuous product of the system, available at all times. Comparatives with previous years will also be carried out automatically as well as profitability ratios and other ratios, such as liquidity ratios.

Although the system will no longer use the simple form of the general ledger, the double entry principle will still be involved as the analysis sheets themselves will be in double entry form. Ledger accounts will be replaced by analysis sheet columns and all calculations will be done automatically once we have set up a spreadsheet. Furthermore, the spreadsheet can be used again and again, year after year, and even for different kinds of businesses, with a few adjustments.

All spreadsheets will be contained in a single workbook. You can have as many worksheets and reports as you require. In this book, we will deal with twenty spreadsheets. They are as follows.

1. Guide to the workbook
2. Opening balances
3. Income sheet Q1
4. Outgoings sheet Q1
5. Income sheet Q2
6. Outgoings sheet Q2
7. Income sheet Q3
8. Outgoings sheet Q3
9. Income sheet Q4
10. Outgoings sheet Q4
11. Income summary
12. Outgoings summary
13. VAT return
14. Assets summary
15. Liability summary
16. Trial balance
17. Profit and loss account
18. Balance sheet

19.   Debtors
20.   Creditors

You have to start with what is known as an abridged list of ledger accounts. This includes the categories into which the figures will be classified in the final accounts. The abridged list we are going to use here is as follows. You can add or subtract to this as necessary.

1	Turnover
2	Other income
3	Incomings Suspense Account
4	Purchases
5	Other direct costs
6	Wages, salaries and other employment cc
7	Rent
8	Repairs and renewals
9	Administration expenses
10	Travelling expenses
11	Advertising and promotion
12	Professional fees and charges
13	Bad debts
14	Bank charges
15	Depreciation costs
16	Loss (or profit) on asset disposals
17	Other expenses
18	Non-allowable expenses
19	Outgoings suspense account
20	Fixed assets
21	Stock
22	Trade debtors
23	Cash at bank
24	Cheques issued
25	Cash in hand
26	Other current assets
27	Trade creditors
28	VAT payable
29	PAYE and NI
30	Credit card
31	Other current liabilities inl accr
32	Business loan
33	Capital
34	Drawings

Figure 30 Abridged list of ledger accounts

The opening balances spreadsheet is, of course, for opening balances. These are the monetary values of the various classes of assets, liabilities and capital with which the current accounting period of the business started.

The asset classes include such things as: land and buildings, motor vehicles, machinery and equipment, stock in trade, office consumables, cash in bank, cash in hand and trade debtors. The various classes of liability include: trade creditors, bank overdraft and long-term loans. This sheet will be balanced according to the equation:

$$\text{Assets} - \text{Liabilities} = \text{Capital}$$

	Opening Balances		
20	Fixed assets		
	Land and buildings		
	Motor vehicles		
	Machinery and equipment		
	Current Assets		
21	Stock		
22	Trade debtors		
23	Cash at bank		
25	Cash in hand		
26	Other current assets		
	Prepayments		
	Deposits		
27	Trade creditors		
28	VAT payable		
29	PAYE and NI		
30	Credit card		
32	Accruals		
33	Net wages and salaries		
	Bank loan		
	capital		

Figure 31 Example of an opening balances spreadsheet

This is how to set up the opening balances spreadsheet. Unless otherwise stated, it will be assumed that the ribbon is opened at the home tab.

1. Left-click on the 'File' tab at the far left of the ribbon and select the 'Save as' option.
2. In the filename box, enter your business name.
3. In the file type box select the Excel workbook option.
4. Right-click on the first sheetname tag at the bottom of the screen. This will highlight it.
5. Type '1. Guide to the spreadsheet'.
6. Now right-click on the second nametag in the row and rename it in the same way, this time type '2. Opening balances'.
7. The final sheet relating to this nametag will now be open. Move the cursor to cell B1 and type 'Opening balances', then left-click on the B (bold icon on the ribbon) and U (underline icon) to embolden and underline the title.
8. In cell C1 type 'Financial year'.
9. In cell D1 type 'Date from'.
10. In cell D2 type 'Date to'.
11. Right-align the last two entries by highlighting the cells with the cursor and clicking on the right-align icon on the ribbon.

The following tells you what to type in various cells.

Cell reference		What to type in
A	5	Fixed assets
B	5	Land and buildings
B	6	Other fixed assets
A	8	21
B	8	Stock
A	9	22
B	9	Trade debtors
A	10	23
B	10	Cash at bank
A	11	24
B	11	Uncleared cheques
A	12	25
B	12	Cash in hand
A	13	26
B	13	Other current assets

Cell reference		What to type in
B	14	Prepayments
B	15	Deposits
A	18	27
B	18	Trade creditors
A	19	28
B	19	VAT payable
A	20	29
B	20	PAYE and NI payable
A	21	30
B	21	Credit card
A	22	31
B	22	Other current liabilities
B	23	Accruals
B	24	Net wages and salaries
A	28	32
B	28	Bank loan
A	29	33
B	29	Capital

12. Now insert a formula in cell C7 to sum the contents of cells D4 to D6 so as to arrive at the total value of fixed assets. The formula to enter is =SUM(C4:C6). You can simply type in this formula but there is an even quicker way. Click on the destination cell, where the sum is to be placed once calculated, click on the sigma icon near the top right-hand corner of the ribbon, highlight the cells to be summed (D4 and D6, in this case) and then press enter. The formula will automatically be placed in the cell concerned.

13. Enter a similar formula in cell D16 to sum the contents of cells C8 to C13 and deduct the contents of cells D15 and D16. You need to enter a similar formula in cell D25 to calculate the total current liabilities from the values in cells C18 to C21 minus cells D23 and D24.

14. Insert a formula in cell C29 to calculate the capital figure. The capital will be a minus figure and therefore you need to supersede the formula with a minus sign. The computation derives from deducting all of the liabilities in the opening balances spreadsheet from the total of the assets. The formula is therefore '=-SUM(C7+C8+C10+C11+C12+C13-D14-D15-C18-C19-C20-C21+D23+D24-C28)'.

15. A 15 per cent grey shading can be applied to sales in which figures are to be recorded. Do this by highlighting the cells, i.e. C6, C7, D8, D9, D10, D11,

D12, C14, C15, C16, C17, D18, D19, D20, D21, C23, C24, C25, C26, C27 and D28. You can highlight all of these together if you hold down the control key and click on each one in turn. When you have done this, click on the shading icon in the font group on the ribbon and select the third option down on the left.

Incomings Analysis			Total debits	3000	3,000.00	Total credits														
			Dr/Cr Error	0																

1st Quarter		Dr. income categories			VAT relevant columns							Cr. Net income analysis columns								
		1	2	3	4	5	6	7	8	9	10	11	12	13	14	15	16	17	18	19	20	21
Date	particulars	Doc. No.	cash received	bank lodgments	cheques received	credit income	VAT on sales	Net sales in UK, or non-EU countries	Net sales in EU countries other than UK	Sales turnover	Other income	Cash withdrawals	Cash deposited in the bank	Cheques deposited in the bank	Payments received from trade debtors	Capital investments	Security deposits and reserves	VAT refunds	PAYE and NI refunds	Other current liabilities	Loans to the business	Income from sale of fixed assets	Suspense account

Date	particulars	Doc. No.	cash received	bank lodgments	cheques received	credit income	VAT on sales	Net sales UK/non-EU	Net sales EU other	Sales turnover	Other income	Cash withdrawals	Cash deposited	Cheques deposited	Payments from trade debtors	Capital investments	Security deposits	VAT refunds	PAYE NI refunds	Other current liabilities	Loans to business	Income sale fixed assets	Suspense account
2013	TOTALS		0	3000	0	0	0	0	0	1200	800	0	0	0	1000	0	0	0	0	0	0	0	0
Feb-21	J Smith Rent			550						550													
28	B Roberts Rent			650						650													
29	Buggins Sec Dep			800							800												
29				1000											1000								

Figure 32 Example of an incomings analysis sheet

The incoming analysis sheet is where we record in detail all of the amount of income the business receives. Income is not only in the form of cash. It includes payments by cheque and income in the form of debt owed to the business, where a customer has purchased goods on credit.

Businesses usually do their VAT accounting quarterly, therefore a separate incomings analysis sheet will be done for each quarter.

There is a limit to how much can be seen on a computer screen and, therefore, we split the analysis sheet up into three parts. The first part contains columns for the date, the details and the particulars of each transaction, and a column for the document number relating to the transaction.

The four columns (columns D to G) analyse the category of income concerned, for example, cash, bank deposits, cheques received and credit income.

Then we have four columns for information necessary for VAT accounting. These only need to be completed if the business is registered for VAT. The rest of the columns are analysis columns such as are found in the daybooks of a manual accounting system (see *Mastering Book-keeping*, ninth edition for a full treatment of this subject).

In column 5, we record the VAT content of the income. Column 6 is for recording the amount net of VAT for a transaction with a customer in the UK or any country outside of the EU. Column 7 is for recording the net amount of any transaction with a customer based outside the UK but in the EU.

The analysis columns

Now we turn to the analysis columns. These are for recording the net figures, after deducting the VAT. The first one, column 8, is headed 'Turnover', and this column will contain the net amounts for every sale transaction. We need this so that we can provide the total sales figure for the nominal ledger and, in turn, the profit and loss account.

Column 9 is for non-sales income. This will include such items as commissions received, interest received, rents received and any other income that is not from sales.

Column 10 is for analysing funds withdrawn from the bank to be used for cash payments and column 11 is for the opposite kind of transaction, IDE, where cash in hand is deposited in the bank. Column 12 serves a similar purpose, in dealing with cheques that have been lodged in the bank. Column 13 is for recording income from trade debtors settling their debts with the business. Column 14 is for recording income from the proprietor investing his own funds in the business. Column 15 is for income represented by deposits, for example, landlord security deposits in the case of a property company or advance payments required for work the business is going to carry out for a customer. Column 16 is for VAT refunds and column 17 is for PAYE and National Insurance refunds. Column 18 is where we will record any other kinds of income. Column 19 is for funds received by the business in the form of loans. Column 20 is for income from the sale of fixed assets and column 21, headed 'Suspense account', is for analysing any items for which the category is at present undecided or uncertain.

Formatting the sheet

Here's how we go about formatting the sheet.

Click on the third sheetname tag at the bottom of the screen. This will highlight the tag and open the sheet. Rename the tag '3IncmsQ1'. The Q1 stands for the first quarter of the year.

Type the following texts in the cells as indicated below:

Cell reference		What to type in
B	1	Incomings analysis
E	1	Total debits
H	1	Total credits
F	2	DrCr error
B	5	1st Quarter

Now centre each of these in their respective cells by placing the curser in each cell in turn and clicking on the centre align icon in the paragraph group on the ribbon.

Now we're going to number all the columns that affect the accounts. To start with, type the figure '1' in cell D4 and the figure '2' in cell E4. Centre both entries by highlighting them and clicking on the centre align icon in the paragraph group on the ribbon. Click the cursor on the bottom right-hand corner of the pair of highlighted cells and a small + sign will appear. Left-click and hold the button down, while you drag your cursor along to the last column required. This is a quick way of consecutively numbering all the analysis columns.

In cell D5, type 'Income category'. Now highlight cells D5 to G5 and click on the shading icon, in the font group on the ribbon. Select what you feel is a suitable colour for this heading. I have chosen yellow. Now click on the merge and centre icon at the bottom-right of the alignment group on the ribbon.

Now we are going to head the VAT columns in the same way. Type 'VAT relevant columns' in cell H5. Apply a shade and merge and centre the title in the same way as before, this time highlighting cells H5 to J5 and using a different colour, perhaps a light shade of blue.

Next, we are going to head the net income analysis columns. In cell K5, type 'Cr. – income analysis columns'. Now, shade, merge and centre the title across cells K5 to X5 in the same way as before, this time using a different colour, perhaps light green.

The next twenty-four steps refer to what to type in various cells:

Cell reference		What to type in
A	6	Date
B	6	Particulars
C	6	Doc no.
D	6	Cash received
E	6	Bank lodgements
F	6	Cheques received
G	6	Credit income
H	6	VAT on sales
I	6	Net sales in UK or non-EU countries
J	6	Net sales in EU countries other than UK
K	6	Sales turnover
L	6	Other income
M	6	Cash withdrawals
N	6	Cash deposited in the bank
O	6	Cheques deposited in the bank
P	6	Payments received from trade debtors
Q	6	Capital investments
R	6	Security deposits and reserves
S	6	VAT refunds
T	6	PAYE and NI refunds
U	6	Other current liabilities
V	6	Loans to the business
W	6	Income from sale of fixed assets
X	6	Suspense account

You will have noticed how continuous stationery used in computer printers has horizontal stripes. This is to make it easier to track along particular lines. Otherwise it is difficult to do so when there are many lines of data on a page. For the same reason, it would be a good idea to shade alternate rows in this spreadsheet to make it easier to read. To do this, place the cursor in cell A7, hold down the shift key and click on cell X50. This will highlight the whole area. Now click on the fill colour icon in the font group on the ribbon and select what you feel is a suitable colour. I have used 'Blue accent 1'. To make the striped effect, hold down the control key and click on all the even row numbers from 8 to 50, then click on the fill colour icon again but this time select the no fill option.

Click on the number 6 at the beginning of that row. This will highlight the whole row of titles. Now click on the format option in the cells group, towards the right of the ribbon, and choose 'Format cells' from the menu. A dialogue box will appear in which you must click on the 'Alignment' tab and then tick the box labelled 'Wrap text'. This will give the row sufficient height to show all the column titles in full. You may still need to make slight adjustments if some of the words in the titles have too many characters for the lines. If you have to do this, simply place the curser on the column border at the top of the sheet and wait for a symbol that looks like a cross with arrowheads pointing horizontally outwards. When this appears click the left mouse button and drag the border to allow for the displaced letters to rejoin the words to which they belong.

Click into cell B7 and Type 'TOTALS', then embolden it by clicking on the bold icon in the fonts group on the left-hand side of the ribbon.

Place the cursor in cell D7 to highlight it. Click on the sigma icon in the editing group at the right of the ribbon. Change the cell references in the formula to D8:D100 and press enter.

Place the cursor in cell D7, right-click the mouse, select the copy option and then left-click. Place the cursor in cell E7, hold down the shift key and place the cursor in cell X7, then right-click, select the paste option and left-click to complete the installation in the whole row.

The next thing is to install a formula in cell F1, which will sum the totals in cells D7 to G7. That formula is '=SUM(D7:G7)' and the quickest way of doing this is simply to place the cursor in cell D7, left-click on the sigma icon in the editing group at the right of the ribbon, left-click with the cursor in cell D7, hold down the shift key, click into cell G7 and finally press the enter key on your keypad to complete the installation.

Next, we need to insert a formula in cell C1 that will add together the values in cell H7 and all the cells from K7 to W7. You will be aware that cells I7 and J7 have been missed out. This is because they are not part of the double entry system. Place the cursor in cell G1 and left-click, then left-click on the sigma icon in the editing group to the right of the ribbon. Next, left-click with the cursor in cell H7, hold down the control key and left-click in cell K7. Hold down the shift key and left-click in cell W7. Finally, press the return key on your keypad to complete the installation.

Shade cell G2 in a different colour to the other cells to make it stand out, as it is this cell that will alert you immediately to errors made in the recording process. I have chosen a dark pink colour from the colour palettes. I have already explained how to shade cells; if you are unsure then reread the previous instructions in Chapter 54.

We now need to insert the formula in this cell that will alert us immediately to a double entry error in the recording. Place the cursor in cell G2 and type '= s'. The moment you get this far, a functions menu will appear. Select the sign option and double-click with the left mouse button. Now left-click on cell G1, type in a minus sign, left-click on cell F1 and finally press enter on your keyboard to complete the installation.

Now we have to set the decimal place formatting. Highlight the column headings: D7 to X7. Left-click on the down arrow at the right of the number group on the ribbon, left-click on the number option in the category pane of the dialogue box that appears and set the number of decimal places to 2. Left-click on the separate tickbox to ensure that thousands are separated with commas in the data you enter and, finally, left-click the 'OK' box or press the return key on your keyboard, both of which serve the same purpose.

In order to be extra sure that inappropriate numbers are not placed in the column numbers boxes, highlight this row in the usual way by left-clicking on the number 4, at the left of the screen. Left-click on the down arrow again in the number group on the ribbon, left-click on the number option in the category pane and, this time, set the number of decimal places to zero. Finally, press the return key or left-click on the 'OK' button.

Preparing the incomings analysis sheet for the other three quarters of the year

This is a pretty simple process. We can just duplicate the first one and make a few changes. Here is how to go about it.

Right-click on the sheetname tag '3IncmsQ1'. Left-click on the move or copy option on the menu that appears. Left-click on the move to end option on the menu that appears next, select the box labelled 'Create a copy' and then click on the 'OK' button (or press the return key on your keyboard).

Rename the filename tag of the duplicated file: '5incmsQ2'. The reason we do not give it the number 4 is that the number is reserved for the outgoings analysis sheet for Q1.

Now repeat the process twice in order to produce incomings analysis sheets for Q3 and Q4, naming them '7IncmsQ3' and '9IncmsQ4' respectively.

All you have to do now is open each of the duplicated sheets in turn and replace 1st with 2nd, 3rd and 4th respectively in cell A1 of the second, third and fourth duplicated incomings analysis sheets. You can superscript the 'st', 'nd', 'rd' and 'th' by highlighting these parts, left-clicking on the down arrow in the font group on the ribbon, left-clicking the superscript box and then left-clicking the 'OK' button.

Outgoings analysis — Total credit 1000 — 1000 Total debit

Dr/Cr Error 0

1st Quarter

Date	Particulars/Doc No.	1	2	3	4	5	6	7	8	9	10	11	12	13	14
		Outgoings category					VAT relevant columns				Cr.				
Date	Particulars/Doc No.	Cash paym	Bank payment	Payments fr	Payment i	Purchases	VAT on purchases	VAT exempted	Net purchases from UK or non-EU	Net purchases from the EU, but non UK	Purchases	Other direct costs	Wages, salaries and other employment costs	Rent costs	Repairs and renewals
	TOTALS	0	1000	0	0	0	0	0	0	0	0	0	0	0	1000
2013															
Feb-22	Brewer Roof rep		1000												1000

Date	Particulars/Doc No.	15	16	17	18	19	20	21	22	23	24	25	26	27	28	29	30	31	32	33	34	35	36	37
		Cr.																						
Date	Particulars/Doc No.	Administration expenses	Travelling expenses	Advertising and promotion	Professional fees and charges	Bad debt	Bank charges	Depreciation costs	Other allowable expenses	Non-allowable expenses	Fixed asset disposals	Fixed assets purchased	Cumulative depreciation	Adjustments to stock	Trade debts written off	Other current assets purchased	Payments are trade creditors	Payments to HMRC in respect of VAT	PAYE and NI paid and accrued	Repayments on credit card	Other current liabilities	Loan repayment, including interest	Drawings	Suspense account
	TOTALS	0	0	0	0	0	0	0	0	0	0	0	0	0	0	0	0	0	0	0	0	0	0	0
2013																								
Feb-22	Brewer Roof rep																							

Figure 33 Example of an outgoings analysis sheet

The outgoing analysis sheet is for recording all outgoings of the business. This includes cash and bank payments. It also includes purchases on credit, since the moment we make such purchases, the assets of the business are reduced by the amount that will inevitably have to be paid for them.

Again, the analysis is done on a quarterly basis.

As with the incomings analysis sheet, there is more detail to record than can be seen easily all at once on a standard-size computer screen. Therefore, we need to split the sheet up. In this case, we split it into five parts.

The way the sheet is divided is the same as for the incoming sheet. The first three columns are for the date, particulars and document number.

The next five columns (columns D to H) analyse the categories of outgoings, for example, payments by cash, cheque banking, electronic banking, purchases on credit and all purchases made by the proprietor out of their own personal funds. The latter column can be renamed 'Directors loan a/c' if the business is a limited company and this change should be made all the way through to accommodate this type of transaction.

Then we have four columns (columns I to L) for information necessary for VAT accounting. They only need to be completed if the business is registered for VAT. The rest of the columns are analysis columns such as are found in the daybooks of a manual accounting system (see *Mastering Book-keeping*, ninth edition, for a full treatment of this subject).

In column 5, we record the VAT content of the outgoings. Column 6 is for recording the unpaid VAT on a purchase from a supplier outside of the UK, but in the EU. Although such purchases are exempt from VAT, the unpaid VAT content must nevertheless be recorded. Column H is for recording the net amount of a purchase transaction with a supplier based in the UK or a non-EU country. Column I is for recording the net amount of a purchase transaction with a EU country outside of the UK.

The analysis columns

Now we turn to the analysis columns. These are for recording the net figures of all transactions. Consequently, where the transactions are purchases, the VAT content will be excluded. Other transactions – for example, bank payments – will not involve VAT content in the first place. They may be payments for purchases, but the VAT on them will have been dealt with when the purchase on credit was recorded; if we record it again when the goods are paid for, we will be recording it twice.

Column 10 is headed 'Purchases', and this column will contain the net amounts for every purchase transaction. We need this to provide the total purchases figure for the nominal ledger and, in turn, the profit and loss account.

Column 11 is for non trading outgoings. These will include such items as carriage, postage and packing, discounts allowed, direct labour, commissions and any other expenditure that must be reflected in the trading account.

Column 12 is for recording employee wages and salaries, and any other costs directly related to the employment of staff.

Column 13 is for recording rent costs incurred by the business.

Column 14 is for recording the costs of repairs and renewals.

Column 15 is for recording administration expenses, e.g. postage, telephone, stationery, etc.

Column 16 is for the recording motor and travelling expenses.

Column 17 is for recording costs relating to advertising and promotion.

Column 18 is for recording professional fees and charges.

Column 19 is for recording bad debts written off. These are outgoings because they reduce the recorded assets of a business.

Column 20 is for recording bank charges.

Column 21 is for recording depreciation of fixed assets.

Column 22 is for recording any expenses, allowable against tax, that do not fall into the other categories.

Column 23 is for recording any expenses that are not allowable against tax, e.g. expenses which cannot be proved because the documentation has been lost.

Column 24 is for recording the net book value of fixed assets that have been disposed of. These are outgoings because they reduce the total assets of the business.

Column 25 is for recording the values of fixed assets purchased in the current year.

Column 26 is for recording new material depreciation on fixed assets.

Column 27 is for recording adjustments to stock values, e.g. opening and closing stock.

Column 28 is for recording trade debts written off. You will have noticed this has also been mentioned for an earlier analysis column. That column recorded the expense of the write-offs. This one deals with the reduction in asset values. Figures are therefore entered here as minus figures. This will also be the case for entries in columns 24 and 26.

Column 29 is for recording prepayments and deposits paid.

Column 30 is for recording payments to trade creditors.

Column 31 is for recording payments to HMRC for net VAT collected.

Column 32 is for recording payments to HMRC in respect of PAYE (Pay As You Earn) and NI (National Insurance).

Column 33 is for recording repayments of credit card expenditure.

Column 34 is for recording repayments of a loan, including interest.

Column 35 is for recording proprietors drawings.

Column 36 is the suspense, wherein we record items if we are temporarily unsure of the correct category.

Formatting the sheet

Here's how we go about formatting the sheet.

Click on the 'Insert new worksheet' icon at the bottom of the spreadsheet. This will highlight the sheetname tag and open the new sheet. Rename it '4OutgngsQ1' (standing for sheet 4, Outgoings, first-quarter of the year).

Type the following texts in the cells indicated below:

Cell reference		What to type in
B	1	Outgoings analysis
F	1	Total credit
I	1	Total debit
G	2	DrCr error
B	5	1st Quarter

Now centre each of these in their respective cells by placing the curser in each cell in turn and clicking on the centre align icon in the paragraph group on the ribbon.

Now we're going to number all the columns that affect the accounts. To start with, type the figure 1 in cell D4 and the figure 2 in cell E4. Centre both entries by highlighting them and clicking on the centre align icon in the paragraph group on the ribbon while both cells are highlighted. When the cursor is on the bottom right-hand corner of the pair of highlighted cells, a small + sign will appear. Left-click and hold the button down, while you drag your cursor along to column the final column you require. This is a quick way of consecutively numbering all the analysis columns.

In cell D5, type 'Outgoings category'. Now highlight cells D5 to H5 and click on the shading icon in the font group on the ribbon. Select what you feel is a suitable colour for this heading. I have chosen yellow. Now click on the merge and centre icon at the bottom-right of the alignment group on the ribbon. Now click on the borders icon, fourth from the left in the font group on the ribbon. Select the outside borders option and press return on your keypad.

Now we are going to head the VAT-relevant columns in the same way. Type 'VAT relevant columns' in cell I5. Merge and centre the title in the same way as before, this time highlighting cells H5 to L5 and applying a different fill colour, perhaps a light shade of blue. Insert borders, as before, by selecting the outside borders option from the borders menu, which is accessed by clicking on the borders icon in the fonts group on the ribbon.

Next, we are going to head the net outgoings analysis columns. In cell M5, type 'Cr. – Outgoings analysis columns'. Now, shade, merge and centre the title across cells M5 to AN5 in the same way as before, this time using a different colour, perhaps, light green.

The next twenty-four steps refer to what to type in various cells:

Cell reference	What to type in	
A	6	Date
B	6	Particulars
C	6	Doc no.
D	6	Cash payments
E	6	Bank payments
F	6	Payments from proprietors personal funds
G	6	Payment by credit card
H	6	Purchases on credit
I	6	VAT on purchases
J	6	VAT exempted
K	6	Net purchases from UK or non-EU
L	6	Net purchases from the EU, but non-UK
M	6	Purchases
N	6	Other direct costs
O	6	Wages, salaries and other employment costs
P	6	Rent costs
Q	6	Repairs and renewals
R	6	Administration expenses
S	6	Travelling expenses
T	6	Advertising and promotion
U	6	Professional fees and charges
V	6	Bad debts
W	6	Bank charges
X	6	Depreciation costs
Y	6	Other allowable expenses
Z	6	Non-allowable expenses
AA	6	Fixed asset disposals
AB	6	Fixed assets purchased
AC	6	Cumulative depreciation
AD	6	Adjustments to stock
AE	6	Trade debts written off
AF	6	Other current assets purchased
AG	6	Payments are trade creditors
AH	6	Payments to HMRC in respect of VAT
AI	6	PAYE and NI paid and accrued
AJ	6	Repayments on credit card
AK	6	Other current liabilities
AL	6	Loan repayment, including interest
AM	6	Drawings
AN	6	Suspense account

The titles you have inserted in the aforementioned forty cells are wider than the standard cells can accommodate. In order to make the full titles visible, we must now make the following adjustment. Click on the row number at the far left of row 6 to highlight the whole row. Next, click on the format option in the cells group on the ribbon. Select the format cells option from the menu that will appear. Click on the alignment tab, tick the wrap text tickbox and press the return key on your keyboard. The full titles will now be visible in all columns. You may still need to make slight adjustments if some of the words in the titles have too many characters for the lines. If you have to do this simply place the curser on the column border at the top of the sheet and wait for a symbol that looks like a cross with arrowheads pointing horizontally outwards. When this appears click the left mouse button and drag the border over to allow for the displaced letters to rejoin the words to which they belong.

In cell B7, type 'TOTALS'. Embolden and centre it.

For ease of reading it would be a good idea to shade alternate rows in exactly the same way as was suggested in respect of the incomings analysis sheet (see Chapter 54 Incomings analysis sheet).

Now we start entering formulae. In cell D7, insert the formula '=SUM(D8:D50)'. The quick way to do this is by clicking into cell D7, clicking on the sigma icon in the editing group on the ribbon, then clicking on cell D8, inserting a colon, clicking on cell D50 and, finally, pressing the return key on your keyboard. The D50 limitation is arbitrary. You do not need to use this specific cell number; the cell range you use will depend on how many transactions you assume you are going to need to enter in the quarter. For example, if there is no likelihood that the number of transactions is going to exceed thirty, then use D30, while, on the other hand, if you expect to make as many as 100 transactions in the quarter, then you may need to use cell D100 in this process.

Next, you need to copy this formula into all cells to the right on that row. To do this, place the cursor in cell D7, right-click the mouse, select the copy option and then left-click. Place the cursor in cell E7, hold down the shift key and place the cursor in cell AN7, then right-click, select the paste option and left-click to complete the installation in the whole row.

The next thing is to install a formula in cell G1, which will sum the totals in cells D7 to H7. That formula is '=SUM(D7:H7)' and the quickest way of doing this is simply to place the cursor in cell G1, left-click on the sigma icon in the editing group at the right of the ribbon, left-click with the cursor in cell D7, hold down the shift key, left-click with the cursor in cell H7 and, finally, press the enter key on your keypad to complete the installation.

Next, we need to insert a formula in cell H1 that will add together the values in cell I7 and all the cells from M7 to AN7. You will be aware that cells J7 to L7 have been missed out. This is because they are not part of the double entry system. Place the cursor in cell H1 and left-click, then left-click on the sigma icon in the editing group to the right of the ribbon. Next, left-click with the cursor in cell I7, hold down the control key and left-click in cell M7. Hold down the shift key and left-click in cell AN7. Finally, press the return key on your keypad to complete the installation.

Shade cell G2 in a different colour to other cells to make it stand out, as it is this cell that will alert you immediately to errors made in the recording process, and you want to be alerted to this as early as possible. I have chosen a dark pink colour from the colour palettes. I have already explained how to shade cells; if you are unsure then reread the previous instructions in Chapter 54.

We now need to insert the formula in this cell that will alert us immediately to a double entry error in the recording. Place the cursor in cell H2 and type '=G1-H1'.

Highlight the column headings: D7 to AN7. Left-click on the down arrow to the right of the number group on the ribbon, left-click on the number option in the category pane of the dialogue box that appears and set the number of decimal places to 2. Left-click on the 'Separate' tickbox to ensure that thousands are separated with commas in the data you enter and, finally, left-click the 'OK' box or press the return key on your keyboard, both of which serve the same purpose.

In order to be extra sure that inappropriate numbers are not placed in the column numbers boxes, highlight this row in the usual way by left-clicking on the number 4 at the left of the screen. Left-click on the down arrow again in the number group on the ribbon, left-click on the number option in the category pane and, this time, set the number of decimal places to zero. Finally, press the return key or left-click on the 'OK' button.

Preparing the outgoings analysis sheet for the other three quarters of the year

Preparing the outgoings analysis sheets for the remaining three quarters of the year is a pretty simple process. We can just duplicate the first one and make a few changes. Here is how to go about it.

Right-click on the sheetname tag '4OutgngsQ1'. Left-click on the move or copy option on the menu that appears. Left-click on the move to end option on the menu that appears next, choose the box labelled 'Create a copy' and then click on the 'OK' button (or press the return key on your keyboard).

Rename the filename tag of the duplicated file: '6OutgngsQ2'. The reason we do not give it the number 5 is that that the odd numbers are reserved for the incomings analysis sheets.

Now repeat the process twice in order to produce outgoings analysis sheets for Q3 and Q4, naming them '8IncmsQ3' and '10InmcsQ4' respectively.

Move the sheetname tags as appropriate to make them appear consecutively numbered at the bottom of the workbook. You can do this by simply clicking on a sheetname tag, holding the button down and dragging it into the required position.

All you have to do now is open each of the duplicated sheets in turn and replace 1st with 2nd, 3rd and 4th, respectively in cell A1 of the second third and fourth of the duplicated outgoings analysis sheets. You can superscript the 'st', 'nd', rd and 'th' by highlighting these parts, left-clicking on the down arrow in the font group on the ribbon, left-clicking the superscript box and then left-clicking the 'OK' button.

Incomings summary

#		Q1 Dr.	Q1 Cr.	Q2 Dr.	Q2 Cr.	Q3 Dr.	Q3 Cr.	Q4 Dr.	Q4 Cr.	Annual Dr.	Annual Cr.
		Category	Class	Category	Class	Category	Class	Category	Class	Category	Class
	TOTALS	3000	3000	2000	2000	5000	5000	750	750	10750	#REF
	DIFFERENCE	0		0		0		0		#REF!	
1	Cash received	0		0		0		0		0	
2	Bank lodgements	3000		2000		0		750		5750	
3	Cheques received	0		0		5000		0		5000	
4	Credit income	0		0		0		0		0	
5	VAT on sales	0	0	0		0		0			0
6	Net sales in UK, or non-EU countries		0	0		0		0			0
7	Net sales in EU countries other than UK	0	0	0		0		0			0
8	Sales turnover		1200		2000		0		750		#REF!
9	Other income		800		0		5000		0		#REF!
10	Cash withdrawals		0		0		0		0		#REF!
11	Cash deposited in the bank		0		0		0		0		#REF!
12	Cheques deposited in the bank		0		0		0		0		#REF!
13	Payments received from trade debtors		1000		0		0		0		#REF!
14	Capital investments		0		0		0		0		#REF!
15	Security deposits and reserves		0		0		0		0		#REF!
16	VAT refunds		0		0		0		0		#REF!
17	PAYE and NI refunds		0		0		0		0		#REF!
18	Other current liabilities		0		0		0		0		#REF!
19	Loans to the business		0		0		0		0		#REF!
20	Income from sale of fixed assets		0		0		0		0		#REF!
21	Suspense account		0		0		0		0		#REF!

Figure 34 Example of an incomings summary

The summary of all incomings analyses the categories vertically and the different quarters horizontally. This is so that the summary can be seen at a glance on a single page. We do not need to make direct entries on to the sheet as the data arrives automatically by way of links from the quarterly incomings analysis sheets as long as we put the appropriate formulae in the right places.

The annual figures are computed automatically in this sheet by way of formulae and links between themselves relevant cells.

This is how to go about formatting, the incoming summary:

Click on the 'Insert new worksheet' icon at the bottom of the workbook and rename it '11IncmsSmry'.

Type the following in the cells indicated:

Cell reference		What to type in
B	1	Incomings summary
B	9	Totals
B	10	Difference
A	11	1
A	12	2

Embolden and underline the first three of these entries, using the bold and underline icons in the fonts group on the ribbon.

Highlight cells A11 and A12, point the cursor at the bottom right-hand corner and when the + appears hold down the left mouse button and drag the cursor to cell B21. This consecutively numbers all of those cells in a fraction of the time it would take you to number each one individually.

Open sheet '9IncmsQ4' by clicking on the relevant sheetname tag at the foot of the workbook.

Highlight cells D6 to X6, right-click and select copy, then left-click. Return to sheet '11Incms3Smry', click on the cell C11. Now click on the downward facing arrow below the paste icon at the far left of the ribbon and then select the transpose option; it is the icon on the right in the second row of the palette. This will reproduce the range of column headings in the quarterly analysis sheets as row headings in the summary sheet.

Now we need to head the four quarterly summaries. Therefore, type the following in the cells indicated:

Cell reference		What to type in
C	4	Q1
F	4	Q2
I	4	Q3
L	4	Q4
O	4	Annual

As these are titles of the different sections, we need to make them stand out. Therefore, for each of these cells in turn, highlight the cell, together with its right adjacent cell, click on the bold icon, then on the borders icon, selecting the outside borders option from the menu that will appear and then click on the merge and centre icon in the alignment group on the ribbon.

We need some space between the different quarterly panes in order to clearly separate them, but it doesn't have to be much, and we don't have that much width to play with if we want to see all the pains on a single screen. Therefore, the next thing to do is to click on the tops of columns E, H, K and N, holding down the control key as we do so, so that the process does not also highlight those columns in between. Then click on the format option in the cells group on the right of the ribbon, select 'Column width' on the menu that will appear and change the width value to 1 pixel.

In cell C5, type 'Category'. Highlight this and embolden it, by clicking on the bold icon on the ribbon. Now copy and paste this into cells F5, I5, L5 and O5.

In cell, D5, type, 'Incomings classification'.

Now highlight D5, click on the borders icon in the fonts group on the ribbon, and press the return key on your keyboard. Now copy and paste this into cells G5, J5, M5 and P5, in the same way as you performed the previous operation in row 5.

Next, to designate the debit and credit columns in each pane, type 'Dr.' and 'Cr.' in cells C8 and D8 respectively. Embolden these entries, in the usual way, to show they are titles. Copy and paste these into cells, F8, I8, L8 and O8.

Now we come to the formulae stage. The first formula we need to enter is in cell C9 to sum the values in cells C11 to C14. The formula is '=SUM(C11:C14)' but, hopefully you will remember that there is a quicker way to enter this formula than typing it out. You just click the cursor into cell C9, click on the sigma icon on the right of the ribbon, click the cursor into cell C11, hold down the shift key, click the cursor into cell C14 and then press the return key on your keyboard. Click on the borders icon in the fonts group on the ribbon and select the outside borders option.

Now, copy and paste the formula into cells F9, I9, L9 and O9. The cell references will be changed automatically as appropriate.

Now, we need a formula in cell D9 to sum all of the analysis columns. That formula is '=SUM(D15,D18:D31)'. By now, you will hardly need me to remind you that all you have to do for this is to place the cursor in cell D9, click on the sigma icon, click the cursor into cell D15, then (and only then) hold down the control key and click the cursor into cell D18. Let go of the control key, hold down the shift key, click the cursor into cell D31 and then press the return key.

Now, paste it into cells G9, J9, M9 and P9. Again, the cell references will be changed automatically as appropriate.

Now we have to insert the formula that will alert us to any error in the double entry accounting. Therefore, in cell C10, type '=C9-D9'. As we want to be alerted to any error as soon as it occurs, it would be a good idea to make this cell very noticeable. Therefore, highlight it and place a border around it by clicking on the borders icon in the fonts group on the ribbon, and then click on the fill icon, in the same group, and select what you feel is a suitable colour.

Now, to make the different columns easily distinguishable from each other, it would be a good idea to highlight cells B11 to B31 and place a border around them by clicking on the borders icon in the fonts group on the ribbon, and selecting the outside borders option on the menu that will appear. Do the same with cells C11 to D31, F11 to G31, I11 to J31, L11 to M31 and O11 to P31.

You may wish treat the surface of these sheets in the same way as suggested for the quarterly analysis sheets to make them easier to read. Alternately shaded rows make it easier for a reader to track along particular lines when there are many lines of data on a page. To do this, place the cursor in cell A11, hold down the shift key and click on cell X31. This will highlight the whole area. Now click on the fill colour icon in the font group on the ribbon and select what you feel is a suitable colour. I will use 'blue accent 1'. To make the striped effect, hold down the control key and click on all the even row numbers from 12 to 30, then click on the fill colour icon again but, this time, select the no fill option.

Linking the sheets

Now we come to linking up the quarterly sheets with the annual summary sheet.

All you have to do here is click into each destination cell in the annual summary sheet, type '=' and then open the source sheet, click into the source cell and press enter on your keyboard.

Therefore, make the following links in the manner described:

Click into cell	Type	Open source sheet	Click into cell	Press on your keyboard
C11	=	3IncmsQ1	D7	Return key
C12	=	3IncmsQ1	E7	Return key
C13	=	3IncmsQ1	F7	Return key
C14	=	3IncmsQ1	G7	Return key
D15	=	3IncmsQ1	H7	Return key
D16	=	3IncmsQ1	I7	Return key
D17	=	3IncmsQ1	J7	Return key
D18	=	3IncmsQ1	K7	Return key
D19	=	3IncmsQ1	L7	Return key
D20	=	3IncmsQ1	M7	Return key
D21	=	3IncmsQ1	N7	Return key
D22	=	3IncmsQ1	O7	Return key
D23	=	3IncmsQ1	P7	Return key
D24	=	3IncmsQ1	Q7	Return key
D25	=	3IncmsQ1	R7	Return key
D26	=	3IncmsQ1	S7	Return key

Click into cell	Type	Open source sheet	Click into cell	Press on your keyboard
D27	=	3IncmsQ1	T7	Return key
D28	=	3IncmsQ1	U7	Return key
D29	=	3IncmsQ1	V7	Return key
D30	=	3IncmsQ1	W7	Return key
D31	=	3IncmsQ1	X7	Return key
F11	=	5IncmsQ2	D7	Return key
F12	=	5IncmsQ2	E7	Return key
F13	=	5IncmsQ2	F7	Return key
F14	=	5IncmsQ2	G7	Return key
G15	=	5IncmsQ2	H7	Return key
G16	=	5IncmsQ2	I7	Return key
G17	=	5IncmsQ2	J7	Return key
G18	=	5IncmsQ2	K7	Return key
G19	=	5IncmsQ2	L7	Return key
G20	=	5IncmsQ2	M7	Return key
G21	=	5IncmsQ2	N7	Return key
G22	=	5IncmsQ2	O7	Return key
G23	=	5IncmsQ2	P7	Return key
G24	=	5IncmsQ2	Q7	Return key
G25	=	5IncmsQ2	R7	Return key
G26	=	5IncmsQ2	S7	Return key
G27	=	5IncmsQ2	T7	Return key
G28	=	5IncmsQ2	U7	Return key
G29	=	5IncmsQ2	V7	Return key
G30	=	5IncmsQ2	W7	Return key
G31	=	5IncmsQ2	X7	Return key
I11	=	7IncmsQ3	D7	Return key
I12	=	7IncmsQ3	E7	Return key
I13	=	7IncmsQ3	F7	Return key
I14	=	7IncmsQ3	G7	Return key
J15	=	7IncmsQ3	H7	Return key
J16	=	7IncmsQ3	I7	Return key
J17	=	7IncmsQ3	J7	Return key
J18	=	7IncmsQ3	K7	Return key
J19	=	7IncmsQ3	L7	Return key

Click into cell	Type	Open source sheet	Click into cell	Press on your keyboard
J20	=	7IncmsQ3	M7	Return key
J21	=	7IncmsQ3	N7	Return key
J22	=	7IncmsQ3	O7	Return key
J23	=	7IncmsQ3	P7	Return key
J24	=	7IncmsQ3	Q7	Return key
J25	=	7IncmsQ3	R7	Return key
J26	=	7IncmsQ3	S7	Return key
J27	=	7IncmsQ3	T7	Return key
J28	=	7IncmsQ3	U7	Return key
J29	=	7IncmsQ3	V7	Return key
J30	=	7IncmsQ3	W7	Return key
J31	=	7IncmsQ3	X7	Return key
L11	=	9IncmsQ4	D7	Return key
L12	=	9IncmsQ4	E7	Return key
L13	=	9IncmsQ4	F7	Return key
L14	=	9IncmsQ4	G7	Return key
M15	=	9IncmsQ4	H7	Return key
M16	=	9IncmsQ4	I7	Return key
M17	=	9IncmsQ4	J7	Return key
M18	=	9IncmsQ4	K7	Return key
M19	=	9IncmsQ4	L7	Return key
M20	=	9IncmsQ4	M7	Return key
M21	=	9IncmsQ4	N7	Return key
M22	=	9IncmsQ4	O7	Return key
M23	=	9IncmsQ4	P7	Return key
M24	=	9IncmsQ4	Q7	Return key
M25	=	9IncmsQ4	R7	Return key
M26	=	9IncmsQ4	S7	Return key
M27	=	9IncmsQ4	T7	Return key
M28	=	9IncmsQ4	U7	Return key
M29	=	9IncmsQ4	V7	Return key
M30	=	9IncmsQ4	W7	Return key
M31	=	9IncmsQ4	X7	Return key

The above operations will put all the quarterly totals on the same screen. Now we have to insert formulae to sum the quarterly totals to arrive at a single annual figure for each category. Here's how to do it:

To begin with, we'll insert a formula into cell O11 to sum the four quarterly totals of cash received. Do this by clicking into cell O11, then clicking on the sigma icon on the right of the ribbon, then, with the control key held down, clicking into each of cells C11, F11, I11 and L11 in turn and finally pressing the return key on your keypad.

Now copy and paste the contents of cell O11 into cells O12, O13 and O14 to sum the rest of the different forms in which income may have been received.

Next, we have to deal with the VAT figures. Insert a formula to sum cells D15, G15, J15 and M15. The formula is '=SUM(D15,G15,J15,M15)', so click into cell P15, click on the sigma icon, hold down the control key and click into the cells you are going to add together, and then press the return key on your keyboard.

Now copy and paste the contents of cell P15 into all the cells from P16 to P31 so that all the other quarterly totals will also be summed and presented on the annual summary.

	Outgoings Classification		Outgoings Classification		Outgoings Classification		Outgoings Classification		Outgoings Classification	
Incomings summary	Dr.	Cr.	Dr.	Cr.	Dr.	Cr.	Dr.	Cr.	Dr.	Cr.
TOTALS	1000	1000	100	100	600	600	2000	2000	3700	3700
DIFFERENCE	0		0		0		0		0	
Cash payments	0		40		0		0		40	0
Bank payments	1000		60		600		2000		3660	
Payments from proprietors personal funds	0		0		0		0		0	
Payment by credit card	0		0		0		0		0	
Purchases on credit	0		0		0		0		0	
VAT on purchases		0		0		0		0		0
VAT exempted		0		0		0		0		0
Net purchases from UK or non-EU		0		0		0		0		0
Net purchases from the EU, but non-UK		0		0		0		0		0
Purchases		0		60		0		0		60
Other direct costs		0		0		0		0		0
Wages, salaries and other employment costs		0		0		0		0		0
Rent costs		0		0		0		0		0
Repairs and renewals		1000		40		600		0		1640
Administration expenses		0		0		0		0		0
Travelling expenses		0		0		0		0		0
Advertising and promotion		0		0		0		2000		2000
Professional fees and charges		0		0		0		0		0
Bad debts		0		0		0		0		0
Bank charges		0		0		0		0		0
Depreciation costs		0		0		0		0		0
Other allowable expenses		0		0		0		0		0
Non-allowable expenses		0		0		0		0		0
Fixed asset disposals		0		0		0		0		0
Fixed assets purchased		0		0		0		0		0
Cumulative depreciation		0		0		0		0		0
Adjustments to stock		0		0		0		0		0
Trade debts written off		0		0		0		0		0
Other current assets purchased		0		0		0		0		0
Payments are trade creditors		0		0		0		0		0
Payments to HMRC in respect of VAT		0		0		0		0		0

Incomings summary	Outgoings Classification		Outgoings Classification		Outgoings Classification		Outgoings Classification		Outgoings Classification	
	Dr.	Cr.	Dr.	Cr.	Dr.	Cr.	Dr.	Cr.	Dr.	Cr.
PAYE and NI paid and accrued		0		0		0		0		0
Repayments on credit card		0		0		0		0		0
Other current liabilities		0		0		0		0		0
Loan repayment, including interest		0		0		0		0		0
Drawings		0		0		0		0		0
Suspense account		0		0		0		0		0

Figure 35 Example of an outgoings summary

The summary of outgoings analyses the categories vertically and the different quarters horizontally. This is so that all columns can all be seen at a glance on a single page. We do not need to make direct entries on to the summary sheet; the data arrives automatically by way of links from the quarterly outgoings analysis sheets, as long as we put the appropriate formulae in the right places.

The annual figures are computed automatically in this sheet by way of formulae and links between the relevant cells.

This is how to go about formatting the outgoings summary:

Click on the 'Insert new worksheet' icon at the bottom of the workbook and rename it '12OutgngsSmry'.

Type the following in the cells indicated:

Cell reference		What to type in
B	1	Outgoings summary
B	9	Totals
B	10	Difference
A	11	1
A	12	2

Embolden and underline the first three of these entries, using the bold and underline icons in the fonts group on the ribbon.

A quick way of doing the last four steps in two simple operations is simply to open sheet 11IncmsSmry, click into cell A1, hold down the shift key and drag the cursor down to cell B12 to highlight all the cells you want to copy, together with the blank cells between them as spacers. Next, return to sheet 12OutgngsSmry and paste into cell B1, then highlight cells B11 and B12, right-click, select the clear contents option and left-click.

Highlight cells A11 and A12, point the cursor at the bottom right-hand corner and when the + appears hold down the left mouse button and drag the cursor to cell B37. This consecutively numbers all of those cells in a fraction of the time it would take you to number each one individually.

Open sheet 10OutgngsQ4 by clicking on the relevant sheetname tag at the foot of the workbook.

Highlight cells D6 to AN6, right-click and select copy, then left-click. Return to sheet 12Incms3Smry and click on the cell C11. Now click on the downward facing arrow below the paste icon at the far left of the ribbon and then select the transpose option from the palate of options that are offered. It is the icon on the right in the second row. This will reproduce the range of column headings in the quarterly analysis sheets as row headings in the summary sheet.

Now we need to head the four quarterly summaries. Therefore, type the following in the cells indicated:

Cell reference		What to type in
C	4	Q1
F	4	Q2
I	4	Q3
L	4	Q4
O	4	Annual

As these are titles of the different panes, we need to make them stand out. Therefore, for each of these cells in turn, highlight the cell, together with its right adjacent cell, click on the bold icon, then on the borders icon, selecting the outside borders option from the menu that will appear and then click on the merge and centre icon in the alignment group on the ribbon.

Alternatively, you can just open sheet 11IncmsQ4, highlight cells C4 to P4, return to sheet 12OutgngsSmry and paste the material into cell C4 there. That way the headings, the emboldenings and borderings, and the merging and centring will all be done together in the process of copying the cells from one sheet to the other.

Although we need some space between the different quarterly panes, it doesn't have to be much and we don't have that much width to play with, if we want to see all the panes on a single screen. Therefore, the next thing to do is to click on the tops of columns E, H, K and N, holding down the control key so that the process does not also highlight those columns in between. Then click on the format option in the cells group on the right of the ribbon, select 'Column width' from the menu that will appear and change the width value to 1 pixel.

In cell C5, type 'Category'. Highlight this and embolden it by clicking on the bold icon on the ribbon. Now copy and paste this into cells F5, I5, L5 and O5.

In cell, D5, type 'Outgoings'.

In cell D6 type 'Classification'.

Now highlight D5 and D6, click on the borders icon in the fonts group on the ribbon, and select the outside borders option, then press the return key on your keyboard to complete the process. Adjust the column width to accommodate the width of the word 'classification' by clicking on the column edge at the top of the column and dragging the cursor sideways as much as necessary.

Now copy and paste the contents of these two cells into cells G5, J5, M5 and P5, in the same way as you performed the previous operation in row 5. Adjust the column widths, as necessary, just as you did in the previous operation.

Next, to designate the debit and credit columns in each pane, type 'Dr.' and 'Cr.' in cells C8 and D8 respectively. Embolden these entries, in the usual way, to show they are titles.

Copy and paste these into cells F8, I8, L8 and O8.

Now we come to the formulae stage. The first formula we need to enter is in cell C9 to sum the values in cells C11 to C15. The formula is '=SUM(C11:C15)', but you will remember that there is a quicker way to enter this formula than typing it out. You just click the cursor into cell C9, click on the sigma icon on the right of the ribbon, click the cursor into cell C11, hold down the shift key, click the cursor into cell C15 and then press the return key on your keyboard.

Click on the borders icon in the fonts group on the ribbon and select the 'Outside borders' option.

Now copy and paste it into cells F9, I9, L9 and O9. The cell references will be changed automatically as appropriate.

Now, we need a formula in cell D9 to sum all of the analysis columns. That formula is '=SUM(D16,D20:D47)'. You will hardly need me to remind you that all you have to do for this is to place the cursor in cell D9, click on the sigma icon, click the cursor into cell D15, then (and only then) hold down the control key and click the cursor into cell D18. Let go of the control key, hold down the shift key and click the cursor into cell D31, and then press the return key on your keypad. Place a border around this cell, as we did with cell C9.

Now, paste the formula into cells G9, J9, M9 and P9. Again, the cell references will be changed automatically as appropriate.

Now we have to insert the formula that will alert us to any error in the double entry accounting. Therefore, in cell C10, type '=C9-D9'. As we want to be alerted to any error immediately it occurs, it would be a good idea to make this cell very noticeable. Therefore, highlight it and place a border around it by clicking on the borders icon in the fonts group on the ribbon, and then click on the fill icon, in the same group, and select what you feel is a suitable colour.

Now, to make the different columns easily distinguishable from each other, it would be a good idea to highlight cells B11 to B31 and place a border around them by clicking on the borders icon in the fonts group on the ribbon, and selecting the outside borders option on the menu that will appear. Do the same with cells C11 to D31, F11 to G31, I11 to J31, L11 to M31 and O11 to P31.

You may wish treat the surface of these sheets in the same way as suggested for the quarterly analysis sheets to make them easier to read. Alternately shaded rows make it easier for a reader to track along particular lines when there are many lines of data on a page. To do this, place the cursor in cell A11, hold down the shift key and click on cell X31. This will highlight the whole area. Now click on the fill colour icon in the font group on the ribbon and select what you feel is a suitable colour. I will use 'blue accent 1'. To make the striped effect, hold down the control key and click on all the even row numbers from 12 to 30, then click on the fill colour icon again but, this time, select the no fill option.

Linking the sheets

Now we come to linking up the quarterly sheets with the annual summary sheet.

All you have to do here is click into each destination cell in the annual summary sheet, type '=' and then open the source sheet, click into the source cell and press enter on your keyboard.

Therefore, make the following links in the manner described:

Click into cell	Type	Open source sheet	Click into cell	Press on your keyboard
C11	=	4OutgngsQ1	D7	Return key
C12	=	4OutgngsQ1	E7	Return key
C13	=	4OutgngsQ1	F7	Return key
C14	=	4OutgngsQ11	G7	Return key
C15	=	4OutgngsQ1	H7	Return key
D16	=	4OutgngsQ1	I7	Return key
D17	=	4OutgngsQ1	J7	Return key
D18	=	4OutgngsQ1	K7	Return key
D19	=	4OutgngsQ1	L7	Return key
D20	=	4OutgngsQ1	M7	Return key
D21	=	4OutgngsQ1	N7	Return key
D22	=	4OutgngsQ1	O7	Return key
D23	=	4OutgngsQ1	P7	Return key
D24	=	4OutgngsQ1	Q7	Return key
D25	=	4OutgngsQ1	R7	Return key
D26	=	4OutgngsQ1	S7	Return key
D27	=	4OutgngsQ1	T7	Return key
D28	=	4OutgngsQ1	U7	Return key
D29	=	4OutgngsQ1	V7	Return key
D30	=	4OutgngsQ1	W7	Return key

Click into cell	Type	Open source sheet	Click into cell	Press on your keyboard
D31	=	4OutgngsQ1	X7	Return key
D32	=	4OutgngsQ1	Y7	Return key
D33	=	4OutgngsQ1	Z7	Return key
D34	=	4OutgngsQ1	AA7	Return key
D35	=	4OutgngsQ1	AB7	Return key
D36	=	4OutgngsQ1	AC7	Return key
D37	=	4OutgngsQ1	AD7	Return key
D38	=	4OutgngsQ1	AE7	Return key
D39	=	4OutgngsQ1	AF7	Return key
D40	=	4OutgngsQ1	AG7	Return key
D41	=	4OutgngsQ1	AH7	Return key
D42	=	4OutgngsQ1	AI7	Return key
D43	=	4OutgngsQ1	AJ7	Return key
D44	=	4OutgngsQ1	AK7	Return key
D45	=	4OutgngsQ1	AL7	Return key
D46	=	4OutgngsQ1	AM7	Return key
D47	=	4OutgngsQ1	AN7	Return key
F11	=	6OutgngsQ2	D7	Return key
F12	=	6OutgngsQ2	E7	Return key
F13	=	6OutgngsQ2	F7	Return key
F14	=	6OutgngsQ2	G7	Return key
F15	=	6OutgngsQ2	H7	Return key
G16	=	6OutgngsQ2	I7	Return key
G17	=	6OutgngsQ2	J7	Return key
G18	=	6OutgngsQ2	K7	Return key
G19	=	6OutgngsQ2	L7	Return key
G20	=	6OutgngsQ2	M7	Return key
G21	=	6OutgngsQ2	N7	Return key
G22	=	6OutgngsQ2	O7	Return key
G23	=	6OutgngsQ2	P7	Return key
G24	=	6OutgngsQ2	Q7	Return key
G25	=	6OutgngsQ2	R7	Return key
G26	=	6OutgngsQ2	S7	Return key
G27	=	6OutgngsQ2	T7	Return key
G28	=	6OutgngsQ2	U7	Return key

Click into cell	Type	Open source sheet	Click into cell	Press on your keyboard
G29	=	6OutgngsQ2	V7	Return key
G30	=	6OutgngsQ2	W7	Return key
G31	=	6OutgngsQ2	X7	Return key
G32	=	6OutgngsQ2	Y7	Return key
G33	=	6OutgngsQ2	Z7	Return key
G34	=	6OutgngsQ2	AA7	Return key
G35	=	6OutgngsQ2	AB7	Return key
G36	=	6OutgngsQ2	AC7	Return key
G37	=	6OutgngsQ2	AD7	Return key
G38	=	6OutgngsQ2	AE7	Return key
G39	=	6OutgngsQ2	AF7	Return key
G40	=	6OutgngsQ2	AG7	Return key
G41	=	6OutgngsQ2	AH7	Return key
G42	=	6OutgngsQ2	AI7	Return key
G43	=	6OutgngsQ2	AJ7	Return key
G44	=	6OutgngsQ2	AK7	Return key
G45	=	6OutgngsQ2	AL7	Return key
G46	=	6OutgngsQ2	AM7	Return key
G47	=	6OutgngsQ2	AN7	Return key
I11	=	8OutgngsQ3	D7	Return key
I12	=	8OutgngsQ3	E7	Return key
I13	=	8OutgngsQ3	F7	Return key
I14	=	8OutgngsQ3	G7	Return key
I15	=	8OutgngsQ3	H7	Return key
J16	=	8OutgngsQ3	I7	Return key
J17	=	8OutgngsQ3	J7	Return key
J18	=	8OutgngsQ3	K7	Return key
J19	=	8OutgngsQ3	L7	Return key
J20	=	8OutgngsQ3	M7	Return key
J21	=	8OutgngsQ3	N7	Return key
J22	=	8OutgngsQ3	O7	Return key
J23	=	8OutgngsQ3	P7	Return key
J24	=	8OutgngsQ3	Q7	Return key
J25	=	8OutgngsQ3	R7	Return key
J26	=	8OutgngsQ3	S7	Return key

Click into cell	Type	Open source sheet	Click into cell	Press on your keyboard
J27	=	8OutgngsQ3	T7	Return key
J28	=	8OutgngsQ3	U7	Return key
J29	=	8OutgngsQ3	V7	Return key
J30	=	8OutgngsQ3	W7	Return key
J31	=	8OutgngsQ3	X7	Return key
J32	=	8OutgngsQ3	Y7	Return key
J33	=	8OutgngsQ3	Z7	Return key
J34	=	8OutgngsQ3	AA7	Return key
J35	=	8OutgngsQ3	AB7	Return key
J36	=	8OutgngsQ3	AC7	Return key
J37	=	8OutgngsQ3	AD7	Return key
J38	=	8OutgngsQ3	AE7	Return key
J39	=	8OutgngsQ3	AF7	Return key
J40	=	8OutgngsQ3	AG7	Return key
J41	=	8OutgngsQ3	AH7	Return key
J42	=	8OutgngsQ3	AI7	Return key
J43	=	8OutgngsQ3	AJ7	Return key
J44	=	8OutgngsQ3	AK7	Return key
J45	=	8OutgngsQ3	AL7	Return key
J46	=	8OutgngsQ3	AM7	Return key
J47	=	8OutgngsQ3	AN7	Return key
L11	=	10OutgngsQ4	D7	Return key
L12	=	10OutgngsQ4	E7	Return key
L13	=	10OutgngsQ4	F7	Return key
L14	=	10OutgngsQ4	G7	Return key
L15	=	10OutgngsQ4	H7	Return key
M16	=	10OutgngsQ4	I7	Return key
M17	=	10OutgngsQ4	J7	Return key
M18	=	10OutgngsQ4	K7	Return key
M19	=	10OutgngsQ4	L7	Return key
M20	=	10OutgngsQ4	M7	Return key
M21	=	10OutgngsQ4	N7	Return key
M22	=	10OutgngsQ4	O7	Return key
M23	=	10OutgngsQ4	P7	Return key
M24	=	10OutgngsQ4	Q7	Return key

Click into cell	Type	Open source sheet	Click into cell	Press on your keyboard
M25	=	10OutgngsQ4	R7	Return key
M26	=	10OutgngsQ4	S7	Return key
M27	=	10OutgngsQ4	T7	Return key
M28	=	10OutgngsQ4	U7	Return key
M29	=	10OutgngsQ4	V7	Return key
M30	=	10OutgngsQ4	W7	Return key
M31	=	10OutgngsQ4	X7	Return key
M32	=	10OutgngsQ4	Y7	Return key
M33	=	10OutgngsQ4	Z7	Return key
M34	=	10OutgngsQ4	AA7	Return key
M35	=	10OutgngsQ4	AB7	Return key
M36	=	10OutgngsQ4	AC7	Return key
M37	=	10OutgngsQ4	AD7	Return key
M38	=	10OutgngsQ4	AE7	Return key
M39	=	10OutgngsQ4	AF7	Return key
M40	=	10OutgngsQ4	AG7	Return key
M41	=	10OutgngsQ4	AH7	Return key
M42	=	10OutgngsQ4	AI7	Return key
M43	=	10OutgngsQ4	AJ7	Return key
M44	=	10OutgngsQ4	AK7	Return key
M45	=	10OutgngsQ4	AL7	Return key
M46	=	10OutgngsQ4	AM7	Return key
M47	=	10OutgngsQ4	AN7	Return key

The above operations will put all the quarterly totals on the same screen. Now we have to insert formulae to sum the quarterly totals to arrive at a single annual figure for each category. Here's how to do it:

To begin with, we'll insert a formula into cell O11 to sum the four quarterly totals of types of payments made. Do this by clicking into cell O11, then clicking on the sigma icon on the right of the ribbon, then, with the control key held down, clicking into each of cells C11, F11, I11 and L11 in turn and finally pressing the return key.

Now copy and paste the contents of cell O11 into cells O12, O13 and O14 to sum the rest of the different forms in which payments have been made.

Next we have to deal with the VAT figures. Insert a formula to sum cells D15, G15, J15 and M15. The formula is '=SUM(D15,G15,J15,M15)', so click into cell

P15, click on the sigma icon, hold down the control key and click into the cells you are going to add together, and then press the return key on your keyboard.

Now copy and paste the contents of cell P15 into all the cells from P16 to P31, so that all the other quarterly totals will also be summed and presented on the annual summary.

VAT RETURN DETAILS

	Box	Q1	Q2	Q3	Q4	Annual
VAT due on all sales	1	0	0	0	0	0
VAT exempted on acquisitions from other EU states	2	0	0	0	0	0
Total VAT due	3	0	0	0	0	0
VAT reclaimed the purchases	4	0	0	0	0	0
VAT be paid (or reclaimed)	5	0	0	0	0	0
Total value of sales excluding VAT	6	0	0	0	0	0
Total value purchases and excluding	7					0
Total value of sales to the EU exclud	8	0	0	0	0	0
Total value of the EU purchases excl	9	0	0	0	0	0

Figure 36 Spreadsheet page for automatic compilation of VAT return details

With the right preparation of the workbook the VAT return details can be completed automatically. First we need to construct a replica of the standard VAT form. This is how we do it.

Click on the 'Insert new worksheet' icon at the foot of the spreadsheet and name it '13VAT'.

Give the sheet a title by clicking into cell B1 and typing 'VAT return details', embolden and underline the title, and then type the following details into the cells indicated.

Cell reference		What to type in
A	5	VAT due on all sales
A	7	VAT exempted on acquisitions from other EU states
A	10	Total VAT due
A	12	VAT reclaimed the purchases
A	14	VAT be paid (or reclaimed)
A	16	Total value of sales excluding VAT
A	18	Total value purchases and excluding VAT
A	20	Total value of sales to the EU excluding VAT
A	22	Total value of the EU purchases excluding VAT
B	5	1

B	8	2
B	10	3
B	12	4
B	14	5
B	16	6
B	18	7
B	20	8
B	22	9
B	4	Box
C	4	Q1
D	4	Q2
E	4	Q3
F	4	Q4
G	4	Annual

Embolden and centre align the last fifteen cells you have just filled, from cell B5 in the list onwards. Use the bold icon in the fonts group and the centre align icon in the paragraph group.

Now, to complete the replication of the VAT form, click on cell A5, hold down the left mouse button and drag sideways to cell G5 in order to highlight all the cells between. Insert a shade, similar to that found on the paper VAT form, and place a border around each of these cells by clicking on the borders icon in the fonts group on the ribbon, this time selecting the all borders option from the drop-down menu.

Repeat the last operation on cells A10 to G10, A12 to G12, A14 to G14, A16 to G16, A18 to G18, A20 to G20 and A22 to G22.

Now highlight cells A7 to A8, insert a shade in the same way as in the previous operation and place a border around them, this time selecting the outside borders option from the drop-down menu.

Repeat the latter operation on cells B7 to B8, C7 to C8, D7 to D8, E7 to E8, F7 to F8 and G7 to G8.

Now it's time to start entering some links. Make the following links in the manner described:

Click into cell	Type	Open source sheet	Click into cell	Press on your keyboard
C5	=	3IncmsQ1	H7	Return key
D5	=	5IncmsQ2	H7	Return key
E5	=	7IncmsQ3	H7	Return key
F5	=	9IncmsQ4	H7	Return key
C8	=	4OutgngsQ1	J7	Return key
D8	=	6OutgngsQ2	J7	Return key
E8	=	8OutgngsQ3	J7	Return key
F8	=	10OutgngsQ4	J7	Return key

Now it's time for some automatic calculations to compute the VAT due.

Click on to cell		Click on to	Click into cell	Hold down	Click into cell	Press	Formula that will be automatically inserted
C	10	Sigma icon	C5	Ctrl key	C8	Return key	=SUM(C5,C8)
D	10	Sigma icon	D5	Ctrl key	D8	Return key	=SUM(D5,D8)
E	10	Sigma icon	E5	Ctrl key	E8	Return key	=SUM(E5,E8)
F	10	Sigma icon	F5	Ctrl key	F8	Return key	=SUM(F5,F8)

The next bit, getting the purchase figures, is a simple linking matter. Make the following links in the manner described:

Click into cell	Type	Open source sheet	Click into cell	Press on your keyboard
C12	=	4OutgngsQ1	I7	Return key
D12	=	6OutgngsQ2	I7	Return key
E12	=	8OutgngsQ3	I7	Return key
F12	=	10OutgngsQ4	I7	Return key

Net VAT to be paid (or reclaimed)

If the input tax is greater than the output tax there will be a balance to be paid over to HMRC, while if the opposite is the case there will be a refund to be claimed. Here is how to make the calculation take place automatically:

Click into cell		Formula to type
C	14	=C10-C12
D	14	=D10-D12
E	14	=E10-E12
F	14	=F10-F12

Now we need to compute the figures for the section of the VAT return that deals with Total Sales excluding VAT. Insert the following formulae in the cells indicated below:

Click into cell	Type	Click on	Open source sheet	Click into cell	Hold down	Click into cell	Press on your keyboard
C16	=	Sigma icon	3IncmsQ1	I7	Shift key	J7	Return key
D16	=	Sigma icon	5IncmsQ2	I7	Shift key	J7	Return key
E16	=	Sigma icon	7IncmsQ3	I7	Shift key	J7	Return key
F16	=	Sigma icon	9IncmsQ4	I7	Shift key	J7	Return key

Now we need to enter formulae to compute the total purchases excluding VAT. To do so, proceed as follows:

Click into cell	Open source sheet	Click into cell	Press on your keyboard
C18	4OutgngsQ1	J7	Return key
D18	6OutgngsQ2	J7	Return key
E18	8OutgngsQ3	J7	Return key
F18	10OutgngsQ4	J7	Return key

Now we come to the section of the form that deals with net sales to non-EU countries. The following links need to be made:

Click into cell	Open source sheet	Click into cell	Press on your keyboard
C20	3IncmsQ1	J7	Return key
D20	5IncmsQ2	J7	Return key
E20	7IncmsQ3	J7	Return key
F20	9IncmsQ4	J7	Return key

That one quickly dealt with, now the only links that are left to do are for the EU purchases excluding VAT and this will be just as quick and simple to do as the last lot. Here are the instructions:

Click into cell	Open source sheet	Click into cell	Press on your keyboard
C22	4OutgngsQ1	L7	Return key
D22	6OutgngsQ2	L7	Return key
E22	8OutgngsQ3	L7	Return key
F22	10OutgngsQ4	L7	Return key

We will now configure the spreadsheet automatically to provide an annual summary of the VAT figures and that will be the VAT section completely set up. This involves inserting nine different formulae and here are the instructions:

Click into cell	Click on to	Click into cell	Hold down	Click into cell	Press	Formula that will be automatically inserted
G5	Sigma icon	C5	Shift key	F5	Return key	=SUM(C5:F5)
G8	Sigma icon	C8	Shift key	F8	Return key	=SUM(C8:F8)
G10	Sigma icon	C10	Shift key	F10	Return key	=SUM(C10:F10)
G12	Sigma icon	C12	Shift key	F12	Return key	=SUM(C12:F12)
G14	Sigma icon	C14	Shift key	F14	Return key	=SUM(C14:F14)
G16	Sigma icon	C16	Shift key	F16	Return key	=SUM(C16:F16)
G18	Sigma icon	C18	Shift key	F18	Return key	=SUM(C18:F18)
G20	Sigma icon	C20	Shift key	F20	Return key	=SUM(C20:F20)
G22	Sigma icon	C22	Shift key	F22	Return key	=SUM(C22:F22)

That is the VAT section completed. All we have to do now, each time we complete the VAT return, is copy the figures over from the screen to the VAT form.

Summary of Fixed Asset Disposals

NVB of disposals Q1	0
Sale proceeds Q1	0
Profit or loss Q1	0
NBV of disposals Q2	0
Sale proceeds Q2	0
Profit or loss Q2	0
NVB of disposals Q3	0
Sale proceeds Q3	0
Profit or loss Q3	0
NVB of disposals Q4	0
Sale proceeds Q4	0
Profit or loss Q4	0

21 Stock Summary

Balance b/d	750
Net adjustments Q1	0
Balance b/d	750
Net adjustments Q2	0
Balance b/d	750
Net adjustments Q3	0
Balance b/d	750
Net adjustments Q4	0
Closing stock Q4	

22 Trade debtors account

Opening Balance	1000
Credit Sales Q1	0
Amount paid Q1	-1000
Trade debts written off Q1	0
Balance c/d Q1	0
Credit Sales Q2	0
Amount paid Q2	0
Trade debts written off Q2	0
Balance c/d	0
Credit Sales Q3	0
Amount paid Q3	0
Trade debts written off Q3	0
Balance c/d	0
Credit Sales Q4	0
Amount paid Q4	0
Trade debts written off Q4	0
Balance c/d Q4	0

23 Bank Summary

Opening Balance	2000
Lodgements Q1	3000
Withdrawals Q1	0
Payments Q1	-1000
Balance c/d Q1	4000
Lodgements Q2	2000
Withdrawals Q2	0
Payments Q2	-60
Balance c/d Q2	3940
Lodgements Q3	0
Withdrawals Q3	0
Payments Q3	-600
Balance c/d Q3	5340
Lodgements Q4	750
Withdrawals Q4	0
Payments Q4	-2000
Balance c/d Q4	4090

24 Bank receipts Summary

Opening balance b/d	100
Cheques received Q1	0
Cheques deposited Q1	0
Balance c/d Q1	100
Cheques received Q2	0
Cheques deposited Q2	0
Balance c/d Q2	100
Cheques received Q3	5000
Cheques deposited Q3	0
Balance c/d Q3	5100
Cheques received Q4	0
Cheques deposited Q4	0
Balance c/d Q4	5100

25 Cash summary

Opening balance b/d	
Cash received Q1	
Cash deposited Q1	
Cash payments Q1	
Balance c/d Q1	
Cash received Q2	
Cash deposited Q2	
Cash payments Q2	
Cash received Q3	
Cash deposited Q3	
Cash payments Q3	
Balance c/d Q3	
Cash received Q4	
Cash deposited Q4	
Cash payments Q4	
Balance c/d Q4	

26 Other Current Assets

Opening balance b/d	50
Additions to Other current assets Q1	0
Disposals of Other Current Assets Q1	0
Balance c/d Q1	50
Additions to Other current assets Q2	0
Disposals of Other Current Assets Q2	0
Balance c/d Q2	-40
Additions to Other current assets Q3	10
Disposals of Other Current Assets Q3	0
Balance c/d Q3	0
Additions to Other current assets Q4	10
Disposals of Other Current Assets Q4	0
Balance c/d Q4	10

Figure 37 Example of an assets summary

The assets summary takes the place of the assets accounts in the nominal ledger of the traditional accounting system.

Fixed assets

The first thing you have to do is configure the worksheet. Click on the 'Insert new worksheet' icon at the bottom of the spreadsheet. Name it '14Assets'.

Cell reference		What to type in
B	1	Summary of assets
B	4	Fixed assets

Embolden and underline each of these as they are titles and change the font of the latter to italics to distinguish it from the other, more general title.

A	4	Fixed assets
C	6	Balance b/d
C	7	Purchased in Q1
C	8	Accumulated depreciation Q1
C	9	Balance Q1
C	10	Purchased in Q2
C	11	Accumulated depreciation Q2
C	12	Balance Q2
C	13	Purchased in Q3
C	14	Accumulated depreciation Q3
C	15	Balance Q3
C	16	Purchased in Q4
C	17	Accumulated depreciation Q4
C	18	Balance Q4

Click on cell B8 and then on to the format icon in the cells group on the ribbon. Select the auto-fit column width option and press the return key.

Now we need to make some links:

Click into cell	Type	Open source sheet	Click into cell	Press on your keyboard
C6	=	2 O B s	C6	Return key
C7	=	4OutgngsQ1	AB7	Return key
C8	=	4OutgngsQ1	AC7	Return key
C10	=	6OutgngsQ2	AB7	Return key
C11	=	6OutgngsQ2	AC7	Return key
C13	=	8OutgngsQ3	AB7	Return key
C14	=	8OutgngsQ3	AC7	Return key
C16	=	10OutgngsQ4	AB7	Return key
C17	=	10OutgngsQ4	AC7	Return key

Now there are four formulae to put in:

Click into cell	Click on to	Click into cell	Hold down	Click into cell	Press	Formula that will be automatically inserted
C9	Sigma icon	C6	Shift key	C8	Return key	=SUM(C6:C8)
C12	Sigma icon	C9	Shift key	C11	Return key	=SUM(C9:C11)
C15	Sigma icon	C12	Shift key	C14	Return key	=SUM(C12:C14)
C18	Sigma icon	C15	Shift key	C17	Return key	=SUM(C15:C17)

The final thing to do in order to complete this report is to highlight cells C8, C11 and C14 by holding down the control key while clicking into each cell and then insert a bottom border by clicking on the borders icon in the fonts group on the ribbon and selecting the bottom border option. Now click on cell C18 and insert both top and bottom borders into that cell by selecting the top and bottom border option.

Now we need to deal with asset disposals: if fixed assets have been disposed of their net book value will have to be removed from the fixed assets account and any profit or loss entered into the profit and loss account.

The first thing you have to do is configure two more columns on the assets worksheet. Proceed as follows:

Cell reference		What to type in
E	4	Summary of fixed asset disposals
E	6	NVB of disposals Q1
E	7	Sale proceeds Q1
E	8	Profit or loss Q1
E	9	NBV of disposals Q2
E	10	Sale proceeds Q2
E	11	Profit or loss Q2
E	12	NVB of disposals Q3
E	13	Sale proceeds Q3
E	14	Profit or loss Q3
E	15	NVB of disposals Q4
E	16	Sale proceeds Q4
E	17	Profit or loss Q4

Embolden and underline the contents of cell E4, by clicking on the bold and underline icons in the fonts group on the ribbon, because it is the title of the sheet.

Now we need to make some links. This is how to do it:

Click into cell	Type	Open source sheet	Click into cell	Press on your keyboard
F6	=	4OutgngsQ1	AA7	Return key
F7	=	3IncmsQ1	W7	Return key
F9	=	6OutgngsQ2	AA7	Return key
F10	=	5IncmsQ2	W7	Return key
F12	=	8OutgngsQ3	AA7	Return key
F13	=	7IncmsQ3	W7	Return key
F15	=	10OutgngsQ4	AA7	Return key
F16	=	9IncmsQ4	W7	Return key

Now there are four formulae to put in:

Cell reference		What to type in
F	8	=F6-F7
F	11	=F9-F10
F	14	=F12-F13
F	17	=F15-F16

Closing stock

Now we are going to deal with the closing stock account.

The first thing we have to do is configure two more columns on the assets worksheet. Proceed as follows.

Cell reference		What to type in
G	4	21
H	4	Stock summary
H	6	Balance b/d
H	7	Net adjustments Q1
H	8	Balance b/d
H	9	Net adjustments Q2
H	10	Balance b/d
H	11	Net adjustments Q3
H	12	Balance b/d
H	13	Net adjustments Q4
H	14	Closing stock Q4

Embolden and underline the contents of cell H5, by clicking on the bold and underline icons in the fonts group on the ribbon, because it is the title of the sheet.

Now we need to make some links. This is how to do it:

Click into cell	Type	Open source sheet	Click into cell	Press on your keyboard
I6	=	2 O B s	C8	Return key
I7	=	4OutgngsQ1	AD7	Return key
F9	=	6OutgngsQ2	AD7	Return key
I11	=	8OutgngsQ3	AD7	Return key
I13	=	10OutgngsQ4	AD7	Return key

Now there are four formulae to put in:

Click into cell	Click on to	Click into cell	Hold down	Click into cell	Press	Formula that will be automatically inserted
I8	Sigma icon	I6	Shift key	I7	Return key	=SUM(I6:I7)
I10	Sigma icon	I8	Shift key	I9	Return key	=SUM(I8:I9)
I12	Sigma icon	I10	Shift key	I11	Return key	=SUM(I10:I11)
I14	Sigma icon	I12	Shift key	I13	Return key	=SUM(I12:I13)

Trade debtors account

Now we are going to deal with the trade debtors account.

The first thing we have to do is configure two more columns on the assets worksheet. Proceed as follows:

Cell reference		What to type in
J	4	22
K	4	Trade debtors account
K	6	Opening balance
K	7	Credit sales Q1
K	8	Amount paid Q1
K	9	Trade debts written off Q1
K	10	Balance c/d Q1
K	11	Credit sales Q2
K	12	Amount paid Q2
K	13	Trade debts written off Q2
K	14	Balance c/d Q2
K	15	Credit sales Q3
K	16	Amount paid Q3
K	17	Trade debts written off Q3
K	18	Balance c/d Q3
K	19	Credit sales Q4
K	20	Amount paid Q4
K	21	Trade debts written off Q4
K	22	Balance c/d Q4

Embolden and underline the contents of cell K4, by clicking on the bold and underline icons in the fonts group on the ribbon, because it is the title of the sheet.

Now we need to make some links. This is how to do it:

Click into cell	Type	Open source sheet	Click into cell	Press on your keyboard
L6	=	2 O B s	C10	Return key
L7	=	3IncmsQ1	G7	Return key
L8	=-	3IncmsQ1	P7	Return key
L9	=	4OutgngsQ1	AE7	Return key
L11	=	5IncmsQ2	G7	Return key
L12	=-	5IncmsQ2	P7	Return key
L13	=	6OutgngsQ2	AE7	Return key
L15	=	7IncmsQ3	G7	Return key
L16	=-	7IncmsQ3	P7	Return key
L17	=	8OutgngsQ3	AE7	Return key
L19	=-	9IncmsQ4	G7	Return key
L20	=	9IncmsQ4	P7	Return key
L21	=	10OutgngsQ4	AE7	Return key

Note: There are minus signs after the equals sign in L8, L12, L16 and L19.

Now there are four formulae to put in:

Click into cell	Click on to	Click into cell	Hold down	Click into cell	Press	Formula that will be automatically inserted
L10	Sigma icon	L6	Shift key	L9	Return key	=SUM(I6:I7)
L14	Sigma icon	L10	Shift key	L13	Return key	=SUM(I8:I9)
L18	Sigma icon	L14	Shift key	L17	Return key	=SUM(I10:I11)
L22	Sigma icon	L18	Shift key	L21	Return key	=SUM(I12:I13)

Bank payments summary

Now we are going to deal with payments out of the bank account.

The first thing we have to do is configure two more columns on the assets worksheet. Proceed as follows:

Cell reference		What to type in
M	4	23
N	4	Bank payments summary
N	6	Opening balance
N	7	Lodgements Q1
N	8	Withdrawals Q1
N	9	Payments Q1
N	10	Balance c/d Q1
N	11	Lodgements Q2
N	12	Withdrawals Q2
N	13	Payments Q2
N	14	Balance c/d Q2
N	15	Lodgements Q3
N	16	Withdrawals Q3
N	17	Payments Q3
N	18	Balance c/d Q3
N	19	Lodgements Q4
N	20	Withdrawals Q4
N	21	Payments Q4
N	22	Balance c/d Q4

Embolden and underline the contents of cell N5, by clicking on the bold and underline icons in the fonts group on the ribbon, because it is the title of the sheet.

Now we need to make some links. This is how to do it:

Click into cell	Type	Open source sheet	Click into cell	Press on your keyboard
O7	=	3IncmsQ1	E7	Return key
O8	=-	3IncmsQ1	M7	Return key
O9	=-	4OutgngsQ1	E7	Return key
O11	=-	5IncmsQ2	E7	Return key
O12	=-	5IncmsQ2	M7	Return key
O13	=-	6OutgngsQ2	E7	Return key
O15	=	7IncmsQ3	E7	Return key
O16	=-	7IncmsQ3	M7	Return key
O17	=-	8OutgngsQ3	E7	Return key
O19	=	9IncmsQ4	E7	Return key
O20	=-	9IncmsQ4	M7	Return key
O21	=-	10OutgngsQ4	E7	Return key

Note: There are minus signs after the equals sign in O8, O9, O11, O12, O13, O16, O17, O20 and O21.

Now there are four formulae to put in:

Click into cell	Click on to	Click into cell	Hold down	Click into cell	Press	Formula that will be automatically inserted
O10	Sigma icon	O6	Shift key	O9	Return key	=SUM(O6:O7)
O14	Sigma icon	O10	Shift key	O13	Return key	=SUM(O10:O13)
O18	Sigma icon	O14	Shift key	O17	Return key	=SUM(O14:O17)
O22	Sigma icon	O18	Shift key	O21	Return key	=SUM(O18:O21)

Bank receipts summary

Now we are going to deal with into the bank account.

The first thing you have to do is configure two more columns on the assets worksheet. Proceed as follows:

Cell reference		What to type in
P	4	24
Q	4	Bank receipts summary
Q	6	Opening balance b/d
Q	7	Cheques received Q1
Q	8	Cheques deposited Q1
Q	9	Balance c/d Q1
Q	10	Cheques received Q2
Q	11	Cheques deposited Q2
Q	12	Balance c/d Q2
Q	13	Cheques received Q3
Q	14	Cheques deposited Q3
Q	15	Balance c/d Q3
Q	16	Cheques received Q4
Q	17	Cheques deposited Q4
Q	18	Balance c/d Q4

Embolden and underline the contents of cells Q4 and Q5, by clicking on the bold and underline icons in the fonts group on the ribbon, because together they constitute the title of the sheet.

Now we need to make some links. This is how to do it:

Click into cell	Type	Open source sheet	Click into cell	Press on your keyboard
R6	=	2 O B s	C11	Return key
R7	=	3IncmsQ1	F7	Return key
R8	=-	3IncmsQ1	O7	Return key
R10	=	5IncmsQ2	F7	Return key
R11	=-	5IncmsQ2	O7	Return key
R13	=	7IncmsQ3	F7	Return key
R14	=-	7IncmsQ3	O7	Return key
R16	=	9IncmsQ4	F7	Return key
R17	=-	9IncmsQ4	O7	Return key

Note: There are minus signs after the equals sign in R8, R11, R14 and R17.

Now there are four formulae to put in:

Click into cell	Click on to	Click into cell	Hold down	Click into cell	Press	Formula that will be automatically inserted
R9	Sigma icon	R6	Shift key	R8	Return key	=SUM(R6:R8)
R12	Sigma icon	R9	Shift key	R11	Return key	=SUM(R9:R11)
R15	Sigma icon	R12	Shift key	R14	Return key	=SUM(R12:R14)
R18	Sigma icon	R15	Shift key	R17	Return key	=SUM(R15:R17)

Cash account summary

Now we are going to deal with the cash account.

The first thing we have to do is configure two more columns on the assets worksheet. Proceed as follows:

Cell reference		What to type in
S	4	25
T	4	Cash summary
T	6	Opening balance b/d
T	7	Cash received Q1
T	8	Cash deposited Q1
T	9	Cash payments Q1

Cell reference		What to type in
T	10	Balance c/d Q1
T	11	Cash received Q2
T	12	Cash deposited Q2
T	13	Cash payments Q2
T	14	Balance c/d Q2
T	15	Cash received Q3
T	16	Cash deposited Q3
T	17	Cash payments Q3
T	18	Balance c/d Q3
T	19	Cash received Q4
T	20	Cash deposited Q4
T	21	Cash payments Q4
T	22	Balance c/d Q4

Embolden and underline the contents of cell T5, by clicking on the bold and underline icons in the fonts group on the ribbon, because it is the title of the sheet.

Now we need to make some links. This is how to do it:

Click into cell	Type	Open source sheet	Click into cell	Press on your keyboard
U6	=	2 O B s	C12	Return key
U7	=	3IncmsQ1	D7	Return key
U8	=-	3IncmsQ1	N7	Return key
U9	=-	4OutgngsQ1	D7	Return key
U11	=	5IncmsQ2	D7	Return key
U12	=-	5IncmsQ2	N7	Return key
U13	=-	6OutgngsQ2	D7	Return key
U15	=	7IncmsQ3	D7	Return key
U16	=-	7IncmsQ3	N7	Return key
U17	=-	8OutgngsQ3	D7	Return key
U19	=	9IncmsQ4	D7	Return key
U20	=-	9IncmsQ4	N7	Return key
U21	=-	10OutgngsQ4	D7	Return key

Note: There are minus signs after the equals sign in U8, U9, U12, U13, U16, U17, U20 and U21.

Now there are four formulae to put in:

Click into cell	Click on to	Click into cell	Hold down	Click into cell	Press	Formula that will be automatically inserted
U10	Sigma icon	U6	Shift Key	U9	Return key	=SUM(U6:U9)
U14	Sigma icon	U10	Shift Key	U13	Return key	=SUM(U10:U13)
U18	Sigma icon	U14	Shift key	U17	Return key	=SUM(U14:U17)
U22	Sigma icon	U18	Shift key	U21	Return key	=SUM(U18:U21)

Other current assets summary

Now we are going to deal with the account for current assets.

The first thing we have to do is configure two more columns on the assets worksheet. Proceed as follows:

Cell reference		What to type in
V	4	26
W	4	Other current assets
W	6	Opening balance b/d
W	7	Additions to other current assets Q1
W	8	Disposals of other current assets Q1
W	9	Balance c/d Q1
W	10	Additions to other current assets Q2
W	11	Disposals of other current assets Q2
W	12	Balance c/d Q2
W	13	Additions to other current assets Q3
W	14	Disposals of other current assets Q3
W	15	Balance c/d Q3
W	16	Additions to other current assets Q4
W	17	Disposals of other current assets Q4
W	18	Balance c/d Q4

Embolden and underline the contents of cell W4, by clicking on the bold and underline icons in the fonts group on the ribbon, because it is the title of the sheet.

Now we need to make some links. This is how to do it:

Click into cell	Type	Open source sheet	Click into cell	Press on your keyboard
X6	=	2 O B s	C13	Return key
X7	=	4OutgngsQ1	AF7	Return key
X8	=-	3IncmsQ1	R7	Return key
X10	=	6OutgngsQ2	AF7	Return key
X11	=-	5IncmsQ2	R7	Return key
X13	=	8OutgngsQ3	AF7	Return key
X14	=-	7IncmsQ3	R7	Return key
X16	=	10OutgngsQ4	AF7	Return key
X17	=-	9IncmsQ4	R7	Return key

Note: There are minus signs after the equals sign in X8, X11, X14 and X17.

Now there are four formulae to put in:

Click into cell	Click on to	Click into cell	Hold down	Click into cell	Press	Formula that will be automatically inserted
X9	Sigma icon	X6	Shift key	X8	Return key	=SUM(X6:X8)
X12	Sigma icon	X9	Shift key	X11	Return key	=SUM(X9:X11)
X15	Sigma icon	X12	Shift key	X14	Return key	=SUM(X12:X14)
X18	Sigma icon	X15	Shift key	X17	Return key	=SUM(X15:X17)

Liabilities and drawings summaries

27

Trade creditors account	
Opening balance b/d	1,800
Credit purchases Q1	0
Payments to creditors Q1	0
Balance c/d Q1	1200
Credit purchases Q2	0
Payments to creditors Q2	0
Balance c/d Q2	1500
Credit purchases Q3	0
Payments to creditors Q3	0
Balance c/d Q3	1200
Credit purchases Q4	0
Payments to creditors Q4	0
Balance c/d Q4	1200

26 VAT Account summary	
Opening balance b/d	1000
VAT on sales Q1	0
VAT refund Q1	0
VAT on purchases Q1	0
VAT paid Q1	0
VAT owed or due Q1	1000
VAT on sales Q2	0
VAT refund Q2	0
VAT on purchases Q2	0
VAT paid Q2	0
VAT owed or due Q2	1000
VAT on sales Q3	0
VAT refund Q3	0
VAT on purchases Q3	0
VAT paid Q3	1000
VAT owed or due Q3	0
VAT on sales Q4	0
VAT refund Q4	0
VAT on purchases Q4	0
VAT paid Q4	0
VAT owed or due Q4	1000

24 PAYE & NI Account Summary	
Opening balance b/d	250
Amount due and paid Q1	0
Balance owed Q1	0
Amount due and paid Q2	0
Balance owed Q2	250
Amount due and paid Q3	0
Balance owed Q3	0
Amount due and paid Q4	0
Balance owed Q4	0

30 Credit Card Summary	
Opening balance b/d	250
Credit card payments Q1	0
Credit card repayments Q1	250
Balance c/d Q1	0
Credit card payments Q2	250
Credit card repayments Q2	0
Balance c/d Q2	250
Credit card payments Q3	0
Credit card repayments Q3	0
Balance c/d Q3	250
Credit card payments Q4	0
Credit card repayments Q4	0
Balance c/d Q4	250

31 Summary of Other Current Liabilities	
Opening balance b/d	500
Net OCL on T&mQ1	0
Net OCL on XCharge Q1	0
Balance c/d Q1	500
Net OCL on T&mQ2	0
Net OCL on XCharge Q2	0
Balance c/d Q2	500
Net OCL on T&mQ3	0
Net OCL on XCharge Q3	0
Balance c/d Q3	500
Net OCL on XCharge Q4	0
Balance c/d Q4	500

32 Loan Account Summary	
Opening balance b/d	10000.00
Loan funds invested Q1	0
Loan funds repaid incl. interest Q1	0
Balance c/d Q1	10000
New Capital invested Q2	0
Loan funds repaid incl. interest Q2	0
Balance c/d Q2	10000
Loan funds received Q3	0
Loan funds repaid incl. interest Q3	0
Balance c/d Q3	10000
Loan funds received Q4	0
Loan funds repaid incl. interest Q4	0
Balance c/d Q4	10000

33 Capital Account Summary	
Opening balance b/d	102200
New Capital invested Q1	0
Profit/loss Q1	1500
Capital Owed Q1	103700
New Capital invested Q2	0
Profit/loss Q2	1500
Capital Owed Q2	105500
New Capital invested Q3	0
Profit/loss Q3	110300
Capital Owed Q3	0
New Capital invested Q4	-5300
Profit/loss Q4	-1250
Capital Owed Q4	103750

34 Drawings Account Summary	
Opening balance b/d	0
Drawings Q1	0
Balance c/d Q1	0
Drawings Q2	0
Balance c/d Q2	0
Drawings Q3	0
Balance c/d Q3	0
Drawings Q4	0
Balance c/d Q4	0

Figure 38 Example of a liabilities summary

Now we are going to deal with the liabilities. There are several categories. Each one will be summarized on the same worksheet. We will start with the trade creditors account.

The first thing we have to do is configure a couple of columns on the liabilities worksheet. Proceed as follows:

Cell reference		What to type in
A	4	27
B	4	Trade creditors account
B	6	Opening balance b/d
B	7	Credit purchases Q1
B	8	Payments to creditors Q1
B	9	Balance c/d Q1
B	10	Credit purchases Q2
B	11	Payments to creditors Q2
B	12	Balance c/d Q2
B	13	Credit purchases Q3
B	14	Payments to creditors Q3
B	15	Balance c/d Q3
B	16	Credit purchases Q4
B	17	Payments to creditors Q4
B	18	Balance c/d Q4

Embolden and underline the contents of cell B4, by clicking on the bold and underline icons in the fonts group on the ribbon, because it is the title of the sheet.

Now we need to make some links. This is how to do it:

Click into cell	Type	Open source sheet	Click into cell	Press on your keyboard
C6	=	2 O B s	C18	Return key
C7	=-	4OutgngsQ1	H7	Return key
C8	=	4OutgngsQ1	AG7	Return key
C10	=-	6OutgngsQ2	H7	Return key
C11	=	6OutgngsQ2	AG7	Return key
C13	=-	8OutgngsQ3	H7	Return key
C14	=	8OutgngsQ3	AG7	Return key
C16	=-	10OutgngsQ4	H7	Return key
C17	=	9IncmsQ4	AG7	Return key

Note: There are minus signs after the equals sign in C7, C10, C13 and C16.

Now there are four formulae to put in:

Click into cell	Click on to	Click into cell	Hold down	Click into cell	Press	Formula that will be automatically inserted
C9	Sigma icon	C6	Shift key	C8	Return key	=SUM(C6:C8)
C12	Sigma icon	C9	Shift key	C11	Return key	=SUM(C9:C11)
C15	Sigma icon	C12	Shift key	C14	Return key	=SUM(C12:C14)
C18	Sigma icon	C15	Shift key	C17	Return key	=SUM(C15:C17)

VAT account summary

Now we are going to deal with the VAT account. It is assumed that there will usually be liabilities to HMRC rather than regular refunds so VAT is dealt with here as a liability.

The first thing we have to do is configure two more columns on the liabilities worksheet. Proceed as follows:

Cell reference		What to type in
D	4	28
E	4	VAT account summary
E	6	Opening balance b/d
E	7	VAT on sales Q1
E	8	VAT refund Q1
E	9	VAT on purchases Q1
E	10	VAT paid Q1
E	11	VAT owed or due Q1
E	12	VAT on sales Q2
E	13	VAT refund Q2
E	14	VAT on purchases Q2
E	15	VAT paid Q2
E	16	VAT owed or due Q2
E	17	VAT on sales Q3
E	18	VAT refund Q3
E	19	VAT on purchases Q3
E	20	VAT paid Q3

Cell reference		What to type in
E	21	VAT owed or due Q3
E	22	VAT on sales Q4
E	23	VAT refund Q4
E	24	VAT on purchases Q4
E	25	VAT paid Q4
E	26	VAT owed or due Q4

Embolden and underline the contents of cell E5, by clicking on the bold and underline icons in the fonts group on the ribbon, because it is the title of the sheet.

Now we need to make some links. This is how to do it:

Click into cell	Type	Open source sheet	Click into cell	Press on your keyboard
F6	=	2 O B s	C19	Return key
F7	=-	3IncmsQ1	H7	Return key
F8	=-	3IncmsQ1	S7	Return key
F9	=	4OutgngsQ1	I7	Return key
F10	=	4OutgngsQ1	AH7	Return key
F12	=-	5IncmsQ2	H7	Return key
F13	=-	5IncmsQ2	S7	Return key
F14	=	6OutgngsQ2	I7	Return key
F15	=	6OutgngsQ2	AH7	Return key
F17	=-	7IncmsQ3	H7	Return key
F18	=-	7IncmsQ3	S7	Return key
F19	=	8OutgngsQ3	I7	Return key
F20	=	8OutgngsQ3	AH7	Return key
F22	=-	9IncmsQ4	H7	Return key
F23	=-	9IncmsQ4	S7	Return key
F24	=	10OutgngsQ4	I7	Return key
F25	=	10OutgngsQ4	AH7	Return key

Note: There are minus signs after the equals sign in F7, F8, F12, F13, F17, F18, F22 and F23.

Now there are four formulae to put in:

Click into cell	Click on to	Click into cell	Hold down	Click into cell	Press	Formula that will be automatically inserted
F11	Sigma icon	F6	Shift key	F10	Return key	=SUM(F6:F108)
F16	Sigma icon	F11	Shift key	F15	Return key	=SUM(F11:F151)
F21	Sigma icon	F16	Shift key	F20	Return key	=SUM(F16:F20)
F26	Sigma icon	F21	Shift key	F25	Return key	=SUM(F21:F25)

PAYE and NI account

Now we are going to deal with the PAYE and NI account.

The first thing we have to do is configure two more columns on the liabilities worksheet. Proceed as follows:

Cell reference		What to type in
G	4	24
H	4	PAYE & NI account summary
H	6	Opening balance b/d
H	7	Amount due and paid Q1
H	8	Balance owed Q1
H	9	Amount due and paid Q2
H	10	Balance owed Q2
H	11	Amount due and paid Q3
H	12	Balance owed Q3
H	13	Amount due and paid Q4
H	14	Balance owed Q4

Embolden and underline the contents of cell H5, by clicking on the bold and underline icons in the fonts group on the ribbon, because it is the title of the sheet.

Now we need to make some links. This is how to do it:

Click into cell	Type	Open source sheet	Click into cell	Press on your keyboard
I6	=	2 O B s	C20	Return key
I7	=	4OutgngsQ1	AI7	Return key
I9	=	6OutgngsQ2	AI7	Return key
I11	=	8OutgngsQ3	AI7	Return key
I13	=	10OutgngsQ4	AI7	Return key

Now there are four formulae to put in:

Click into cell	Click on to	Click into cell	Hold down	Click into cell	Press	Formula that will be automatically inserted
I8	Sigma icon	I6	Shift key	I7	Return key	=SUM(I6:I7)
I10	Sigma icon	I8	Shift key	I9	Return key	=SUM(I8:I9)
I12	Sigma icon	I10	Shift key	I11	Return key	=SUM(I10:I11)
I14	Sigma icon	I12	Shift key	I13	Return key	=SUM(I12:I13)

Business credit card account

Now we are going to deal with the business credit card account.

The first thing we have to do is configure two more columns on the liabilities worksheet. Proceed as follows:

Cell reference		What to type in
J	4	30
K	4	Credit card summary
K	6	Opening balance b/d
K	7	Credit card payments Q1
K	8	Credit card repayments Q1
K	9	Balance c/d Q1
K	10	Credit card payments Q2
K	11	Credit card repayments Q2
K	12	Balance c/d Q2
K	13	Credit card payments Q3
K	14	Credit card repayments Q3

Cell reference		What to type in
K	15	Balance c/d Q3
K	16	Credit card payments Q4
K	17	Credit card repayments Q4
K	18	Balance c/d Q4

Embolden and underline the contents of cell K4, by clicking on the bold and underline icons in the fonts group on the ribbon, because it is the title of the sheet.

Now we need to make some links. This is how to do it:

Click into cell	Type	Open source sheet	Click into cell	Press on your keyboard
L6	=	2 O B s	C21	Return key
L7	=-	4OutgngsQ1	G7	Return key
L8	=	4OutgngsQ1	AJ7	Return key
L10	=-	6OutgngsQ2	G7	Return key
L11	=	6OutgngsQ2	AJ7	Return key
L13	=-	8OutgngsQ3	G7	Return key
L14	=	8OutgngsQ3	AJ7	Return key
L16	=-	10OutgngsQ4	G7	Return key
L17	=	10OutgngsQ4	AJ7	Return key

Note: There are minus signs after the equals sign in L7, L10, L13 and L16.

Now there are four formulae to put in:

Click into cell	Click on to	Click into cell	Hold down	Click into cell	Press	Formula that will be automatically inserted
L9	Sigma icon	L6	Shift key	L8	Return key	=SUM(L6:L8)
L12	Sigma icon	L9	Shift key	L11	Return key	=SUM(L9:L11)
L15	Sigma icon	L12	Shift key	L14	Return key	=SUM(L12:R14)
L18	Sigma icon	L15	Shift key	L17	Return key	=SUM(L15:L17)

Summary of other current liabilities

Now we are going to deal with other current liabilities.

The first thing we have to do is configure two more columns on the liabilities worksheet. Proceed as follows:

Cell reference		What to type in
N	4	31
O	4	Summary of other current liabilities
O	6	Opening balance b/d
O	7	Net OCL on 3IncmsQ1
O	8	Net OCL on 4OutgngsQ1
O	9	Balance c/d Q1
O	10	Net OCL on 5IncmsQ2
O	11	Net OCL on 6OutgngsQ2
O	12	Balance c/d Q2
O	13	Net OCL on 7IncmsQ3
O	14	Net OCL on 8OutgngsQ3
O	15	Balance c/d Q3
O	16	Net OCL on 9IncmsQ4
O	17	Net OCL on 10OutgngsQ4
O	18	Balance c/d Q4

Embolden and underline the contents of cell O4, by clicking on the bold and underline icons in the fonts group on the ribbon, because it is the title of the sheet.

Now we need to make some links. This is how to do it:

Click into cell	Type	Open source sheet	Click into cell	Press on your keyboard
P6	=	2 O B s	C22	Return key
P7	=-	3IncmsQ1	U7	Return key
P8	=	4OutgngsQ1	AK7	Return key
P10	=-	5IncmsQ2	U7	Return key
P11	=	6OutgngsQ2	AK7	Return key
P13	=-	7IncmsQ3	U7	Return key
P14	=	8OutgngsQ3	AK7	Return key
P16	=-	9IncmsQ4	U7	Return key
P17	=	10OutgngsQ3	AK7	Return key

Note: There are minus signs after the equals sign in P7, P10, P13 and P16.

Now there are four formulae to put in:

Click into cell	Click on to	Click into cell	Hold down	Click into cell	Press	Formula that will be automatically inserted
P9	Sigma icon	P6	Shift key	P8	Return key	=SUM(P6:P8)
P12	Sigma icon	P9	Shift key	P11	Return key	=SUM(P9:P11)
P15	Sigma icon	P12	Shift key	P14	Return key	=SUM(P12:P14)
P18	Sigma icon	P15	Shift key	P17	Return key	=SUM(P15:P17)

Business loan summary

Now we are going to deal with the business loan account.

The first thing you have to do is configure two more columns on the liabilities worksheet. Proceed as follows:

Cell reference		What to type in
Q	4	32
R	4	Loan account summary
R	6	Opening balance b/d
R	7	Loan funds received Q1
R	8	Loan funds repaid incl. interest Q1
R	9	Balance c/d Q1
R	10	Loan funds received Q2
R	11	Loan funds repaid incl. interest Q2
R	12	Balance c/d Q2
R	13	Loan funds received Q3
R	14	Loan funds repaid incl. interest Q3
R	15	Balance c/d Q3
R	16	Loan funds received Q4
R	17	Loan funds repaid incl. interest Q4
R	18	Balance c/d Q4

Embolden and underline the contents of cell R5, by clicking on the bold and underline icons in the fonts group on the ribbon, because it is the title of the sheet.

Now we need to make some links. This is how to do it:

Click into cell	Type	Open source sheet	Click into cell	Press on your keyboard
S6	=	2 O B s	C28	Return key
S7	=-	3IncmsQ1	V7	Return key
S8	=	4OutgngsQ1	AL7	Return key
S10	=-	5IncmsQ2	V7	Return key
S11	=	6OutgngsQ2	AL7	Return key
S13	=-	7IncmsQ3	V7	Return key
S14	=	8OutgngsQ3	AL7	Return key
S16	=-	9IncmsQ4	V7	Return key
S17	=	10OutgngsQ4	AL7	Return key

Note: There are minus signs after the equals sign in S7, S10, S13 and S16.

Now there are four formulae to put in:

Click into cell	Click on to	Click into cell	Hold down	Click into cell	Press	Formula that will be automatically inserted
S9	Sigma icon	S6	Shift key	S8	Return key	=SUM(S6:S8)
S12	Sigma icon	S9	Shift key	S11	Return key	=SUM(S9:S11)
S15	Sigma icon	S12	Shift key	S14	Return key	=SUM(S12:S14)
S18	Sigma icon	S15	Shift key	S17	Return key	=SUM(S15:S17)

Capital account summary

Now we are going to deal with the capital account.

The first thing we have to do is configure two more columns on the liabilities worksheet. Proceed as follows:

Cell reference		What to type in
T	4	33
U	4	Capital account summary
U	6	Opening balance b/d
U	7	New capital invested Q1
U	8	Profit/loss Q1
U	9	Capital owed Q1

Cell reference		What to type in
U	10	New capital invested Q1
U	11	Profit/loss Q1
U	12	Capital owed Q1
U	13	New capital invested Q1
U	14	Profit/loss Q1
U	15	Capital owed Q1
U	16	New capital invested Q1
U	17	Profit/loss Q1
U	18	Capital owed Q1

Embolden and underline the contents of cell U5, by clicking on the bold and underline icons in the fonts group on the ribbon, because it is the title of the sheet.

Now we need to make some links. This is how to do it:

Click into cell	Type	Open source sheet	Click into cell	Press on your keyboard
V6	=	2 O B s	C29	Return key
V7	=-	3IncmsQ1	Q7	Return key
V8	=	17PL	C29	Return key
V10	=-	5IncmsQ2	Q7	Return key
V11	=	17PL	D294	Return key
V13	=-	7IncmsQ3	Q7	Return key
V14	=	17PL	E29	Return key
V16	=-	9IncmsQ4	Q7	Return key
V17	=	17PL	F29	Return key

Note: There are minus signs after the equals sign in cells V7, V10, V13 and V16.

Now there are four formulae to put in:

Click into cell	Click on to	Click into cell	Hold down	Click into cell	Press	Formula that will be automatically inserted
V9	Sigma icon	V6	Shift key	V8	Return key	=SUM(V6:V8)
V12	Sigma icon	V9	Shift key	V11	Return key	=SUM(V9:V11)
V15	Sigma icon	V12	Shift key	V14	Return key	=SUM(V12:V14)
V18	Sigma icon	V15	Shift key	V17	Return key	=SUM(V15:V17)

Drawings account summary

Now we are going to deal with into the drawings account.

The first thing we have to do is configure two more columns on the liabilities worksheet. Proceed as follows:

Cell reference		What to type in
W	4	34
X	4	Drawings account summary
X	6	Opening balance b/d
X	7	Drawings Q1
X	8	Balance c/d Q1
X	9	Drawings Q2
X	10	Balance c/d Q2
X	11	Drawings Q3
X	12	Balance c/d Q3
X	13	Drawings Q4
X	14	Balance c/d Q4

Embolden and underline the contents of cell X5, by clicking on the bold and underline icons in the fonts group on the ribbon, because it is the title of the sheet.

Now we need to make some links. This is how to do it:

Click into cell	Type	Open source sheet	Click into cell	Press on your keyboard
Y7	=	4OutgngsQ1	AM7	Return key
Y8	=	6OutgngsQ2	AM7	Return key
Y10	=	8OutgngsQ3	AM7	Return key
Y11	=	10OutgngsQ4	AM7	Return key

Now there are four formulae to put in:

Click into cell	Click on to	Click into cell	Hold down	Click into cell	Press	Formula that will be automatically inserted
Y8	Sigma icon	Y6	Shift key	Y7	Return key	=SUM(Y6:Y7)
Y10	Sigma icon	Y8	Shift key	Y9	Return key	=SUM(Y8:Y9)
Y12	Sigma icon	Y10	Shift key	Y11	Return key	=SUM(Y10:Y11)
Y14	Sigma icon	Y12	Shift key	Y13	Return key	=SUM(Y13:Y14)

Trial Balance

		Q1	Q2	Q3	Q4	Year to date
1	Turnover	-1,200.00	-2000.00	0.00	-750.00	-3950.00
2	Other income	-800.00	0.00	-5000.00	0.00	-5800.00
3	Incomings Suspense Account	0.00	0.00	0.00	0.00	0.00
4	Purchases	0.00	60.00	0.00	0.00	60.00
5	Other direct costs	0.00	0.00	0.00	0.00	0.00
6	Wages, salaries and other employment costs	0.00	0.00	0.00	0.00	0.00
7	Rent	0.00	0.00	0.00	0.00	0.00
8	Repairs and renewals	1,000.00	40.00	600.00	0.00	1640.00
9	Administration expenses	0.00	0.00	0.00	0.00	0.00
10	Travelling expenses	0.00	0.00	0.00	0.00	0.00
11	Advertising and promotion	0.00	0.00	0.00	2000.00	2000.00
12	Professional fees and charges	0.00	0.00	0.00	0.00	0.00
13	Bad debts	0.00	0.00	0.00	0.00	0.00
14	Bank charges	0.00	0.00	0.00	0.00	0.00
15	Depreciation costs	0.00	0.00	0.00	0.00	0.00
16	Loss (or profit) on asset disposals	0.00	0.00	0.00	0.00	0.00
17	Other expenses	0.00	0.00	0.00	0.00	0.00
18	Non-allowable expenses	0.00	0.00	0.00	0.00	0.00
19	Outgoings suspense account	0.00	0.00	0.00	0.00	0.00
20	Fixed assets	112,000.00	112,000.00	112,000.00	112,000.00	112,000.00
21	Stock	750.00	750.00	750.00	750.00	750.00
22	Trade debtors	0.00	0.00	0.00	0.00	0.00
23	Cash at bank	4,000.00	5940.00	5340.00	4090.00	4090.00
24	Cheques issued	100.00	100.00	5100.00	5100.00	5100.00
25	Cash in hand	50.00	10.00	10.00	10.00	10.00
26	Other current assets	0.00	0.00	0.00	0.00	0.00
27	Trade creditors	-1,200.00	-1,200.00	-1,200.00	-1200.00	-1200.00
28	VAT payable	-1,000.00	-1,000.00	-1000.00	-1000.00	-1000.00
29	PAYE and NI	-250.00	-250.00	-250.00	-250.00	-250.00
30	Credit card	-250.00	-250.00	-250.00	-250.00	-250.00
31	Other current liabilities inl accr	-500.00	-500.00	-500.00	-500.00	-500.00
32	Business loan	-10,000.00	-10,000.00	-10000.00	-10000.00	-10000.00
33	Capital	-102,700.00	-103,700.00	-105600.00	-110000.00	-102700.00
34	Drawings	0.00	0.00	0.00	0.00	0.00
	Error	0.00	0.00	0.00	0.00	0.00
	Suspense account, to clear	0.00	0.00	0.00	0.00	0.00

Figure 39 Example of a trial balance

Now we are going to deal with the trial balance. This is how to configure the spreadsheet page for this.

First we need to create a new worksheet by clicking on the new worksheet icon at the bottom of the page and renaming it '16TB'.

Then we need to fill cells A5 to A40 with consecutive numbers from 1 to 34. The quick way of doing this is to type the figure 1 in cell A5 and 2 in cell A6, highlight both and hold the mouse over the bottom right-hand corner until the small + appears, then hold down the left mouse button, drag the cursor down to cell A38 and release it.

Cell reference		What to type in
B	2	Trial balance
B	5	Turnover
B	6	Other income
B	7	Incomings suspense account
B	8	Purchases
B	9	Other direct costs
B	10	Wages, salaries and other employment costs
B	11	Rent
B	12	Repairs and renewals
B	13	Administration expenses
B	14	Travelling expenses
B	15	Advertising and promotion
B	16	Professional fees and charges
B	17	Bad debts
B	18	Bank charges
B	19	Depreciation costs
B	20	Loss (or profit) on asset disposals
B	21	Other expenses
B	22	Non-allowable expenses
B	23	Outgoings suspense account
B	24	Fixed assets
B	25	Stock
B	26	Trade debtors
B	27	Cash at bank
B	28	Cheques issued
B	29	Cash in hand
B	30	Other current assets
B	31	Trade creditors
B	32	VAT payable
B	33	PAYE and NI
B	34	Credit card
B	35	Other current liabilities
B	36	Business loan
B	37	Capital
B	38	Drawings
B	39	Error
C	4	Q1
D	4	Q2
E	4	Q3
F	4	Q4
G	4	Year-to-date

Note: A super-quick way to fill cells B8 to B19 is to click on sheet 4OutgngsQ1, highlight cells M6 to X6, copy and paste this into cell B8 of sheet 16TB, click the down arrow below the paste icon, select the transpose option, then unwrap, remove borders, unbold and press the return key.

Embolden and underline the contents of cell B1, B39 and B40, by clicking on the bold and underline icons in the fonts group on the ribbon, because the content of the first of these is the title of the sheet while special attention needs to be drawn to the contents of the other two.

It would be a good idea to shade alternate rows in this spreadsheet as it is easier to read in this form. To do this, place the cursor in cell A5, hold down the shift key and click on cell G41. This will highlight the whole area. Now click on the fill colour icon in the font group on the ribbon and select what you feel is a suitable colour. I will use 'blue accent 1'. To make the striped effect, hold down the control key and click on all the even row numbers from 6 to 40, then click on the fill colour icon again but, this time, select the no fill option.

Now we need to make some links. This is how to do it:

Click into cell		Type	Open source sheet	Click into cell	Press on your keyboard
C	5	=-	3IncmsQ1	K7	Return key
C	6	=-	3IncmsQ1	L7	Return key
C	7	=-	3IncmsQ1	X7	Return key
C	8	=	4OutgngsQ1	M7	Return key
C	9	=	4OutgngsQ1	N7	Return key
C	10	=	4OutgngsQ1	O7	Return key
C	11	=	4OutgngsQ1	P7	Return key
C	12	=	4OutgngsQ1	Q7	Return key
C	13	=	4OutgngsQ1	R7	Return key
C	14	=	4OutgngsQ1	S7	Return key
C	15	=	4OutgngsQ1	T7	Return key
C	16	=	4OutgngsQ1	U7	Return key
C	17	=	4OutgngsQ1	V7	Return key
C	18	=	4OutgngsQ1	W7	Return key
C	19	=	4OutgngsQ1	X7	Return key
C	20	=	14Assets	F8	Return key
C	21	=	4OutgngsQ1	Y7	Return key
C	22	=	4OutgngsQ1	Z7	Return key
C	23	=	4OutgngsQ1	AN7	Return key
C	24	=	14Assets	C9	Return key
C	25	=	14Assets	II8	Return key
C	26	=	14Assets	L10	Return key
C	27	=	14Assets	O10	Return key

Click into cell		Type	Open source sheet					Click into cell	Press on your keyboard
C	28	=	14Assets					R9	Return key
C	29	=	14Assets					U10	Return key
C	30	=	14Assets					X9	Return key
C	31	=	15Liabs					C9	Return key
C	32	=	15Liabs					F11	Return key
C	33	=	15Liabs					I8	Return key
C	34	=	15Liabs					L9	Return key
C	35	=	15Liabs					P9	Return key
C	36	=	15Liabs					S9	Return key
C	37	=	14Assets					V9	Return key
C	38	=	15Liabs					Y8	Return key
D	5	=-	5IncmsQ2					K7	Return key
D	6	=-	5IncmsQ2					L7	Return key
D	7	=-	5IncmsQ2					X7	Return key
D	8	=	6OutgngsQ2					M7	Return key
D	9	=	6OutgngsQ2					N7	Return key
D	10	=	6OutgngsQ2					O7	Return key
D	11	=	6OutgngsQ2					P7	Return key
D	12	=	6OutgngsQ2					Q7	Return key
D	13	=	6OutgngsQ2					R7	Return key
D	14	=	6OutgngsQ2					S7	Return key
D	15	=	6OutgngsQ2					T7	Return key
D	16	=	6OutgngsQ2					U7	Return key
D	17	=	6OutgngsQ2					V7	Return key
D	18	=	6OutgngsQ2					W7	Return key
D	19	=	6OutgngsQ2					X7	Return key
D	20	=	14Assets					F11	Return key
D	21	=	6OutgngsQ2					Y7	Return key
D	22	=	6OutgngsQ2					Z7	Return key
D	23	=	6OutgngsQ2					AN	Return key
D	24	=	14Assets					C12	Return key
D	25	=	14Assets					I10	Return key
D	26	=	14Assets					L14	Return key
D	27	=	14	Assets	O14	-	14 Assets	O10	Return key

Click into cell		Type	Open source sheet						Click into cell	Press on your keyboard
D	28	=	14Assets						R12	Return key
D	29	=	14Assets						U14	Return key
D	30	=	14Assets						X12	Return key
D	31	=	15Liabs						C12	Return key
D	32	=	15Liabs						F16	Return key
D	33	=	15Liabs						I10	Return key
D	34	=	15Liabs						L12	Return key
D	35	=	15Liabs						P12	Return key
D	36	=	15	Liabs	S12	-	15	Liabs	S9	Return key
D	37	=	15	Liabs	V9	-	15	Liabs	V6	Return key
D	38	=	15Liabs						Y10	Return key
E	5	=-	7IncmsQ3						K7	Return key
E	6	=-	7IncmsQ3						L7	Return key
E	7	=-	7IncmsQ3						X7	Return key
E	8	=	8OutgngsQ3						M7	Return key
E	9	=	8OutgngsQ3						N7	Return key
E	10	=	8OutgngsQ3						O7	Return key
E	11	=	8OutgngsQ3						P7	Return key
E	12	=	8OutgngsQ3						Q7	Return key
E	13	=	8OutgngsQ3						R7	Return key
E	14	=	8OutgngsQ3						S7	Return key
E	15	=	8OutgngsQ3						T7	Return key
E	16	=	8OutgngsQ3						U7	Return key
E	17	=	8OutgngsQ3						V7	Return key
E	18	=	8OutgngsQ3						W7	Return key
E	19	=	8OutgngsQ3						X7	Return key
E	20	=	14Assets						F14	Return key
E	21	=	8OutgngsQ3						Y7	Return key
E	22	=	8OutgngsQ3						Z7	Return key
E	23	=	8OutgngsQ3						AN7	Return key
E	24	=	14Assets						C15	Return key
E	25	=	14Assets						I12	Return key
E	26	=	14Assets						L18	Return key
E	27	=	14	Assets	O14	-	14	Assets	O14	Return key

Click into cell		Type	Open source sheet						Click into cell	Press on your keyboard
E	28	=	14Assets						R15	Return key
E	29	=	14Assets						U18	Return key
E	30	=	14Assets						X15	Return key
E	31	=	15Liabs						C15	Return key
E	32	=	15Liabs						F21	Return key
E	33	=	15Liabs						I12	Return key
E	34	=	15Liabs						L15	Return key
E	35	=	15Liabs						P15	Return key
E	36	=	15	Liabs	S15	-	15	Liabs	S12	Return key
E	37	=	15	Liabs	V12	-	15	Liabs	V9	Return key
E	38	=	15Liabs						Y12	Return key
F	5	=	9IncmsQ4						K7	Return key
F	6	=	9IncmsQ4						L7	Return key
F	7	=	9IncmsQ14						X7	Return key
F	8	=	8OutgngsQ4						M7	Return key
F	9	=	10OutgngsQ4						N7	Return key
F	10	=	10OutgngsQ4						O7	Return key
F	11	=	10OutgngsQ4						P7	Return key
F	12	=	10OutgngsQ4						Q7	Return key
F	13	=	10OutgngsQ4						R7	Return key
F	14	=	10OutgngsQ4						S7	Return key
F	15	=	10OutgngsQ4						T7	Return key
F	16	=	10OutgngsQ4						U7	Return key
F	17	=	10OutgngsQ4						V7	Return key
F	18	=	10OutgngsQ4						W7	Return key
F	19	=	10OutgngsQ4						X7	Return key
F	20	=	14Assets						F17	Return key
F	21	=	10OutgngsQ4						Y7	Return key
F	22	=	10OutgngsQ4						Z7	Return key
F	23	=	10OutgngsQ4						AN7	Return key
F	24	=	14Assets						C18	Return key
F	25	=	14Assets						I14	Return key
F	26	=	14Assets						L22	Return key
F	27	=	14	Assets	O14	-	14	Assets	O18	Return key

Click into cell		Type	Open source sheet						Click into cell	Press on your keyboard
F	28	=	14Assets						R18	Return key
F	29	=	14Assets						U22	Return key
F	30	=	14Assets						X18	Return key
F	31	=	15Liabs						C18	Return key
F	32	=	15Liabs						F26	Return key
F	33	=	15Liabs						I14	Return key
F	34	=	15Liabs						L18	Return key
F	35	=	15Liabs						P18	Return key
F	36	=	15	Liabs	S18	-	15	Liabs	S15	Return key
F	37	=	15	Liabs	V15	-	15	Liabs	V12	Return key
F	38	=	15Liabs						Y14	Return key

Note: There are minus signs after the equals signs in cells C5, C6, C7, D5, D6, D7, E5, E6 and E7.

Now there are some formulae to put in to compute the annual figures from the quarterly summaries:

Click into cell	Click on to	Click into cell	Hold down	Click into cell	Press	Formula that will be automatically inserted
G5	Sigma icon	C5	Shift Key	F5	Return key	=SUM(C5:F5)
G6	Sigma icon	C6	Shift Key	F6	Return key	=SUM(C6:F6)
G7	Sigma icon	C7	Shift Key	F7	Return key	=SUM(C7:F7)
G8	Sigma icon	C8	Shift Key	F8	Return key	=SUM(C8:F8)
G9	Sigma icon	C9	Shift Key	F9	Return key	=SUM(C9:F9)
G10	Sigma icon	C10	Shift Key	F10	Return key	=SUM(C10:F10)
G11	Sigma icon	C11	Shift Key	F11	Return key	=SUM(C11:F11)
G12	Sigma icon	C12	Shift Key	F12	Return key	=SUM(C12:F12)
G13	Sigma icon	C13	Shift Key	F13	Return key	=SUM(C13:F13)

61 The trial balance—cont.

Click into cell	Click on to	Click into cell	Hold down	Click into cell	Press	Formula that will be automatically inserted
G14	Sigma icon	C14	Shift Key	F14	Return key	=SUM(C14:F14)
G15	Sigma icon	C15	Shift Key	F15	Return key	=SUM(C15:F15)
G16	Sigma icon	C16	Shift Key	F16	Return key	=SUM(C16:F16)
G17	Sigma icon	C17	Shift Key	F17	Return key	=SUM(C17:F17)
G18	Sigma icon	C18	Shift Key	F18	Return key	=SUM(C18:F18)
G19	Sigma icon	C19	Shift Key	F19	Return key	=SUM(C19:F19)
G20	Sigma icon	C20	Shift Key	F20	Return key	=SUM(C20:F20)
G21	Sigma icon	C21	Shift Key	F21	Return key	=SUM(C21:F21)
G22	Sigma icon	C22	Shift Key	F22	Return key	=SUM(C22:F22)
G23	Sigma icon	C23	Shift Key	F23	Return key	=SUM(C23:F23)
G24	Sigma icon	C24	Shift Key	F24	Return key	=SUM(C24:F24)
G25	Sigma icon	C25	Shift Key	F25	Return key	=SUM(C25:F25)
G26	Sigma icon	C26	Shift Key	F26	Return key	=SUM(C26:F26)
G27	Sigma icon	C27	Shift Key	F27	Return key	=SUM(C27:F27)
G28	Sigma icon	C28	Shift Key	F28	Return key	=SUM(C28:F28)
G29	Sigma icon	C29	Shift Key	F29	Return key	=SUM(C29:F29)
G30	Sigma icon	C30	Shift Key	F30	Return key	=SUM(C30:F30)
G31	Sigma icon	C31	Shift Key	F31	Return key	=SUM(C31:F31)
G32	Sigma icon	C32	Shift Key	F32	Return key	=SUM(C32:F32)
G33	Sigma icon	C33	Shift Key	F33	Return key	=SUM(C33:F33)

Click into cell	Click on to	Click into cell	Hold down	Click into cell	Press	Formula that will be automatically inserted
G34	Sigma icon	C34	Shift Key	F34	Return key	=SUM(C34:F34)
G35	Sigma icon	C35	Shift Key	F35	Return key	=SUM(C35:F35)
G36	Sigma icon	C36	Shift Key	F36	Return key	=SUM(C36:F36)
G37	Sigma icon	C37	Shift Key	F37	Return key	=SUM(C37:F37)
G38	Sigma icon	C38	Shift Key	F38	Return key	=SUM(C38:F38)
C39	Sigma icon A	C5	Shift Key	C38	Return key	=SUM(C5:C38)
D39	Sigma icon A	D5	Shift Key	D38	Return key	=SUM(D5:D38)
E39	Sigma icon A	E5	Shift Key	E38	Return key	=SUM(E5:E38)
F39	Sigma icon A	F5	Shift Key	F38	Return key	=SUM(F5:F38)

Notes: A super-quick way to fill cells G5 to G36 is simply to click into cell G5, click on the copy icon on the ribbon, click into cell G6, hold down the shift key and drag the cursor down to cell G36. Let go of the cursor and press the return key on your keypad.

PROFIT AND LOSS ACCOUNT

#		Q1	Q2	Q3	Q4	YEAR TO DATE	PREV YEAR	CHANGE	% CHANGE
1	Gross profit/loss	-1,200.00	-1,940.00	0.00	-750.00	-3,890.00	60.00	3,950.00	3,950.00
2	Gross profit/loss margin	100%	97%	#DIV/0!	100%	98%	#DIV/0!	#DIV/0!	#DIV/0!
3	Net profit/loss margin	50%	#DIV/0!	587%	-32%	#DIV/0!	54%	#DIV/0!	#DIV/0!
4	Return on capital employed	0.0097371	0.018322083	0.04166667	-0.0113636	#DIV/0!	#DIV/0!	#DIV/0!	#DIV/0!
5									
6	Turnover	-1,200.00	-2,000.00	0.00	-750.00	-3,950.00		3,950.00	#DIV/0!
7	Other income	-800.00	0.00	-5,000.00	0.00	-5,800.00		5,800.00	#DIV/0!
8	TOTAL INCOME	-2,000.00	-2,000.00	-5,000.00	-750.00		0.00	0.00	#DIV/0!
9	Purchases	0.00	50.00	0.00	0.00	60.00	50.00	10.00	20.00%
10	Other direct costs	0.00	0.00	0.00	0.00	0.00	10.00	-10.00	-100.00%
11	Wages, salaries and other employment costs	0.00	0.00	0.00	0.00	0.00	10.00	-10.00	-100.00%
12	Rent	0.00	0.00	0.00	0.00	0.00	5.00	-5.00	-100.00%
13	Repairs and renewals	1,000.00	40.00	600.00	0.00	1,640.00	1,000.00	640.00	64.00%
14	Administration expenses	0.00	0.00	0.00	0.00	0.00	5.00	-5.00	-100.00%
15	Travelling expenses	0.00	0.00	0.00	0.00	0.00	5.00	-5.00	-100.00%
16	Advertising and promotion	0.00	0.00	0.00	2,000.00	2,000.00	1,000.00	1,000.00	100.00%
17	Professional fees and charges	0.00	0.00	0.00	0.00	0.00	5.00	-5.00	-100.00%
18	Bad debts	0.00	0.00	0.00	0.00	0.00	5.00	-5.00	-100.00%
19	Bank charges	0.00	0.00	0.00	0.00	0.00	5.00	-5.00	-100.00%
20	Depreciation costs	0.00	0.00	0.00	0.00	0.00	5.00	-5.00	-100.00%
21	Loss (or profit) on asset disposals	0.00	0.00	0.00	0.00	0.00	5.00	-5.00	-100.00%
22	Other expenses	0.00	0.00	0.00	0.00	0.00	5.00	-5.00	-100.00%
23	Non-allowable expenses	0.00	0.00	0.00	0.00	0.00	5.00	-5.00	-100.00%
24	TOTAL EXPENSES	1,000.00	100.00	600.00	2,000.00	3,700.00	2,120.00		
25	NET PROFIT/LOSS	-1,000.00	-1,900.00	-4,400.00	1,250.00	3,700.00	2,120.00	-1,580.00	0.00%
26									
27	Opening capital	-102,700.00	-103,700.00	-105,600.00	-110,000.00				

Figure 40 Example of a profit and loss account

Now we are going to deal with the profit and loss account. This is how to configure the spreadsheet page for this.

First, we need to create a new worksheet by clicking on the new worksheet icon at the bottom of the page and renaming it '17P&L'.

Cell reference		What to type in
B	1	Profit and loss account
B	5	Gross profit/loss
B	6	Gross profit/loss margin
B	7	Net profit/loss margin
B	8	Return on capital employed
A	10	1
B	10	Turnover
A	11	2
B	11	Other income
B	12	TOTAL INCOME
A	13	4
B	13	Purchases
A	14	5
B	14	Other direct costs
A	15	6
B	15	Wages, salaries and other employment costs
A	16	7
B	16	Rent
A	17	8
B	17	Repairs and renewals
A	18	9
B	18	Administration expenses
A	19	10
B	19	Travelling expenses
A	20	11
B	20	Advertising and promotion
A	21	12
B	21	Professional fees and charges
A	22	13
B	22	Bad debts
A	23	14

Cell reference		What to type in
B	23	Bank charges
A	24	15
B	24	Depreciation costs
A	25	16
B	25	Loss (or profit) on asset disposals
A	26	17
B	26	Other expenses
A	27	18
B	27	Non-allowable expenses
B	28	TOTAL EXPENSES
B	29	Net profit/loss
B	31	Opening capital
C	4	Q1
D	4	Q2
E	4	Q3
F	4	Q4
G	4	YEAR-TO-DATE
H	4	PREV YEAR
I	4	CHANGE
J	4	% CHANGE

Note: A super-quick way to fill cells A13 to B27 is to click on sheet 16TB, highlight cells A8 to B22 and copy and paste this range into cell A13 of sheet 17P&L.

Embolden and underline the contents of cell B1, by clicking on the bold and underline icons in the fonts group on the ribbon, because the content of this cell is the title of the sheet. Embolden and right-align the contents of cells B5, B8, B12, B28 and B31 because these are figures to which the reader's attention needs to be particularly drawn. Embolden the contents of cells C4 to J4 and place all borders around each of the cells, by highlighting the range, clicking on the borders icon in the fonts section of the ribbon and selecting the all borders option.

Highlight cells C28 to H28 and place top and double bottom borders around them by clicking on the borders icon and selecting the top and double bottom option.

Now we need to create four links, the first three of which we can simply copy from the trial balance sheet. This is how to do it:

Open sheet	Click into cell		Hold down	Click into cell		Icon to click	Open sheet	Click into cell		Icon to click
16TB	C	5	Shift key	F	6	Copy	17P&L	C	10	Paste link
16TB	C	8	Shift key	F	27	Copy	17P&L	C	13	Paste link
16TB	C	37	Shift key	F	37	Copy	17P&L	C	31	Paste link

Now there are fourteen different formulae to put in:

Open sheet	Click into cell		Click on	Click into cell		Hold down	Click into cell		Press	Resulting formula
P&L	C	12	Sigma icon	C	10	Shift key	C	11	Return key	=SUM(C10:C11)
	D	12	Sigma icon	D	10	Shift key	D	11	Return key	=SUM(D10:D11)
	E	12	Sigma icon	E	10	Shift key	E	11	Return key	=SUM (E10:E11)
	F	12	Sigma icon	F	10	Shift key	F	11	Return key	=SUM(F10:F11)
	G	12	Sigma icon	G	10	Shift key	G	11	Return key	=SUM(G10:G11)
	H	12	Sigma icon	H	10	Shift key	H	11	Return key	=SUM(H10:H11)
	C	28	Sigma icon	C	13	Shift key	C	26	Return key	=SUM(C13:C26)
	D	28	Sigma icon	D	13	Shift key	D	26	Return key	=SUM(D13:D26)
	E	28	Sigma icon	E	13	Shift key	E	26	Return key	=SUM(E13:E26)
	F	28	Sigma icon	F	13	Shift key	F	26	Return key	=SUM(F13:F26)
	G	28	Sigma icon	G	13	Shift key	G	26	Return key	=SUM(G13:G26)
	H	28	Sigma icon	H	13	Shift key	H	26	Return key	=SUM(H13:H26)
	C	29	Sigma icon	C	28	Ctrl key	C	12	Return key	=SUM(C28,C12)
	D	29	Sigma icon	D	28	Ctrl key	D	12	Return key	=SUM(D28,D12)
	E	29	Sigma icon	E	28	Ctrl key	E	12	Return key	=SUM(E28,E12)
	F	29	Sigma icon	F	28	Ctrl key	F	12	Return key	=SUM(F28,F12)
	G	29	Sigma icon	G	28	Ctrl key	G	12	Return key	=SUM(G28,G12)
	H	29	Sigma icon	H	28	Ctrl key	H	12	Return key	=SUM(H28,H12)

Note: A super-quick way to fill cells C12 to H12 is to fill cell D12 as instructed, copy the contents, highlight cells D12 to H12 and then paste.

Click into cell	Click on	Click into cell	Hold down	Click into cell	Hold down	Click into cell	Press	Resulting formula
C 5	Sigma icon	C 10	Ctrl key	C 13	Ctrl key	C 14	Return key	=SUM(C10,C13,C14)
D 5	Sigma icon	D 10	Ctrl key	D 13	Ctrl key	D 14	Return key	=SUM(D10,D13,D14)
E 5	Sigma icon	E 10	Ctrl key	E 13	Ctrl key	E 14	Return key	=SUM(E10,E13,E14)
F 5	Sigma icon	F 10	Ctrl key	F 13	Ctrl key	F 14	Return key	=SUM(F10,F13,F14)
G 5	Sigma icon	G 10	Ctrl key	G 13	Ctrl key	G 14	Return key	=SUM(G10,G13,G14)
H 5	Sigma icon	H 10	Ctrl key	H 13	Ctrl key	H 14	Return key	=SUM(H10,H13,H14)

Note: You can fill cells C28 to H28 by filling cell C28 and then copying and pasting the contents into the other cells in the range. You can take the same shortcut to fill cell ranges C5 to H5, C6 to H6, C7 to H7 and C8to H8 with the content in the tables below.

Click into cell	Click on	Click into cell	Click on	Click into cell	Press	Resulting formula
C 6	=	C 5	/	C 10	Return key	=C5/C10
D 6	=	D 5	/	D 10	Return key	=D5/D10
E 6	=	E 5	/	E 10	Return key	=E5/E10
F 6	=	F 5	/	F 10	Return key	=F5/F10
G 6	=	G 5	/	G 10	Return key	=G5/G10
H 6	=	H 5	/	H 10	Return key	=H5/H10
C 7	=	C 29	/	C 10	Return key	=C29/C10
D 7	=	D 29	/	D 10	Return key	=D29/D10
E 7	=	E 29	/	E 10	Return key	=E29/E10
F 7	=	F 29	/	F 10	Return key	=F29/F10
G 7	=	G 29	/	G 10	Return key	=G29/G10
H 7	=	H 29	/	H 10	Return key	=H29/H10
C 8	=	C 29	/	C 31	Return key	=C29/C31
D 8	=	D 29	/	D 31	Return key	=D29/D31
E 8	=	E 29	/	E 31	Return key	=E29/E31
F 8	=	F 29	/	F 31	Return key	=F29/F31
G 8	=	G 29	/	G 31	Return key	=G29/G31
H 8	=	H 29	/	H 31	Return key	=H29/H31

Now we need to sum the quarterly profit and loss figures to arrive at the annual figures. This is how to do it:

Click into cell	Click on to	Click into cell	Hold down	Click into cell	Hold down	Click into cell	Hold down	Click into cell	Press	Formula that will be automatically inserted
G 10	Sigma icon	C 10	Ctrl key	D 10	Ctrl key	E 10	Ctrl key	F 10	Return key	=SUM(C10,D10, E10,F10)
G 11	Sigma icon	C 11	Ctrl key	D 11	Ctrl key	E 11	Ctrl key	F 11	Return key	=SUM(C11,D11, E11,F11)
G 13	Sigma icon	C 13	Ctrl key	D 13	Ctrl key	E 13	Ctrl key	F 13	Return key	=SUM(C13,D13, E13,F13)
G 14	Sigma icon	C 14	Ctrl key	D 14	Ctrl key	E 14	Ctrl key	F 14	Return key	=SUM(C14,D14, E14,F14)
G 15	Sigma icon	C 15	Ctrl key	D 15	Ctrl key	E 15	Ctrl key	F 15	Return key	=SUM(C15,D15, E15,F15)
G 16	Sigma icon	C 16	Ctrl key	D 16	Ctrl key	E 16	Ctrl key	F 16	Return key	=SUM(C16,D16, E16,F16)
G 17	Sigma icon	C 17	Ctrl key	D 17	Ctrl key	E 17	Ctrl key	F 17	Return key	=SUM(C17,D17, E17,F17)
G 18	Sigma icon	C 18	Ctrl key	D 18	Ctrl key	E 18	Ctrl key	F 18	Return key	=SUM(C18,D18, E18,F18)
G 19	Sigma icon	C 19	Ctrl key	D 19	Ctrl key	E 19	Ctrl key	F 19	Return key	=SUM(C19,D19, E19,F19)
G 20	Sigma icon	C 20	Ctrl key	D 20	Ctrl key	E 20	Ctrl key	F 20	Return key	=SUM(C20,D20, E20,F20)
G 21	Sigma icon	C 21	Ctrl key	D 21	Ctrl key	E 21	Ctrl key	F 21	Return key	=SUM(C21,D21, E21,F21)
G 22	Sigma icon	C 22	Ctrl key	D 22	Ctrl key	E 22	Ctrl key	F 22	Return key	=SUM(C22,D22, E22,F22)
G 23	Sigma icon	C 23	Ctrl key	D 23	Ctrl key	E 23	Ctrl key	F 23	Return key	=SUM(C23,D23, E23,F23)
G 24	Sigma icon	C 24	Ctrl key	D 24	Ctrl key	E 24	Ctrl key	F 24	Return key	=SUM(C24,D24, E24,F24)
G 25	Sigma icon	C 25	Ctrl key	D 25	Ctrl key	E 25	Ctrl key	F 25	Return key	=SUM(C25,D25, E25,F25)
G 26	Sigma icon	C 26	Ctrl key	D 26	Ctrl key	E 26	Ctrl key	F 26	Return key	=SUM(C26,D26, E26,F26)
G 27	Sigma icon	C 27	Ctrl key	D 27	Ctrl key	E 27	Ctrl key	F 27	Return key	=SUM(C27,D27, E27,F27)

Note: A super-quick way to fill cells G10 to G27 is to fill G10 as described above, then while still in G10, copy the contents, highlight cells G11 to G27 and paste.

Comparatives

Now we need to make provision for the insertion of comparative figures from the previous year and for the actual and percentage changes to be computed and displayed.

Column H in the profit and loss sheet is designated for the previous year's figures and it is useful to make this column look different to the others to indicate that it is a column wherein content is to be entered manually. A common way to do this is to light shade the cells in this column. Shading can be applied by clicking on the arrow at the right of the fill icon in the fonts section of the ribbon, while the 'Home' tab is open. Choose from the various shades of grey running downwards from light to dark. The 5 per cent shade is really too light as it hardly contrasts with unshaded cells at all, while those shades greater than 15 per cent obscure the clarity of the figures in the cells: 15 per cent is therefore the best option. To shade these cells proceed as follows:

Click into cell	Hold down	Click into cell	Hold down	Click into cell	Hold down	Click into cell	Click on icon	Select	Press
H10	Shift key	H11	Ctrl key	H13	Shift key	H27	Fill colour	15% grey	Return key

To ensure that these cells are formatted appropriately highlight cells C5 to I5. Click on the small arrow at the bottom right-hand corner of the number section of the ribbon (close to the middle when the 'Home' tab is open). In the dialogue box that will appear:

- Select the number option from the menu in the left-hand pane;
- select '2' as the number of decimal places;
- tick the '000s' separators box;
- select the option that shows minus figures being preceded by a minus sign in the negative numbers pane.

Now highlight cells C10 to I31 and repeat the above process.

Now we need to enter formulae to compute the actual change between the current year's figures and those of the previous year:

Click into cell	Press key	Click into cell	Press key	Click into cell	Press key
I5	=	H5	-	G5	Return

Now copy the formula in cell I5 into cells I10, I11, I12 and I29, as follows:

Click into cell	Right mouse click	Select	Left mouse click	Click into cell	Hold down	Click into	Hold down	Click into	Right mouse click	Select	Left mouse click
I5		Copy option		I10	Shift key	I12	Ctrl key	I29		Copy option	

The next thing to compute is the difference in gross profit margin. To do this we need to place a formula in cell I6. That formula is '=G6-H6', as G6 contains the percentage margin for the current year and H6 for the previous year.

Click into cell	Press key	Click into cell	Press key	Click into cell	Press key
I6	=	G6	-	H6	Return

We can then copy and paste the formula into cells I7 and I8 and the range of cells from I13 to I27 to display differences in all the expenses between the two years.

Click into cell	Right mouse click	Select	Left mouse click	Click into cell	Hold down	Into cell	Hold down	into cell	Hold down	into cell	Right mouse click	Select	Left mouse click
I6		Copy option		I7	Shift key	I8	Ctrl key	I13	Shift key	I27		Paste option	

We can now display these differences as percentages by dividing the amount of change by the value to which it relates in the previous year for each expense category. Proceed as follows:

Click into cell	Press key	Click into cell	Press key	Click into cell	Press key	Type	Press key
J10	=	I10	/	H10	*	100	Return

Now we need to format cell J10 to display the result as a percentage. To do this, click back into J10, click on the small arrow at the bottom right-hand corner of the numbers group on the ribbon, and then select the percentage option in the category pane. Make sure the number of decimal places is set at 2 and adjust as necessary.

If there are no actual values in the cells that are being compared, cell J10 will simply display the formula. Once there are values in the cells it will perform the calculation and display the percentage result.

We now need to place similar formulae into cells J11 to J13. We can begin by copying and pasting from J10: the cell numbers will change accordingly.

Click into cell	Right mouse click	Select	Left mouse click	Click into cell	Hold down	Click into cell	Select	Left mouse click
J10		Copy option		J11	Shift key	J13	Paste option	

Now we can copy and paste the formula in J13 into each of the other expense cells, as follows:

Click into cell	Right mouse click	Select	Left mouse click	Click into cell	Hold down	Click into cell	Select	Left mouse click
J13		Copy option		J14	Shift key	J28	Paste option	

As before, you will need to format the percentage change cells into which you have just pasted formulae to make them present the results as percentages. To do this, click on the arrow in the right-hand corner of the number group on the ribbon to bring up the format dialogue box, select percentages in the category pane and make sure the number of decimal places is set to 2, adjusting as necessary, then click on the 'OK' button.

Balance sheet								
	Q1	Q2	Q3	Q4	YEAR TO DATE	PREV YEAR	CHANGE	% CHANGE
Current assets	4,900.00	6,800.00	11,200.00	9,950.00	9,950.00	3,900.00	6,050.00	155.12821
Current liabilities	-3,200.00	-3,200.00	-3,200.00	-3,200.00	-3,200.00	-3,200.00	0.00	0
Current ratio	1.53125	2.125	3.5	3.109375	3.109375	1.21875	1.89	155.12821
Acid test ratio	1.30	1.89	3.27	2.88	2.88	0.98	1.89	192.06349
							0.00	#DIV/0!
20 Fixed assets	112,000.00	112,000.00	112,000.00	112,000.00	112000	112000	0.00	0
21 Stock	750.00	750.00	750.00	750.00	750.00	750	0.00	0
22 Trade debtors	0.00	0.00	0.00	0.00	0.00	1000	-1,000.00	-100
23 Cash at bank	4,000.00	5940.00	5340.00	4090.00	4090.00	2000	2,090.00	104.5
24 Unbanked cheques	100.00	100.00	5100.00	5100.00	5100.00	100	5,000.00	5000
25 Cash in hand	50.00	10.00	10.00	10.00	10.00	50	-40.00	-80
26 Other current assets	0.00	0.00	0.00	0.00	0.00	0.00	0.00	#DIV/0!
Total assets	116,900.00	118,800.00	123,200.00	121,950.00	121,950.00	115,900.00	6,050.00	5.2200173
27 Trade creditors	-1,200.00	-1,200.00	-1,200.00	-1,200.00	-1,200.00	-1200.00	0.00	0
28 VAT payable	-1,000.00	-1,000.00	-1000.00	-1000.00	-1,000.00	-1000.00	0.00	0
29 PAYE and NI	-250.00	-250.00	-250.00	-250.00	-250.00	-250.00	0.00	0
30 Credit card	-250.00	-250.00	-250.00	-250.00	-250.00	-250.00	0.00	0
31 Other current liabilities	-500.00	-500.00	-500.00	-500.00	-500.00	-500.00	0.00	0
32 Business loan	-10,000.00	-10,000.00	-10000.00	-10000.00	-10,000.00	-10000.00	0.00	0
Total liabilities	-13,200.00	-13,200.00	-13,200.00	-13,200.00	-13,200.00	-13,200.00	0.00	0
Net assets	103,700.00	105,600.00	110,000.00	108,750.00	108,750.00	102,700.00	6,050.00	5.8909445
33 Capital	-102,700.00	-103700.00	-105600.00	-110000.00	-110000.00	-102700	-7,300.00	7.1080818
Net profit/loss	-1000	-1900	-4400	1250	1250.00		1,250.00	#DIV/0!
34 Drawings	0.00	0.00	0.00	0.00	0.00		0.00	#DIV/0!
Owners equity	-103,700.00	-105,600.00	-110,000.00	-108,750.00	-108,750.00	-102,700.00	-6,050.00	5.8909445
Error	0.00	0.00	0.00	0.00	0.00	0.00		

Figure 41 Example of a balance sheet

Now we are going to deal with the balance sheet. This is how to configure the spreadsheet page for this.

First, we need to create a new worksheet by clicking on the new worksheet icon at the bottom of the page and renaming it '18BS'.

Cell reference		What to type in
B	1	Balance sheet
B	5	Current assets
B	6	Current liabilities
B	7	Current ratio
B	8	Acid test ratio
B	17	Total assets
B	24	Total liabilities
B	25	Net assets
A	26	33

Cell reference		What to type in
B	26	Capital
B	27	Net profit/loss
A	28	34
B	28	Drawings
B	29	Owners equity
B	30	Error

Embolden and underline the contents of cell B1, by clicking on the bold and underline icons in the fonts group on the ribbon, because the content of this cell is the title of the sheet. Embolden and right-align the contents of cells B5, B8, B17, B24, B25, B27, B29 and B30 because these are figures to which the reader's attention needs to be particularly drawn and the right alignment is to conform to standard accounting practice.

Now we need to list the asset categories:

- Fixed assets
- Stock
- Trade debtors
- Cash at bank
- Cheques received but not yet banked
- Cash in hand
- Other current assets.

(There may be more categories, depending on the requirements of the business.)

A quick way of doing this is simply to copy and paste the categories from the trial balance. Here's what to do:

Open sheet	Click into cell	Hold down	Click into cell	Right mouse click	Select	Left mouse click	Open sheet	Click into cell	Right mouse click	Select	Left mouse click
16TB	A24	Shift key	B30		Copy		18BS	A10		Paste	

Now we need to list the categories of liabilities:

- Trade creditors
- VAT payable
- PAYE and NI
- Credit card
- Other current liabilities including accruals
- Business loan

Again we can do this quickly by cutting and pasting from the trial balance. Here's how:

Open sheet	Click into cell	Hold down	Click into cell	Right mouse click	Select	Left mouse click	Open sheet	Click into cell	Right mouse click	Select	Left mouse click
16TB	A31	Shift key	B36			Copy		18BS	A18			Paste

Now we need to put in the column headings. As they are the same as in the profit and loss account, we can save time by simply copying them over:

Open sheet	Click into cell	Hold down	Click into cell	Right mouse click	Select	Left mouse click	Open sheet	Click into cell	Right mouse click	Select	Left mouse click
17P&L	C4	Shift key	J4			Copy		18BS	C4			Paste

Now we need to create five links, which we can paste from the trial balance. This is how to do it.

Open sheet	Click into cell		Hold down	Click into cell		Icon to click	Open sheet	Click into cell		Icon to click
16TB	C	24	Shift key	F	30	Copy	18BS	C	10	Paste link
16TB	C	31	Shift key	F	36	Copy	18BS	C	18	Paste link
16TB	C	37	Shift key	F	37	Copy	18BS	C	26	Paste link
16TB	C	38	Shift key	F	38	Copy	18BS	C	28	Paste link
17P&L	C	29	Shift key	G	29	Copy	18BS	C	27	Paste link

Now there are several formulae that we need to put in to sheet 18BS:

Click into cell		Click on	Click into cell		Hold down	Click into cell		Press	Resulting formula
C	17	Sigma icon	C	10	Shift key	C	16	Return key	=SUM(C10:C16)
D	17	Sigma icon	D	10	Shift key	D	16	Return key	=SUM(C10:C11)
E	17	Sigma icon	E	10	Shift key	E	16	Return key	=SUM(C10:C11)
F	17	Sigma icon	F	10	Shift key	F	16	Return key	=SUM(C10:C11)
G	17	Sigma icon	G	10	Shift key	G	16	Return key	=SUM(C10:C11)
H	17	Sigma icon	H	10	Shift key	H	16	Return key	=SUM(C10:C11)
C	24	Sigma icon	C	18	Shift key	C	23	Return key	=SUM(C18:C23)

Click into cell		Click on	Click into cell		Hold down	Click into cell		Press	Resulting formula
D	24	Sigma icon	D	18	Shift key	D	23	Return key	=SUM(D18:D23)
E	24	Sigma icon	E	18	Shift key	E	23	Return key	=SUM(E18:E23)
F	24	Sigma icon	F	18	Shift key	F	23	Return key	=SUM(F18:F23)
G	24	Sigma icon	G	18	Shift key	G	23	Return key	=SUM(G18:G23)
H	24	Sigma icon	H	18	Shift key	H	23	Return key	=SUM(H18:H23)
C	25	Sigma icon	C	17	Ctrl key	C	24	Return key	=SUM(C17,C24)
D	25	Sigma icon	D	17	Ctrl key	D	24	Return key	=SUM(D17,D24)
E	25	Sigma icon	E	17	Ctrl key	E	242	Return key	=SUM(E17,E24)
F	25	Sigma icon	F	17	Ctrl key	F	242	Return key	=SUM(F17,F24)
G	25	Sigma icon	C	25	Shift key	F	25	Return key	=SUM(C25:F25)
H	25	Sigma icon	H	17	Ctrl key	H	24	Return key	=SUM(H17,H24)
C	29	Sigma icon	C	26	Shift key	C	28	Return key	=SUM(C26,C28)
D	29	Sigma icon	D	26	Shift key	D	28	Return key	=SUM(D26,D28)
E	29	Sigma icon	E	26	Shift key	E	28	Return key	=SUM(E26,E28)
F	29	Sigma icon	F	26	Shift key	F	28	Return key	=SUM(F26,F28)
G	29	Sigma icon	G	26	Shift key	G	28	Return key	=SUM(G26,G28)
C	30	Sigma icon	C	25	Ctrl key	C	29	Return key	=SUM(C25,C29)
D	30	Sigma icon	D	25	Ctrl key	D	29	Return key	=SUM(D25,D29)
E	30	Sigma icon	E	25	Ctrl key	E	29	Return key	=SUM(E25,E29)
F	30	Sigma icon	F	25	Ctrl key	F	29	Return key	=SUM(F25,F29)

Click into cell		Click on	Click into cell		Hold down	Click into cell		Press	Resulting formula
G	30	Sigma icon	G	25	Ctrl key	G	29	Return key	=SUM(G25,G29)
H	30	Sigma icon	H	25	Ctrl key	H	29	Return key	=SUM(H25,H29)
C	5	Sigma icon	C	11	Shift key	C	16	Return key	=SUM(C11:D16)
D	5	Sigma icon	D	11	Shift key	D	16	Return key	=SUM(D11:,D16)
E	5	Sigma icon	E	11	Shift key	E	16	Return key	=SUM(E11:E16)
F	5	Sigma icon	F	11	Shift key	F	16	Return key	=SUM(F11:F16)
G	5	Sigma icon	G	11	Shift key	G	16	Return key	=SUM(G11:G16)
H	5	Sigma icon	H	11	Shift key	H	16	Return key	=SUM(H11:H16)
C	6	Sigma icon	C	18	Shift key	C	22	Return key	=SUM(C18:C22)
D	6	Sigma icon	D	18	Shift key	D	22	Return key	=SUM(D18:D22
E	6	Sigma icon	E	18	Shift key	E	22	Return key	=SUM(E18:E22
F	6	Sigma icon	F	18	Shift key	F	22	Return key	=SUM(F18:F22
G	6	Sigma icon	G	18	Shift key	G	22	Return key	=SUM(G18:G22
H	6	Sigma icon	H	18	Shift key	H	22	Return key	=SUM(H18:H22

Notes: A super-quick way to fill cells C17 to H17 is to fill cell C17, as instructed, copy the contents, highlight cells D17 to H17 and then paste. You can fill cells C24 to H24, C25 to H25, C29 to G29, C30 to H30, C5 to H5 and C6 to H6 in the same way by filling the first cell in the range and then copying and pasting the contents into the others.

Click into cell		Press key	Click into cell		Press key	Click into cell		Press key	Resulting formula
C	7	=	C	5	/	C	6	Return key	=C5/C6
D	7	=	D	5	/	D	6	Return key	=D5/D6
E	7	=	E	5	/	E	6	Return key	=E5/E6
F	7	=	F	5	/	F	6	Return key	=F5/F6
G	7	=	G	5	/	G	6	Return key	=G5/G6
H	7	=	H	5	/	H	6	Return key	=H5/H6

Note: You can use the same shortcut as before to fill cells C7 to D7 and C8 to D8. Insert the formula in the first of the range and then copy and paste it into the others. The cell numbers will change as appropriate automatically.

Click into cell		Press key	Press key	Click into cell		Press key	Click into cell		Press key	Press key	Click into cell		Resulting formula
C	8	=	(	C	5	-	C	11	)	/	C	6	=(C5-C11)/C6
D	8	=	(	D	5	-	D	11	)	/	D	6	=(D5-D11)/D6
E	8	=	(	E	5	-	E	11	)	/	E	6	=(E5-E11)/E6
F	8	=	(	F	5	-	F	11	)	/	F	6	=(F5-F11)/F6
G	8	=	(	G	5	-	G	11	)	/	G	6	=(G5-G11)/G6
H	8	=	(	H	5	-	H	11	)	/	H	6	=(H5-H11)/H6

As the last twelve formulae inserted involve division, there may be decimal places in the quotients. We need to make sure that the cells concerned are formatted to a limit of 2 decimal places, otherwise we could have an output that exceeds the column width. Do this by highlighting the cells in which the formulae have been inserted, clicking on the down-facing arrow at the bottom right-hand corner of the number group on the ribbon and selecting the number option in the categories pane, then selecting 2 decimal places.

Now we just need to put in some borders to make the sheet look like a balance sheet would be expected to look like.

Click into cell		Hold down	Click into cell		Click on	Select	Press
C	17	Shift key	H	17	The arrow at the right of the borders icon	Top and double bottom border	Return key
C	24	=	H	24			
C	29	=	H	29			

Now we need to configure column J to compute the percentage change from last year. Proceed as follows.

Click into cell	Click on	Click into cell	Click on	Click into	Click on	Type	Press
J 5	=	I 5	/	H 5	*	100	Return
J 6	=	I 6	/	H 6	*	100	Return
J 7	=	I 7	/	H 7	*	100	Return
J 8	=	I 8	/	H 8	*	100	Return
J 9	=	I 9	/	H 9	*	100	Return
J 10	=	I 10	/	H 10	*	100	Return
J 11	=	I 11	/	H 11	*	100	Return
J 12	=	I 12	/	H 12	*	100	Return
J 13	=	I 13	/	H 13	*	100	Return
J 14	=	I 14	/	H 14	*	100	Return
J 15	=	I 15	/	H 15	*	100	Return
J 16	=	I 16	/	H 16	*	100	Return
J 17	=	I 17	/	H 17	*	100	Return
J 18	=	I 18	/	H 18	*	100	Return
J 19	=	I 19	/	H 19	*	100	Return
J 20	=	I 20	/	H 20	*	100	Return
J 21	=	I 21	/	H 21	*	100	Return
J 22	=	I 22	/	H 22	*	100	Return
J 23	=	I 23	/	H 23	*	100	Return
J 24	=	I 24	/	H 24	*	100	Return
J 25	=	I 25	/	H 25	*	100	Return
J 26	=	I 26	/	H 26	*	100	Return
J 27	=	I 27	/	H 27	*	100	Return
J 28	=	I 28	/	H 28	*	100	Return
J 29	=	I 29	/	H 29	*	100	Return

You can add additional columns to the incomings and outgoings analysis sheets as required. As it is more likely that this will be required for the outgoings than the incomings we will use the former as an example. The process is the same for the incomings analysis sheets. This is how to do it:

Making the changes on the analysis sheets

1. Decide what columns you need to add to the right-hand side of the outgoings analysis sheets and add them by clicking into the previous right-most occupied cell in row 7. Right-click, select copy and then left-click.
2. Left-click into the cell immediately to the right, right-click, select the paste option and then left-click. This will place the appropriate formula for the summing of each row at the top of the column in row 7.
3. Click into the cell immediately above it in row 6 and type the heading (the name of the ledger account concerned).
4. Repeat the above process for as many additional columns as you need.
5. Click into the cell in row 5 immediately above the first of the new category names you have added. Click on to the fill icon on the ribbon, and fill the cell with the same colour as that immediately to its left.
6. If you have added more than one additional category name, copy this cell by right-clicking, selecting the copy option and then left-clicking.
7. Click into the adjacent right cell, hold down the shift key and scroll along to the cell above the right-most newly occupied column. Select the paste option, left-click and release the mouse button.
8. Click the cursor into the first of the newly occupied cells in row 5, hold down the shift key and click into the right-most cell in row 7. Right-click, select the copy option, left-click and release the mouse button.
9. Now paste into the same locations on sheets 6OutgngsQ2, 8OutgngsQ3 and 10OutgngsQ4.
10. Staying on the same sheet, click into the first of the newly occupied cells in row 6. Hold the shift key down and scroll to the right-most of the newly occupied cells in that row.
11. Right-click, select the copy option, left-click and release the mouse button.

Carrying the changes through to the summary sheet

12. Now click into the outgoings summary sheet tag at the bottom of the page.
13. Click into the next unoccupied cell in column B.
14. Click on the home tab at the top the sheet.
15. Click on the downward arrow at the bottom of the paste icon, on the far left of the ribbon, and select the paste special option.

16. Tick the 'Transpose' box and click 'OK'.

17. This will place the new column headings downwards in the next occupied cells in column B.

18. Click into the cell in column D adjacent to the first of the new category names you added into column B. Insert an equals sign.

19. Click on to sheetname tag 4OutgngsQ1. Click into the first of the newly occupied cells in row 7 and press the return key. This will place this cell reference in the destination cell and return us immediately to the outgoings summary sheet in the next cell we have to deal with.

20. Repeat the process for all the cells in this column adjacent to newly added category names and then do the same in columns G, J and M, clicking into sheets 6OutgngsQ1, 8OutgngsQ3 and 10OutgngsQ4 respectively for the source data.

21. Click into the last of the occupied cells in column P, right-click, select the copy option, left-click and release the mouse button.

22. Click into the cell below it, hold down the shift key and scroll to the last of the cells adjacent to the newly added headings. Right-click and select the paste option, left-click and release the mouse button. The formulae will adjust automatically.

Carrying the changes through to the trial balance

23. Click on sheetname tag 16 TB to open it.

24. Insert the required number of additional rows between the last expense item and the error line.

25. Return to worksheet 12OutgngsSmry.

26. Highlight the category names that we added.

27. Right-click, select the copy option, left-click and release the right mouse button.

28. Return to worksheet 16TB.

29. Click into the cell in column B in the first of the newly added rows, right-click, select the paste option and left-click.

30. Tidy up the added material by making the type font and other style issues uniform with the rest of the material in the column and putting back any shading of lines, which may have been corrupted in the process.

31. Save your work so far.

32. Click into the cell in column C adjacent to the first of the new headings.

33. Press the '=' key on your keyboard.

34. Click open the 12OutgngsSmry sheetname tag and click into the cell in column D adjacent to the first of the added headings.

35. Press the return key on your keyboard. This will place the cell reference of the destination cell in sheet 16TB and automatically return you to the latter sheet and place the cursor into the next cell you have to deal with.

36.   Copy the cell that you have just filled with a formula and paste it to all the others adjacent to the newly added headings.

37.   If the latter step does not work, and very occasionally this is the case due to bugs in the system, then deal with each item separately rather than copying and pasting en bloc.

38.   Now copy the whole part of the column into which you have just copied formulae and paste it into the cell in column D adjacent to the first of the added headings.

39.   Click on each cell in turn and change the E to G in each case in the data bar below the ribbon.

40.   Next, highlight and copy both column parts that you have just filled with formulae and paste them into the adjacent cells in columns E and F.

41.   Change the F column references to J and the I column references to M in the formulae that have been installed in the cells.

42.   Now copy the last of the already occupied cells in column G in sheet 16TB (before the additional formulae were added) and paste into all of the cells in column G adjacent to the newly added headings.

43.   Save your work so far.

Carrying the changes through to the profit and loss account

44.   Click on the sheetname tag for 17P&L.

45.   Insert the required number of rows above the non-allowable expenses category to accommodate the added category names.

46.   Click open the sheetname tag 16TB and highlight and copy the block of newly added headings.

47.   Click back into the sheetname tag 17P&L and click into the first of the unoccupied cells in column B of the first empty extra rows you inserted.

48.   Paste the material you have just copied here.

49.   Remove any shading that has been pasted with the material by highlighting the area affected and then clicking on the fill icon on the ribbon and selecting the no fill option.

50.   Click into the cell in column C adjacent to the first of the added-in headings.

51.   Press the '=' key on your keyboard to insert an '=' sign. This tells the system that you are entering a formula here.

52.   Click open the sheetname tag 16TB and click into the corresponding cell (the cell in column C adjacent to the first of the added-in headings).

53.   Press the return key on your keyboard. You will be immediately returned to the 17P&L worksheet, where the formula will be completed in the desired cell.

54.   Copy and paste it into the three adjacent cells. The formula will be automatically adjusted appropriately.

55.   Highlight all four cells in that row that you have just filled. Copy and paste the contents into the cells in columns C, D, E and F adjacent to each of the rest of the added-in headings.

56.   Click into the last of the cells in column G, immediately before the first of those we have just filled in column F. Copy the contents and paste into all of the cells in column G adjacent to the newly added-in headings.

57.   Save your changes.

Adding additional columns to the incomings analysis sheets is done in exactly the same way.

There is space along the bottom of the workbook for up to fifteen tabs representing fifteen worksheets. However, there are eighteen worksheets in the formatting we have done here. They are:

1. Guide to completing the worksheets
2. Opening balances
3. Income Q1
4. Outgoings Q1
5. Income Q2
6. Outgoings Q2
7. Income Q3
8. Outgoings Q3
9. Income Q4
10. Outgoings Q4
11. Annual income summary
12. Annual outgoings summary
13. VAT return
14. Assets summary
15. Liabilities summary
16. Trial balance
17. Profit and loss account
18. Balance sheet

Furthermore, there is a limit to how much we can shorten a label before it becomes difficult to identify, so realistically we could not have anywhere near the fifteen labels visible with each one still being easily identifiable. Therefore, just as in a manual accounting system it is useful to create an index. The advantage of the spreadsheet index is that the moment we select the account in the index the pages are automatically and instantaneously turned for you.

Here's how to create the index.

Select the second tab from the left on the bottom of the worksheet. If there was hitherto such a tab left blank for the purpose in this position, then click on the new worksheet tab at the far right of the tabs and rename it index. Then drag it with the cursor to the second place position from the left.

List the account names in column B, starting from cell B3 to give you room for a page title at the top and a blank line between the title and content of the page. The list in the configuration we have done in this book is as above, but you can modify this to suit your specific requirements.

1. Right-click on each title in turn, to highlight it.
2. Left-click on the hyperlink option at the bottom of the menu that will appear.
3. Left-click on the 'Place in the document' option in the 'Link to' pane on the left-hand side of the dialogue box that will appear.

4. Click on the 'OK' button. The title will immediately turn blue to indicate that it has become a hyperlink.
5. Repeat for each item in the list.

	Index		
	Guide		
	Opening Balances		
	Income Q1		
	Outgoings Q1		
	Income Q2		
	Outgoings Q2		
	Income Q3		
	Outgoings Q3		
	Income Q4		
	Outgoings Q4		
	Incomings summary		
	Outgoings summary		
	Assets		
	Liabilities		
	Trial Balance		
	Profit and Loss Account		
	Balance sheet		

Figure 42 Example of a hyperlink index to the accounts

Now that you have created your spreadsheet you need to protect the structure and formulae in it. Otherwise you or anyone else will all too easily overwrite formulae by mistake and, thereby mess the whole system up. Many people find this a complicated thing to do, but it is really quite simple. The reason people find it complicated and problematic is that newcomers assume the task in hand is to protect the cells bearing formulae when in fact it is the opposite. The task is to unprotect those that don't bear formulae before you click on the protect worksheet icon. That way, those formulae cells are left out of the protection that the protect worksheet icon triggers.

This is how to protect your formulae cells:

Before you protect a worksheet, highlight any data cells. By this I mean any cells into which you want the user to be able to enter data. You can highlight many cells by using the control and shift keys. If you have adjacent cells (vertically or horizontally) to highlight then hold down the shift key while you drag the cursor across and/or down the range). If the cells are not adjacent, but rather there is a gap between them, hold the control key down as you move the cursor between them. If some are adjacent and some not then you can use the shift key for moving between those that are adjacent and the control key for moving between those that are not. The cells you highlight will remain highlighted after you have moved on to the next one. You must make sure that you do not begin to move between any cells without either the control or the shift key depressed.

When you have highlighted all the data cells you wish to leave unprotected for the user to input data into, then click on the home tab on the ribbon, select the format option in the cells group close to the right of the ribbon.

Click on the format cells option at the bottom of the drop-down menu that will appear. The format cells dialogue box will appear.

Click on the 'Locked' box at the top left-hand corner to remove the tick.

Click on the 'OK' button.

Unhighlight the cells.

Click on the review tab on the ribbon.

Click on the protect worksheet icon.

You will be asked to insert a password. You don't have to, but if you don't anyone can undo the protection so it is best to do so.

Click on the 'OK' button when you have done so.

You will be asked to enter the password again. Enter it and click on the 'OK' button.

The formulae in that particular sheet are now protected from accidental or malicious modification.

You will need to protect each sheet in your workbook individually. Only eleven of the sheets (the quarterly incomings and outgoings sheets, plus the opening balances sheet) will have data input cells, though. All the others will simply need a blanket protection by clicking on the protect worksheet icon.

To modify your formulae or constants at any time just unprotect the sheet concerned and make the changes. You will, however, need to go through the full process of unprotecting data cells before protecting the worksheet when you have done so.

Part Four

Examination Papers, Answers and Associated Material

This book is particularly designed for people and businesses who wish to use their existing Microsoft or other spreadsheet software for accounting purposes. With this software and the instructions given in this book powerful systems can be set up. Many public examinations on computerized accounting, however, are focused on the use of packages like Sage, Accountz, Quickbooks, Fusion and Iris. For information and guidance on these kinds of systems the reader should purchase my other book, *Computerised Book-keeping*, which deals specifically with this technology.

Here are some examination materials on computerized accounting, which are reproduced with the kind permission of the examination boards concerned: ICB, AAT and City and Guilds.

THE INSTITUTE
OF CERTIFIED
BOOKKEEPERS

LEVEL II CERTIFICATE IN
COMPUTERISED BOOKKEEPING - <u>MOCK</u>

This final assignment should be completed and posted to the Institute by the date at the bottom of this page. You are advised to obtain proof of posting from The Royal Mail.

Required:

Complete the various tasks and send all the required print outs to the Institute at the address below. Ensure that you include your ICB student/membership number on each section. Do NOT include your name. You may keep the question paper

Deadline Date......N/A - MOCK.............

(Oaklands)
2012

The Institute of Certified Bookkeepers
Victoria House, 64 Paul Street, London EC2A 4NG
Tel: 0845 060 2345   www.bookkeepers.org.uk

Assessment Criteria

This piece of work will be graded at Distinction, Merit, Pass or Fail.

Pass   To gain a Pass, candidates must achieve between 85-89%

Merit   To gain a Merit, candidates must achieve between 90-94%

Distinction   To gain a Distinction, candidates must achieve between 95-100%

Fail   Candidates who achieve less than 85% of the total marks will bo failed.

Any error will lead to a reduction in total marks. An error could include posting to the wrong nominal code, VAT being incorrectly coded, incorrect accounts coded to the wrong section of the chart of accounts etc.

This examination can be completed on any computerised software package, but you need to ensure that the reports submitted contain all of the information requested.

Note – it is important that you keep your own back-up of your data until you are informed that you have successfully completed this assignment.

Scenario

Oaklands Tree Care is owned and run by Scott Lawson, a qualified tree surgeon. He deals with all aspects of tree work for both residential customers and for commercial industries, including Local Schools, Builders and Golf Courses. He also provides hedge cutting and general pruning services as well as selling the by-products such as logs and mulch.

Up until recently his wife has been doing his books but as the business has grown it is taking up too much of her time, so he has asked you to take over the bookkeeping.

The business is VAT registered and uses standard accounting for VAT. The registration number is 742256879. Scott's financial year runs from 1st January to 31st December and his wife has given you the account balances as of 1st January 2012, which she has received from their accountant after completing last year's accounts.

You are asked to set up Oaklands Tree Care in a suitable computerised accounts system, and to complete the accounts for the month of January 2012.

For the purposes of this examination, the VAT rate is 20%.

Instructions to candidates

You are required to complete the tasks as listed below.

Enter the balances using a date of 1st January. As a general rule, unless the task asks for a specific financial report e.g. Trial Balance, Aged Debtors Analysis, Profit & Loss, etc., your report(s) should provide the examiner with sufficient information to show that you have completed the task correctly, so please mark each report with the appropriate task number:

Task	Activity	Marks
1	Amend the nominal ledger	6
2	Set-up customer and supplier account information	11
3	Enter the opening balances	13
4	Reverse the opening prepayments and accruals	3
5	Post supplier invoices and credit notes to the purchase ledger	10
6	Post customer invoices and credit notes to the sales ledger	8
7	Post payments to suppliers and receipts from customers	9
8	Post any sundry payments	5
9	Post the petty cash transactions and maintain the float	9
10	Prepare the VAT return	2
11	Correct the error in the bank payment	1
12	Reconcile the bank account	9
13	Post the wages journals	7
14	Post adjustments and produce month-end reports	6
	An additional mark will be given for presentation	1

Task 1 - Amend the nominal ledger

Required:

i)   Set up the following nominal accounts to customise the system for Oaklands
        Tree Care:

Account name	Account type
Tree services	Sales
Hedge Cutting	Sales
By-product sales	Sales
Waste disposal	Direct Cost

ii)   Provide a report listing these nominal ledger accounts.

iii)   Provide a report showing the layout of the chart of accounts used for this
        company.

Task 2 – Set up customer and supplier account information

Required:

i)   Enter the following customer information into your accounts package:

Customer	Account Reference	Address	Credit Limit	Outstanding balance at 1/1/2012
Heathlands Golf Course	HGC001	43-46 Reading Road Bracknell Berkshire RG12 3RR	£1000	
White House School	WHS001	54 High Street Crowthorne Berkshire RG45 1HS	£1000	
Lord Patrick Groves	LPG001	The Birches Sandy Lane Wargrave Berkshire RG10 2SL	£1000	£480
Mr & Mrs S Smith	SSM001	23 Gordon Road Great Hollands Bracknell Berkshire RG12 1GR	£1000	
E Bryant Construction	EBC001	17 Westfield Close Binfield Berkshire RG42 8WC	£1000	

ii)   Provide a report showing the above customer information. Include, as a
        minimum, name and address and account reference.

Task 2 continued...

iii) Enter the following supplier information into your accounts package:

Supplier	Account Reference	Address	VAT number	Credit Limit	Outstanding balance at 1/1/2012
Waste Recycling Group	WRG001	Longshot Lane Bracknell Berkshire RG12 1LL	789456123	£1000	
Tool Maintenance Ltd	TML001	Unit 5 Western Industrial Area Bracknell Berkshire RG12 6WA	740584406	£1000	£360
Smiths Garden Tools	SMG001	14 High Street Binfield Berkshire RG42 7HS	725612390	£2000	
KT Clothing Company	KTC001	24 Main Avenue Swans Business Park Crowthorne Berkshire RG45 2MA	758041422	£2000	

iv) Provide a report showing the above supplier information. Include, as a minimum, name and address and account reference.

Task 3 - Enter the opening balances

Required:

i) Enter the remaining opening balances as at 1st January from the information shown below; you may need to set up or amend some nominal accounts depending on your accounting software (**note: Debtors and Creditors balances should already be there**):

	Dr	Cr
Motor Vehicles	20000.00	
Motor Vehicle depreciation		8000.00
Tools & Equipment	10000.00	
Tools & Equipment depreciation		2000.00
Bank account	4200.00	
Petty Cash	100.00	
Bank Loan		10000.00
Capital Account		13670.00
Prepayments	250.00	
Accruals		1000.00
Debtors	480.00	
Creditors		360.00

ii) Provide an opening Trial Balance as at January 2012.

Task 4 - Reverse the opening prepayments and accruals

The opening balances above contain a prepayment of £250 for personal indemnity (PI) insurance for the month of January and an accrual of £1000 for accountancy fees incurred last year.

Required:

i)   Post a journal to reverse the accrual and prepayment, using the appropriate expense accounts, as at 1st January.

ii)   Provide a report to show details of your journals.

Task 5 – Post supplier invoices and credit notes to the purchase ledger

Required:

i)   Post the following invoices to the appropriate accounts in the purchase ledger. Use the description as a basis for deciding which nominal account to use.

Supplier	Description	Invoice Number	Invoice Date	Amount (Gross)
Waste Recycling Group	Waste disposal charges	3001	04/01/12	120.00
Tool Maintenance Ltd	Annual service of shredder	65002	06/01/12	288.00
Smiths Garden Tools	New chainsaw	SGT322	11/01/12	192.00
KT Clothing Company	Boots and fleeces	12/504	22/01/12	480.00
Tool Maintenance Ltd	Repairs to hedge cutter	65050	24/01/12	30.00
Smiths Garden Tools	Replace old hedge cutter	SGT374	31/01/12	90.00

ii)   Post the following credit notes to the appropriate purchase ledger accounts.

Supplier	Description	Credit Note Number	Credit Date	Amount (Gross)
KT Clothing Company	Return of damaged fleece	12/504C	24/01/12	36.00
Smiths Garden Tools	Overcharge on chainsaw	SGT322C	25/01/12	12.00

iii)   Provide a report showing details of the above information.

iv)   Provide a report showing an Aged Creditors analysis as at 31st January 2012.

Task 6 – Post customer invoices and credit notes to the sales ledger

Required:

i) Post the following invoices to the appropriate accounts in the sales ledger. Use the description as a basis for deciding which nominal account to use:

Customer	Description	Invoice Number	Invoice Date	Price (inc VAT)
E Bryant Construction	Remove 3 trees from building site	1101	08/01/12	1440.00
Heathlands Golf Course	Replace storm damaged tree	1102	16/01/12	600.00
Mr & Mrs S Smith	Annual hedge cutting 1 Bag of logs	1103	20/01/12	192.00 60.00
Lord Patrick Groves	Reshape large beech tree 3 bags of mulch	1104	29/01/12	480.00 72.00
White House School	Annual hedge cutting	1105	31/01/12	432.00

ii) Post the following credit note to the relevant account in the sales ledger:

Customer	Description	Credit Note Number	Credit Date	Price (inc VAT)
White House School	Overcharged for hedge cutting	C1105	31/01/12	72.00

iii) Provide a report showing details of the above information.

iv) Provide a report showing an Aged Debtors analysis as at 31st January 2012.

Task 7 – Post payments to suppliers and receipts from customers

Required:

i)   Post the following cheques to the purchase ledger:

Supplier	Cheque Number	Date Paid	Invoices Cleared	Cheque Value
Tool Maintenance Ltd	100221	07/01/12	Outstanding balance from previous year	360.00
Waste Recycling Group	100222	11/01/12	3001	120.00
Smiths Garden Tools	100223	26/01/12	SGT322 SGT322C	180.00
Tool Maintenance Ltd	100225	28/01/12	65002 65050	318.00

ii)   Provide a report showing the above supplier payments and cleared invoices.

iii) Post the following receipts from customers to the sales ledger:

Customer	Paying-in Slip Number	Date Paid	Invoices Cleared	Total Paid
Lord Patrick Groves	000401	05/01/12	Outstanding balance from previous year	480.00
E Bryant Construction	000402	15/01/12	1101	1440.00
Heathlands Golf Course	000403	23/01/12	1102	600.00

iv)   Provide a report showing the above customer receipts and cleared invoices.

Task 8 – Post any Sundry Payments

Required:

i)   Post the following payments made from Scott's business bank account:

Date	Cheque Number	Description	Amount paid	VAT rate
04/01/12	100220	PI Insurance	200.00	Exempt
18/01/12	100224	Advertising	120.00	Standard
28/01/12	100226	Accountancy fees	1200.00	Standard
31/01/12	100227	Road tax	300.00	Exempt

ii)   Provide a report showing details of these bank payments.

Task 9 – Post the Petty Cash Transactions and maintain the float

Scott keeps a small amount of petty cash available for incidental expenses. He uses the Imprest system, keeping records in a petty cash voucher book, and maintaining a monthly float of £100.

Required:

i)   Post the following petty cash payments into the ledger:

Date	Description	Voucher Number	Amount paid	VAT Rate
07/01/12	Petrol	40	24.00	Standard
13/01/12	Stamps	41	8.64	Exempt
15/01/12	Petrol	42	21.60	Standard
22/01/12	Sandwiches	43	3.60	Zero
29/01/12	Envelopes	44	4.20	Standard
30/01/12	Coffee	45	4.80	Zero
31/01/12	Stamps	45	3.60	Exempt

ii)   Provide a report showing details of these cash payments.

iii)   Restore the Imprest as at 31/01/12 and provide a report showing the transfer.

Task 10 – Prepare the VAT return

Required:

i)   Prepare the VAT return for the period 01/01/12 to 31/01/12 and print it.

ii)   Provide a report showing the breakdown of each box, including the transactions that made up the totals.

Task 11 – Correct the error in the bank payment

When you receive the bank statement you discover that cheque number 100220 has been posted incorrectly to the accounts. Due to misreading the cheque stub, you have posted this payment for PI insurance for £200 when it should have been for £300.

Required:

i)   Correct the error and provide evidence of the correction.

Task 12 – Reconcile the bank account

Required:

i)   Reconcile the bank account as per the Bank Statement below:

Berkshire Bank PLC
14 The Mall
Bracknell

Account Name: Oaklands Tree Care
Account No: 047230652
Sort Code 31-11-40

Date: 31/01/2012
Statement No: 304

Date	Payment Type	Details	Money Out	Money In	Balance
01 Jan 12		Balance BFD			4200.00
06 Jan 12	Deposit	000401		480.00	4680.00
10 Jan 12	Cheque	100221	360.00		4320.00
11 Jan 12	Cheque	100220	300.00		4020.00
14 Jan 12	Cheque	100222	120.00		3900.00
16 Jan 12	Deposit	000402		1440.00	5340.00
21 Jan 12	Cheque	100223	180.00		5160.00
22 Jan 12	Cheque	100224	120.00		5040.00
24 Jan 12	Deposit	000403		600.00	5640.00
31 Jan 12		Balance CFD			5640.00

ii)   Report on any unreconciled transactions.

Task 13 – Post the wages journals

Scott employs 2 local trainees and his accountant asks you to post the journals for the monthly salaries for January. Scott supports local charities and encourages his staff to participate in the Give As You Earn (GAYE) scheme, where donation to charity is deducted from pre-tax wages, so you may need to set up a suitable nominal account for this deduction.

Required:

i)   Post the following journals on 31st January.

Nominal Account	Dr	Cr
Gross Wages	1200.00	
PAYE deductions		220.00
National Insurance Deductions		100.00
GAYE Deductions		20.00
Net Wages Payable		920.00
Employers NI	60.00	

ii)   Provide a report showing details of the above journals.

Task 14 – Post adjustments and produce the month-end reports

Scott's accountant asks you to post the following adjustments to the January accounts:

The asset depreciation charges for January are:

Motor Vehicle	£150
Tools & Equipment	£60

Required:

i)   Post journals to record the adjustments and provide a report showing the transactions.

ii) Provide a Trading and Profit and Loss account for the month ended 31/01/12.

iii) Provide a Balance Sheet as at 31/01/12.

iv) Provide a Trial Balance as at 31/01/12.

This is the end of the examination

THE INSTITUTE
OF CERTIFIED
BOOKKEEPERS

THE LEVEL II CERTIFICATE IN
COMPUTERISED BOOKKEEPING - <u>MOCK</u>

This final assignment should be completed and posted to the Institute by the date at the bottom of this page. You are advised to obtain proof of posting from The Royal Mail.

Required

Complete the various tasks and send all the required print outs to the Institute at the address below. Ensure that you include your name and enrolment number on each section. You may keep the question paper

N/A - Mock
Deadline Date.....................................

(Orchard Bistro)

The Institute of Certified Bookkeepers
Wolverton Park, Wolverton, Hampshire RG26 5RU
Tel: 0845 060 2345   www.bookkeepers.org.uk

Assessment Criteria

This piece of work will be graded at Distinction, Merit, Pass or Fail.

Pass To gain a Pass, candidates must achieve between 85-89%

Merit To gain a Merit, candidates must achieve between 90-94%

Distinction To gain a Distinction, candidates must achieve between 95-100%

Fail Candidates who achieve less than 85% of the total marks will be failed.

Any error will lead to a reduction in total marks. An error could include posting to the wrong nominal code, VAT being incorrectly coded, incorrect accounts coded to the wrong section of the chart of accounts etc.

This examination can be completed on any computerised software package, but you need to ensure that the reports submitted contain all of the information requested.

Note – it is important that you keep your own back-up of your data until you are informed that you have successfully completed this assignment.

This page is left blank intentionally

The Orchard Bistro
St Nicholas Street
Cayton
Scarborough
YO34 9GT

Scenario

You are the bookkeeper for The Orchard Bistro, a restaurant/café that places an emphasis on local produce and high-welfare farming techniques. The business is registered for VAT and uses standard VAT accounting. You have prepared the books for several years using manual ledgers; however with recent expansion it is felt that from the financial year start date of 1st April 2010, computerised record keeping would be a more efficient approach.

For the purposes of this examination, the VAT rate is 17.5%.

Instructions to candidates

You are required to complete the tasks as listed below:

Task	Activity	Marks
1	Enter the opening balances	11
2	Amend the nominal ledger	4
3	Enter supplier details	8
4	Post supplier invoices and credit notes	21
5	Enter supplier cheques	8
6	Enter sales for the month	10
7	Post the wages journal	6
8	Enter and correct the cash payments	8
9	Set up a new customer and post the invoice	3
10	Prepare the VAT Return	3
11	Reconcile the bank	11
12	Post the month end journals	7

Task 1 – Enter the opening balances

Required:

i)   Enter the opening balances as shown below:

	Dr	Cr
Freehold property	100,000	
Plant and Machinery cost	20,000	
Plant and Machinery depreciation		5,000
Fixtures and Fittings cost	12,000	
Fixtures and Fittings depreciation		2,400
Stock	2,500	
Bank Account	2,020	
Petty Cash	1,300	
Loans		80,000
Capital Account		50,420

ii)   Provide an opening trial balance as at April 2010.

Task 2 - Amend the nominal ledger

Required:

i)   Set up the following nominal accounts to customise the system for The Orchard Bistro:

Nominal Account Name	Nominal Type
Bistro sales	Sales
Food purchases	Direct cost
Drink purchases	Direct cost

ii)   Provide a report listing the nominal ledger accounts and their location within the chart of accounts.

Task 3 – Enter supplier details

Required:

i)   Enter the following suppliers into your accounts package:

Supplier	Account Reference	Address
The Cheese Mouse	CHM01	45 Britain Street Pickering York North Yorkshire NY56 8RD
Cecelia's Salads	CCS01	Church Farm Hunmanby Scarborough North Yorkshire NY34 7GB
Direct Fruit Ltd	DFL01	The Old Barn Treeston Leeds West Yorkshire WS28 1AL
Pavarotti Pasta	PPA01	46 Via Appia Corleone Palermo Sicily 56 XE 78TY Italy
Bob the Baker	BTB01	33 Green Street Bridlington Hull Humberside HU22 3ER
English Wine Co	EWC01	Coal Lane Reighton Lincoln LO9 7OP
Grove Farm Meat	GFM01	46 Maypole Lane Burneston Thirsk North Yorkshire NY5 1EA

ii)   Provide a report showing the above supplier information.

Task 4 – Post Supplier invoices and credit notes

Required:

i) Post the following invoices to the purchase ledger. Use the description as a basis for deciding which nominal account to use:

Supplier	Description	Invoice Number	Invoice Date	Price (inc VAT)	VAT rate
Bob the Baker	Oven bottom loaves	574	02/04/10	70.00	Zero
Bob the Baker	36 seeded rolls	588	20/04/10	50.00	Zero
Bob the Baker	2 sponge cakes	591	25/04/10	47.00	Zero
Cecelia's Salad	32 mixed salads	12/34-1	04/04/10	40.00	Zero
Cecelia's Salad	1 box of tomatoes	12/35-1	09/04/10	20.00	Zero
Cecelia's Salad	Assorted vegetables	12/38-1	25/04/10	39.00	Zero
The Cheese Mouse	Cheese selections	45301	05/04/10	70.00	Zero
The Cheese Mouse	Fruit chutneys	45378	12/04/10	23.50	Standard
The Cheese Mouse	Crackers and biscuits	45399	28/04/10	47.00	Standard
Direct Fruit	2 fruit baskets	341	13/04/10	30.00	Zero
Direct Fruit	3 fruit baskets	344	20/04/10	45.00	Zero
English Wine Co	Mixed merlot case	3789	12/04/10	70.50	Standard
English Wine Co	Mixed white case	3745	20/04/10	141.00	Standard
Grove Farm Meat	Beef fillet	CF1460	02/04/10	167.00	Zero
Grove Farm Meat	Free range chicken	CF1478	13/04/10	190.00	Zero
Pavarotti Pasta	20kg penne	IT5748	20/04/10	150.00	Zero
Pavarotti Pasta	30kg linguine	IT9387	29/04/10	250.00	Zero

ii) Post the following credit notes to the purchase ledger:

Supplier	Description	Credit Note Number	Credit Note Date	Price (inc VAT)	VAT rate
Grove Farm Meat	Credit bad chicken	CF2201	29/04/10	20.00	Zero
English Wine Co	Credit corked merlot	C8894	28/04/10	23.50	Standard

iii) Provide a report showing details of supplier accounts activity.

iv) Provide a report showing aged creditors information as at 30th April 2010.

231

Task 5 – Enter supplier cheques

Required:

i)   Post the following cheques to the purchase ledger:

Supplier	Cheque Number	Date Paid	Invoice Number Paid	Total Amount Paid
Bob the Baker	102346	10/04/10	574	70.00
Cecelia's Salad	102347	15/04/10	12/34-1 12/35-1	60.00
The Cheese Mouse	102348	15/04/10	45301 45378	93.50
Direct Fruit Ltd	102349	15/04/10	341	30.00
English Wine Co	102350	18/04/10	3789	70.50
Grove Farm Meat	102351	30/04/10	CF1460 CF1478 CF2201	337.00
Pavarotti Pasta	102352	30/04/10	IT5748 IT9387	400.00

ii) Provide a report showing the details of the above supplier payments.

Task 6 – Enter sales for the month

Required:

i)   Enter the weekly Bistro sales into the accounts, paying attention to where the cash was deposited. All Bistro sales include VAT.

Week ended	Total Sales	Amount Banked	Paid to petty cash
07/04/10	4589.00	1200.00	3389.00
14/04/10	4893.00	1467.00	3426.00
21/04/10	3845.00	1961.00	1884.00
28/04/10	4354.00	2069.00	2285.00

ii) Provide a report showing details of bank receipts.

iii) Provide a report showing details of cash receipts.

Task 7 - Post the wages journal

Required:

    i)   Post the following journals for April's wages at the end of the month:

Nominal Heading	Dr	Cr
Gross Wages	3487.00	
Employers NI	256.00	
PAYE Deductions		476.00
NI Deductions		389.00
Net Wages Payable		2878.00

    ii)   Provide a report showing details of the above journals.

Task 8 – Enter and correct the cash payments

As the Orchard Bistro receives a lot of cash, it also pays a number of its bills in cash to save bank charges.

Required:

    i)   Post the following cash payments into the accounts:

Date	Description	Amount (inc VAT)	VAT rate
03/04/10	Postage	35.52	Exempt
06/04/10	Rent	500.00	Exempt
20/04/10	Petrol	20.00	Standard
23/04/10	Gas	45.00	5%
30/04/10	Wages payable	2878.00	Non VATable

    ii)   Provide a report showing details of these cash payments.

After reviewing your records you find that the amount paid in cash for rent was actually £600.00. Amend your records appropriately.

    iii)   Provide a new cash payments report to show your correction.

Task 9 – Set up a new customer and post the invoice

A local business has asked you to cater for one of its corporate events.

Required:

Set up a suitable sales account for "Corporate Catering" and set up the customer details as follows:

Business Name	Account Reference	Address	Contact	Credit Limit
Pineapple Marketing Ltd	PMA01	Masonry House Dunstable Bedford Bedfordshire BD25 8OP	Peter Longer	4000.00

    i)   Provide a report showing the customer information.

    ii)   Post the following invoice for the completed work to the accounts:

Customer	Date	Invoice Number	Description	Amount (inc VAT)
Pineapple Marketing Ltd	30/04/10	445/10	Catering at Silverstone event	2350.00

    iii)   Provide a report showing the customer account activity.

Task 10 – Prepare the VAT return

Required:

    i)   Prepare a VAT return for the period 01/04/10 to 30/04/10.
    ii)   Provide a report showing the VAT Return
    iii)   Provide a report showing summary VAT information
    iv)   Provide a report showing detailed VAT information.

Task 11 – Reconcile the bank

Required:

i)   Reconcile the bank account as per the bank statement below

ii)   You will notice that there are bank charges on the statement that have not yet been posted to the accounts. Depending on the facilities offered by your accounts software, enter these during the reconciliation, post them as an adjustment, or post a bank payment in the normal way.

The Leeds Bank PLC
23 Valley Road
York

Account of The Orchard Bistro
Account No. 46378765
Sort Code 34-12-11

Statement No 99

30/4/2010

Date	Details	Paid Out	Paid In	Balance
31/03/10	Balance B/Fwd			2020.00
02/04/10	Bank Charges	37.58		1982.42
07/04/10	Deposit		1200.00	3182.42
13/04/10	102346	70.00		3112.42
14/04/10	Deposit		1467.00	4579.42
17/04/10	102348	93.50		4485.92
17/04/10	102349	30.00		4455.92
18/04/10	102347	60.00		4395.92
20/04/10	102350	70.50		4325.42
21/04/10	Deposit		1961.00	6286.42
28/04/10	Deposit		2069.00	8355.42

iii)   Provide a report showing any unreconciled transactions.

Task 12 – Post the month end journals

The accountant asks you to make some adjustments to the accounts.

Depreciation is to be charged for April in the following amounts:

Plant and Machinery:	£250
Fixtures and Fittings:	£100

Required:

i)   Post journals as per the requested adjustments and provide a report showing details of the transactions.

ii)   Provide a Trading and Profit and Loss account for the month ended 30/04/10.

iii)   Provide a Balance Sheet as at 30/04/10.

iv)   Provide a Trial Balance as at 30/04/10.

This is the end of the examination

This page is left blank intentionally

This page is left blank intentionally

Patron: His Royal Highness Prince Michael of Kent KCVO
Vice President: Leslie T Ellis

Wolverton Park, Wolverton, Hampshire RG26 5RU
0845 060 2345
www.bookkeepers.org.uk

THE INSTITUTE
OF CERTIFIED
BOOKKEEPERS

LEVEL II CERTIFICATE IN COMPUTERISED
BOOKKEEPING
MOCK PAPER ANSWERS

(Orchard Bistro scenario)

To Period: Month 1, April 2010

N/C	Name	Debit	Credit
0010	Freehold Property	100,000.00	
0020	Plant and Machinery	20,000.00	
0021	Plant/Machinery Depreciation		5,000.00
0040	Furniture and Fixtures	12,000.00	
0041	Furniture/Fixture Depreciation		2,400.00
1001	Stock	2,500.00	
1200	Bank Current Account	2,020.00	
1230	Petty Cash	1,300.00	
2300	Loans		80,000.00
3000	Capital		50,420.00
	Totals:	137,820.00	137,820.00

Task 2

N/C From:
N/C To: 99999999

N/C	Name
0010	Freehold Property
0011	Leasehold Property
0020	Plant and Machinery
0021	Plant/Machinery Depreciation
0030	Office Equipment
0031	Office Equipment Depreciation
0040	Furniture and Fixtures
0041	Furniture/Fixture Depreciation
0050	Motor Vehicles
0051	Motor Vehicles Depreciation
1001	Stock
1002	Work in Progress
1003	Finished Goods
1100	Debtors Control Account
1101	Sundry Debtors
1102	Other Debtors
1103	Prepayments
1200	Bank Current Account
1210	Bank Deposit Account
1220	Building Society Account
1230	Petty Cash
1240	Company Credit Card
1250	Credit Card Receipts
2100	Creditors Control Account
2101	Sundry Creditors
2102	Other Creditors
2109	Accruals
2200	Sales Tax Control Account
2201	Purchase Tax Control Account
2202	VAT Liability
2204	Manual Adjustments
2210	P.A.Y.E.
2211	National Insurance
2220	Net Wages
2230	Pension Fund
2300	Loans
2310	Hire Purchase
2320	Corporation Tax
2330	Mortgages
3000	Capital
3010	Preference Shares
3100	Reserves
3101	Undistributed Reserves
3200	Profit and Loss Account
4000	Bistro Sales
4001	Sales Type B
4002	Sales Type C
4009	Discounts Allowed
4100	Sales Type D
4101	Sales Type E
4200	Sales of Assets
4400	Credit Charges (Late Payments)
4900	Miscellaneous Income
4901	Royalties Received
4902	Commissions Received
4903	Insurance Claims
4904	Rent Income
4905	Distribution and Carriage
5000	Food Purchases
5001	Drink Purchases
5002	Miscellaneous Purchases
5003	Packaging

N/C	Name
5009	Discounts Taken
5100	Carriage
5101	Import Duty
5102	Transport Insurance
5200	Opening Stock
5201	Closing Stock
6000	Productive Labour
6001	Cost of Sales Labour
6002	Sub-Contractors
6100	Sales Commissions
6200	Sales Promotions
6201	Advertising
6202	Gifts and Samples
6203	P.R. (Literature & Brochures)
6900	Miscellaneous Expenses
7000	Gross Wages
7001	Directors Salaries
7002	Directors Remuneration
7003	Staff Salaries
7004	Wages - Regular
7005	Wages - Casual
7006	Employers N.I.
7007	Employers Pensions
7008	Recruitment Expenses
7009	Adjustments
7010	SSP Reclaimed
7011	SMP Reclaimed
7100	Rent
7102	Water Rates
7103	General Rates
7104	Premises Insurance
7200	Electricity
7201	Gas
7202	Oil
7203	Other Heating Costs
7300	Fuel and Oil
7301	Repairs and Servicing
7302	Licences
7303	Vehicle Insurance
7304	Miscellaneous Motor Expenses
7350	Scale Charges
7400	Travelling
7401	Car Hire
7402	Hotels
7403	U.K. Entertainment
7404	Overseas Entertainment
7405	Overseas Travelling
7406	Subsistence
7500	Printing
7501	Postage and Carriage
7502	Telephone
7503	Telex/Telegram/Facsimile
7504	Office Stationery
7505	Books etc.
7600	Legal Fees
7601	Audit and Accountancy Fees
7602	Consultancy Fees
7603	Professional Fees
7700	Equipment Hire
7701	Office Machine Maintenance
7800	Repairs and Renewals
7801	Cleaning
7802	Laundry
7803	Premises Expenses

N/C	Name
7900	Bank Interest Paid
7901	Bank Charges
7902	Currency Charges
7903	Loan Interest Paid
7904	H.P. Interest
7905	Credit Charges
7906	Exchange Rate Variance
8000	Depreciation
8001	Plant/Machinery Depreciation
8002	Furniture/Fitting Depreciation
8003	Vehicle Depreciation
8004	Office Equipment Depreciation
8100	Bad Debt Write Off
8102	Bad Debt Provision
8200	Donations
8201	Subscriptions
8202	Clothing Costs
8203	Training Costs
8204	Insurance
8205	Refreshments
9998	Suspense Account
9999	Mispostings Account

Task 3

Supplier From:
Supplier To: *ZZZZZZZZ*

A/C	Name	Contact	Telephone	Fax
BTB01	Bob the Baker 33 Green Street Bridlington Hull Humberside HU22 3ER			
CCS01	Cecelia's Salads Church Farm Hunmanby Scarborough North Yorkshire NY34 7GB			
CHM01	The Cheese Mouse 45 Britain Street Pickering York North Yorkshire NY56 8RD			
DFL01	Direct Fruit Ltd The Old Barn Treeston Leeds West Yorkshire WS28 1AL			
EWC01	English Wine Co Coal Lane Reighton Lincoln LO9 7OP			
GFM01	Grove Farm Meat 46 Maypole Lane Burneston Thirsk North Yorkshire NY5 1EA			
PPA01	Pavarotti Pasta 46 Via Appia Corleone Palermo Sicily 56 XE 78TY			

248

Date From:	01/04/2010		Supplier From:	
Date To:	30/04/2010		Supplier To:	ZZZZZZZZ
Transaction From:	1		N/C From:	
Transaction To:	99,999,999		N/C To:	99999999
Inc b/fwd transaction:	No		Dept From:	0
Exc later payment:	No		Dept To:	999

** NOTE: All report values are shown in Base Currency, unless otherwise indicated **

A/C: BTB01   **Name:** Bob the Baker   **Contact:**   **Tel:**

No	Type	Date	Ref	N/C	Details	Dept	T/C	Value	O/S	Debit	Credit	V	B
17	PI	02/04/2010	574	5000	Oven bottom loaves	0	T0	70.00 *	70.00		70.00	N	-
18	PI	20/04/2010	588	5000	36 seeded rolls	0	T0	50.00 *	50.00		50.00	N	-
19	PI	25/04/2010	591	5000	2 sponge cakes	0	T0	47.00 *	47.00		47.00	N	-
							Totals:	167.00	167.00	0.00	167.00		

Amount Outstanding	167.00
Amount paid this period	0.00
Credit Limit £	0.00
Turnover YTD	167.00

A/C: CCS01   **Name:** Cecelia's Salads   **Contact:**   **Tel:**

No	Type	Date	Ref	N/C	Details	Dept	T/C	Value	O/S	Debit	Credit	V	B
20	PI	04/04/2010	12/34-1	5000	32 mixed salads	0	T0	40.00 *	40.00		40.00	N	-
21	PI	09/04/2010	12/35-1	5000	1 box tomatoes	0	T0	20.00 *	20.00		20.00	N	-
22	PI	01/04/2010	12/38-1	5000	Assorted vegetables	0	T0	39.00 *	39.00		39.00	N	-
							Totals:	99.00	99.00	0.00	99.00		

Amount Outstanding	99.00
Amount paid this period	0.00
Credit Limit £	0.00
Turnover YTD	99.00

A/C: CHM01   **Name:** The Cheese Mouse   **Contact:**   **Tel:**

No	Type	Date	Ref	N/C	Details	Dept	T/C	Value	O/S	Debit	Credit	V	B
23	PI	05/04/2010	45301	5000	Cheese selections	0	T0	70.00 *	70.00		70.00	N	-
24	PI	12/04/2010	45378	5000	Fruit chutneys	0	T1	23.50 *	23.50		23.50	N	-
25	PI	28/04/2010	45399	5000	Crackers & biscuits	0	T1	47.00 *	47.00		47.00	N	-
							Totals:	140.50	140.50	0.00	140.50		

Amount Outstanding	140.50
Amount paid this period	0.00
Credit Limit £	0.00
Turnover YTD	130.00

A/C: DFL01   **Name:** Direct Fruit Ltd   **Contact:**   **Tel:**

No	Type	Date	Ref	N/C	Details	Dept	T/C	Value	O/S	Debit	Credit	V	B
26	PI	13/04/2010	341	5000	2 fruit baskets	0	T0	30.00 *	30.00		30.00	N	-
27	PI	20/04/2010	344	5000	3 fruit baskets	0	T0	45.00 *	45.00		45.00	N	-
							Totals:	75.00	75.00	0.00	75.00		

Amount Outstanding	75.00
Amount paid this period	0.00
Credit Limit £	0.00
Turnover YTD	75.00

A/C: EWC01   Name: English Wine Co   Contact: Tel:

No	Type	Date	Ref	N/C	Details	Dept	T/C	Value	O/S	Debit	Credit	V	B
28	PI	12/04/2010	3789	5001	Mixed merlot case	0	T1	70.50 *	70.50		70.50	N	-
29	PI	20/04/2010	3745	5001	Mixed white case	0	T1	141.00 *	141.00		141.00	N	-
35	PC	28/04/2010	C8894	5001	Credit corked merlot	0	T1	23.50 *	-23.50	23.50		N	-
					Totals:			188.00	188.00	23.50	211.50		

Amount Outstanding	188.00
Amount paid this period	0.00
Credit Limit £	0.00
Turnover YTD	160.00

A/C: GFM01   Name: Grove Farm Meat   Contact: Tel:

No	Type	Date	Ref	N/C	Details	Dept	T/C	Value	O/S	Debit	Credit	V	B
30	PI	02/04/2010	CF1460	5000	Beef fillet	0	T0	167.00 *	167.00		167.00	N	-
31	PI	13/04/2010	CF1478	5000	Free range chicken	0	T0	190.00 *	190.00		190.00	N	-
34	PC	29/04/2010	CF2201	5000	Credit bad chicken	0	T0	20.00 *	-20.00	20.00		N	-
					Totals:			337.00	337.00	20.00	357.00		

Amount Outstanding	337.00
Amount paid this period	0.00
Credit Limit £	0.00
Turnover YTD	337.00

A/C: PPA01   Name: Pavarotti Pasta   Contact: Tel:

No	Type	Date	Ref	N/C	Details	Dept	T/C	Value	O/S	Debit	Credit	V	B
32	PI	20/04/2010	IT5748	5000	20Kg penne	0	T0	150.00 *	150.00		150.00	N	-
33	PI	29/04/2010	IT9387	5000	30Kg linguine	0	T0	250.00 *	250.00		250.00	N	-
					Totals:			400.00	400.00	0.00	400.00		

Amount Outstanding	400.00
Amount paid this period	0.00
Credit Limit £	0.00
Turnover YTD	400.00

Report Date:	30/04/2010	Supplier From:	
Include future transactions:	No	Supplier To:	ZZZZZZZZ
Exclude Later Payments:	No		

** NOTE: All report values are shown in Base Currency, unless otherwise indicated **

A/C	Name	Credit Limit	Turnover	Balance	Future	Current	Period 1	Period 2	Period 3	Older
BTB01	Bob the Baker	£ 0.00	167.00	167.00	0.00	167.00	0.00	0.00	0.00	0.00
CCS01	Cecelia's Salads	£ 0.00	99.00	99.00	0.00	99.00	0.00	0.00	0.00	0.00
CHM01	The Cheese Mouse	£ 0.00	130.00	140.50	0.00	140.50	0.00	0.00	0.00	0.00
DFL01	Direct Fruit Ltd	£ 0.00	75.00	75.00	0.00	75.00	0.00	0.00	0.00	0.00
EWC01	English Wine Co	£ 0.00	160.00	188.00	0.00	188.00	0.00	0.00	0.00	0.00
GFM01	Grove Farm Meat	£ 0.00	337.00	337.00	0.00	337.00	0.00	0.00	0.00	0.00
PPA01	Pavarotti Pasta	£ 0.00	400.00	400.00	0.00	400.00	0.00	0.00	0.00	0.00
		Totals:	1,368.00	1,406.50	0.00	1,406.50	0.00	0.00	0.00	0.00

Task 5

| Date From: | 01/04/2010 | | Bank From: | 1200 |
| DateTo: | 30/04/2010 | | Bank To: | 1200 |

| Transaction From: | 1 | | Supplier From: | |
| Transaction To: | 99,999,999 | | Supplier To: | ZZZZZZZZ |

Bank 1200   Currency   Pound Sterling

No	Type	A/C	Date	Ref	Details	Net £	Tax	£ T/C	Gross £	V	B	Bank Rec. Date
36	PP	BTB01	10/04/2010	102346	Purchase Payment	70.00		0.00 T9	70.00	-	N	
		-	10/04/2010	574	70.00 to PI 17							
37	PP	CCS01	15/04/2010	102347	Purchase Payment	60.00		0.00 T9	60.00	-	N	
		-	15/04/2010	12/34-1	40.00 to PI 20							
		-	15/04/2010	12/35-1	20.00 to PI 21							
38	PP	CHM01	15/04/2010	102348	Purchase Payment	93.50		0.00 T9	93.50	-	N	
		-	15/04/2010	45301	70.00 to PI 23							
		-	15/04/2010	45378	23.50 to PI 24							
39	PP	DFL01	15/04/2010	102349	Purchase Payment	30.00		0.00 T9	30.00	-	N	
		-	15/04/2010	341	30.00 to PI 26							
40	PP	EWC01	18/04/2010	102350	Purchase Payment	70.50		0.00 T9	70.50	-	N	
		-	18/04/2010	3789	70.50 to PI 28							
41	PP	GFM01	30/04/2010	102351	Purchase Payment	337.00		0.00 T9	337.00	-	N	
		-	30/04/2010	CF1460	147.00 to PI 30							
		-	30/04/2010	CF1478	190.00 to PI 31							
42	PP	PPA01	30/04/2010	102352	Purchase Payment	400.00		0.00 T9	400.00	-	N	
		-	30/04/2010	IT5748	150.00 to PI 32							
		-	30/04/2010	IT9387	250.00 to PI 33							
					Totals £	1,061.00		0.00	1,061.00			

Task 6

The Orchard Bistro
Day Books: Bank Receipts (Detailed)

| Date From: | 01/04/2010 | | | Bank From: | 1200 |
| DateTo: | 30/04/2010 | | | Bank To: | 1200 |

| Transaction From: | 1 | | | N/C From: | |
| Transaction To: | 99,999,999 | | | N/C To: | 99999999 |

| Dept From: | 0 |
| Dept To: | 999 |

Bank: 1200 **Currency:** Pound Sterling

No	Type	N/C	Date	Ref	Details	Dept	Net £	Tax £	T/C	Gross £	V	B	Bank Rec. Date
43	BR	4000	07/04/2010	REC001	Sales w/e 7/4/10	0	1,021.28	178.72	T1	1,200.00	N	N	
44	BR	4000	14/04/2010	REC002	Sales w/e 14/4/10	0	1,248.51	218.49	T1	1,467.00	N	N	
45	BR	4000	21/04/2010	REC003	Sales w/e 21/4/10	0	1,668.94	292.06	T1	1,961.00	N	N	
46	BR	4000	28/04/2010	REC004	Sales w/e 28/4/10	0	1,760.85	308.15	T1	2,069.00	N	N	
						Totals £	5,699.58	997.42		6,697.00			

The Orchard Bistro
Day Books: Cash Receipts (Detailed)

Page: 1

| Date From: | 01/04/2010 | | Bank From: | 1230 |
| DateTo: | 30/04/2010 | | Bank To: | 1230 |

| Transaction From: | 1 | | N/C From: | |
| Transaction To: | 99,999,999 | | N/C To: | 99999999 |

| Dept From: | 0 |
| Dept To: | 999 |

Bank: 1230   Currency: Pound Sterling

No	Type	N/C	Date	Ref	Details	Dept	Net £	Tax £ T/C	Gross £ V B	Bank Rec. Date
47	CR	4000	07/04/2010	CASH	Sales w/e 7/4/10	0	2,884.26	504.74 T1	3,389.00 N N	
48	CR	4000	14/04/2010	CASH	Sales w/e 14/4/10	0	2,915.74	510.26 T1	3,426.00 N N	
49	CR	4000	21/04/2010	CASH	Sales w/e 21/4/10	0	1,603.40	280.60 T1	1,884.00 N N	
50	CR	4000	28/04/2010	CASH	Sales w/e 28/4/10	0	1,944.68	340.32 T1	2,285.00 N N	
						Totals £	9,348.08	1,635.92	10,984.00	

Task 7

Date: 19/11/2010
Time: 17:25:25

The Orchard Bistro
Audit Trail (Summary)

Page: 1

Date From:	01/01/1980	
Date To:	31/12/2019	
Transaction From:	51	
Transaction To:	55	
Dept From:	0	
Dept To:	999	
Exclude Deleted Tran:	No	

Customer From:	
Customer To:	ZZZZZZZZ
Supplier From:	
Supplier To:	ZZZZZZZZ
N/C From:	
N/C To:	99999999

No	Type	Date	A/C	N/C	Dept	Ref	Details	Net	Tax	T/C	Pd	Paid	V	B	Bank Rec. Date
51	JD	30/04/2010	7000	7000	0	APRWAG	April Wages	3,487.00	0.00	T9	Y	3,487.00	-	-	
52	JD	30/04/2010	7006	7006	0	APRWAG	April Wages	256.00	0.00	T9	Y	256.00	-	-	
53	JC	30/04/2010	2210	2210	0	APRWAG	April Wages	476.00	0.00	T9	Y	476.00	-	-	
54	JC	30/04/2010	2211	2211	0	APRWAG	April Wages	389.00	0.00	T9	Y	389.00	-	-	
55	JC	30/04/2010	2220	2220	0	APRWAG	April Wages	2,878.00	0.00	T9	Y	2,878.00	-	-	

259

Task 8

The Orchard Bistro
Day Books: Cash Payments (Detailed)

Page: 1

| Date From: | 01/04/2010 | | Bank From: | 1230 |
| DateTo: | 30/04/2010 | | Bank To: | 1230 |

| Transaction From: | 1 | | N/C From: | |
| Transaction To: | 99,999,999 | | N/C To: | 99999999 |

| Dept From: | 0 |
| Dept To: | 999 |

Bank: 1230   Currency: Pound Sterling

No	Type	N/C	Date	Ref	Details	Dept	Net £	Tax £	T/C	Gross £	V	B	Bank Rec. Date
56	CP	7501	03/04/2010	CASHPAY	Postage	0	35.52	0.00	T2	35.52	N	N	
57	CP	7100	06/04/2010	CASHPAY	Rent	0	500.00	0.00	T2	500.00	N	N	
58	CP	7300	20/04/2010	CASHPAY	Petrol	0	17.02	2.98	T1	20.00	N	N	
59	CP	7201	23/04/2010	CASHPAY	Gas	0	42.86	2.14	T5	45.00	N	N	
60	CP	2220	30/04/2010	CASHPAY	Net Wages	0	2,878.00	0.00	T9	2,878.00	-	N	
						Totals £	3,473.40	5.12		3,478.52			

261

The Orchard Bistro
Day Books: Cash Payments (Detailed)

Page: 1

| Date From: | 01/04/2010 | | Bank From: | 1230 |
| DateTo: | 30/04/2010 | | Bank To: | 1230 |

| Transaction From: | 1 | | N/C From: | |
| Transaction To: | 99,999,999 | | N/C To: | 99999999 |

| Dept From: | 0 |
| Dept To: | 999 |

Bank: 1230   **Currency:** Pound Sterling

No	Type	N/C	Date	Ref	Details	Dept	Net £	Tax £	T/C	Gross £	V	B	Bank Rec. Date
56	CP	7501	03/04/2010	CASHPAY	Postage	0	35.52	0.00	T2	35.52	N	N	
57	CP	7100	06/04/2010	CASHPAY	Rent	0	600.00	0.00	T2	600.00	N	N	
58	CP	7300	20/04/2010	CASHPAY	Petrol	0	17.02	2.98	T1	20.00	N	N	
59	CP	7201	23/04/2010	CASHPAY	Gas	0	42.86	2.14	T5	45.00	N	N	
60	CP	2220	30/04/2010	CASHPAY	Net Wages	0	2,878.00	0.00	T9	2,878.00	-	N	
						Totals £	3,573.40	5.12		3,578.52			

Task 9

The Orchard Bistro

Customer Address List

Page: 1

Customer From:
Customer To: ZZZZZZZZ

A/C	Name & Address	Contact Name	Telephone	Fax
PMA01	Pineapple Marketing Ltd Masonry House Dunstable Bedford Bedfordshire BD25 8OP	Peter Longer		

Date From:	01/01/1980	Customer From:	
Date To:	30/04/2010	Customer To:	ZZZZZZZZ
Transaction From:	1	N/C From:	
Transaction To:	99,999,999	N/C To:	99999999
Inc b/fwd transaction:	No	Dept From:	0
Exc later payment:	No	Dept To:	999

** NOTE: All report values are shown in Base Currency, unless otherwise indicated **

A/C: PMA01 Name: Pineapple Marketing Ltd   Contact: Peter Longer   Tel:

No	Type	Date	Ref	N/C	Details	Dept	T/C	Value	O/S	Debit	Credit	V	B
62	SI	30/04/2010	445/10	4001	Catering @ Silverstone Event	0	T1	2,350.00 *	2,350.00	2,350.00		N	-
					Totals:			2,350.00	2,350.00	2,350.00			

Amount Outstanding	2,350.00
Amount Paid this period	0.00
Credit Limit £	4,000.00
Turnover YTD	2,000.00

Task 10

The Orchard Bistro
VAT Return

Date From: 01/04/2010
Date To: 30/04/2010

Inc Current Reconciled: No
Inc Earlier Unreconciled: No

Transaction Number Analysis

Number of reconciled transactions included	0
Number of unreconciled transactions included (within date range)	32
Number of unreconciled transactions included (prior to date range)	0
Total number of transactions included	32

VAT due in this period on sales	1	2,983.34
VAT due in this period on EC acquisitions	2	0.00
Total VAT due (sum of boxes 1 and 2)	3	2,983.34
VAT reclaimed in this period on purchases	4	43.62
Net VAT to be paid to Customs or reclaimed by you	5	2,939.72
Total value of sales, excluding VAT	6	17,047.66
Total value of purchases, excluding VAT	7	2,063.40
Total value of EC sales, excluding VAT	8	0.00
Total value of EC purchases, excluding VAT	9	0.00

| Date From: | 01/04/2010 | | | Inc Current Reconciled: | No |
| Date To: | 30/04/2010 | | | Inc Earlier Unreconciled: | No |

VAT due in this period on sales

Tax Code	Sales Invoice	Sales Credit	Receipts	Journal Crd
T0	0.00	0.00	0.00	0.00
T1	350.00	0.00	2,633.34	0.00
T2	0.00	0.00	0.00	0.00
T3	0.00	0.00	0.00	0.00
T5	0.00	0.00	0.00	0.00
T6	0.00	0.00	0.00	0.00
T20	0.00	0.00	0.00	0.00
Totals	350.00	0.00	2,633.34	0.00

Total for Return - Box   1   2,983.34

Date From: 01/04/2010
Date To: 30/04/2010

Inc Current Reconciled: No
Inc Earlier Unreconciled: No

VAT due in this period on EC acquisitions

Tax Code	Purchase Inv	Purchase Crd	Payments	Journal Dbt
T8	0.00	0.00	0.00	0.00
Totals	0.00	0.00	0.00	0.00

Total for Return - Box 2   0.00

The Orchard Bistro

VAT Report (Summary)

Date From: 01/04/2010
Date To: 30/04/2010

Inc Current Reconciled: No
Inc Earlier Unreconciled: No

VAT reclaimed in this period on purchases

Tax Code	Purchase Inv	Purchase Crd	Payments	Journal Dbt
T0	0.00	0.00	0.00	0.00
T1	42.00	-3.50	2.98	0.00
T2	0.00	0.00	0.00	0.00
T3	0.00	0.00	0.00	0.00
T5	0.00	0.00	2.14	0.00
T6	0.00	0.00	0.00	0.00
T8	0.00	0.00	0.00	0.00
T20	0.00	0.00	0.00	0.00
Totals	42.00	-3.50	5.12	0.00

Total for Return - Box 4   43.62

The Orchard Bistro
VAT Report (Summary)

| Date From: | 01/04/2010 | | Inc Current Reconciled: | No |
| Date To: | 30/04/2010 | | Inc Earlier Unreconciled: | No |

Total value of sales, excluding VAT

Tax Code	Sales Invoice	Sales Credit	Receipts	Journal Crd
T0	0.00	0.00	0.00	0.00
T1	2,000.00	0.00	15,047.66	0.00
T2	0.00	0.00	0.00	0.00
T3	0.00	0.00	0.00	0.00
T4	0.00	0.00	0.00	0.00
T5	0.00	0.00	0.00	0.00
T6	0.00	0.00	0.00	0.00
T20	0.00	0.00	0.00	0.00
Totals	2,000.00	0.00	15,047.66	0.00

Total for Return - Box 6   17,047.66

Date From: 01/04/2010
Date To: 30/04/2010

Inc Current Reconciled: No
Inc Earlier Unreconciled: No

Total value of purchases, excluding VAT

Tax Code	Purchase Inv	Purchase Crd	Payments	Journal Dbt
T0	1,168.00	-20.00	0.00	0.00
T1	240.00	-20.00	17.02	0.00
T2	0.00	0.00	635.52	0.00
T3	0.00	0.00	0.00	0.00
T5	0.00	0.00	42.86	0.00
T6	0.00	0.00	0.00	0.00
T7	0.00	0.00	0.00	0.00
T8	0.00	0.00	0.00	0.00
T20	0.00	0.00	0.00	0.00
Totals	1,408.00	-40.00	695.40	0.00

Total for Return - Box 7   2,063.40

Date From: 01/04/2010   **Inc Current Reconciled:**   No
Date To: 30/04/2010   **Inc Earlier Unreconciled:** No

Total value of EC sales, excluding VAT

Tax Code	Sales Invoice	Sales Credit	Receipts	Journal Crd
T4	0.00	0.00	0.00	0.00
Totals	0.00	0.00	0.00	0.00

Total for Return - Box   8   0.00

Date From: 01/04/2010
Date To: 30/04/2010

Inc Current Reconciled: No
Inc Earlier Unreconciled: No

Total value of EC purchases, excluding VAT

Tax Code	Purchase Inv	Purchase Crd	Payments	Journal Dbt
T7	0.00	0.00	0.00	0.00
T8	0.00	0.00	0.00	0.00
Totals	0.00	0.00	0.00	0.00

Total for Return - Box   9   0.00

| Date From: | 01/04/2010 | | Inc Current Reconciled: | No |
| Date To: | 30/04/2010 | | Inc Earlier Unreconciled: | No |

Transactions Included In:
VAT Box 1   Sales Invoice   Tax Code   T1

No	Type	A/C	N/C	Ref	Date	Details	Amount	VR
62	SI	PMA01	4001	445/10	30/04/2010	Catering @ Silverstone Event	350.00	N
						Total for Tax Code	350.00	

Transactions Included In:
VAT Box 1   Receipts   Tax Code   T1

No	Type	A/C	N/C	Ref	Date	Details	Amount	VR
43	BR	1200	4000	REC001	07/04/2010	Sales w/e 7/4/10	178.72	N
44	BR	1200	4000	REC002	14/04/2010	Sales w/e 14/4/10	218.49	N
45	BR	1200	4000	REC003	21/04/2010	Sales w/e 21/4/10	292.06	N
46	BR	1200	4000	REC004	28/04/2010	Sales w/e 28/4/10	308.15	N
47	CR	1230	4000	CASH	07/04/2010	Sales w/e 7/4/10	504.74	N
48	CR	1230	4000	CASH	14/04/2010	Sales w/e 14/4/10	510.26	N
49	CR	1230	4000	CASH	21/04/2010	Sales w/e 21/4/10	280.60	N
50	CR	1230	4000	CASH	28/04/2010	Sales w/e 28/4/10	340.32	N
						Total for Tax Code	2,633.34	
						Total for Vat Box 1	2,983.34	

Transactions Included In:
VAT Box 4   Purchase Inv   Tax Code   T1

No	Type	A/C	N/C	Ref	Date	Details	Amount	VR
24	PI	CHM01	5000	45378	12/04/2010	Fruit chutneys	3.50	N
25	PI	CHM01	5000	45399	28/04/2010	Crackers & biscuits	7.00	N
28	PI	EWC01	5001	3789	12/04/2010	Mixed merlot case	10.50	N
29	PI	EWC01	5001	3745	20/04/2010	Mixed white case	21.00	N
						Total for Tax Code	42.00	

Transactions Included In:
VAT Box 4   Purchase Crd   Tax Code   T1

No	Type	A/C	N/C	Ref	Date	Details	Amount	VR
35	PC	EWC01	5001	C8894	28/04/2010	Credit corked merlot	-3.50	N
						Total for Tax Code	-3.50	

Transactions Included In:
VAT Box 4   Payments   Tax Code   T1

No	Type	A/C	N/C	Ref	Date	Details	Amount	VR
58	CP	1230	7300	CASHPAY	20/04/2010	Petrol	2.98	N
						Total for Tax Code	2.98	

Transactions Included In:
VAT Box 4   Payments   Tax Code   T5

No	Type	A/C	N/C	Ref	Date	Details	Amount	VR
59	CP	1230	7201	CASHPAY	23/04/2010	Gas	2.14	N
						Total for Tax Code	2.14	
						Total for Vat Box 4	43.62	

Date From: 01/04/2010
Date To: 30/04/2010

Inc Current Reconciled: No
Inc Earlier Unreconciled: No

Transactions Included In:
VAT Box   6   Sales Invoice   Tax Code   T1

No	Type	A/C	N/C	Ref	Date	Details	Amount	VR
62	SI	PMA01	4001	445/10	30/04/2010	Catering @ Silverstone Event	2,000.00	N
						Total for Tax Code	2,000.00	

Transactions Included In:
VAT Box   6   Receipts   Tax Code   T1

No	Type	A/C	N/C	Ref	Date	Details	Amount	VR
43	BR	1200	4000	REC001	07/04/2010	Sales w/e 7/4/10	1,021.28	N
44	BR	1200	4000	REC002	14/04/2010	Sales w/e 14/4/10	1,248.51	N
45	BR	1200	4000	REC003	21/04/2010	Sales w/e 21/4/10	1,668.94	N
46	BR	1200	4000	REC004	28/04/2010	Sales w/e 28/4/10	1,760.85	N
47	CR	1230	4000	CASH	07/04/2010	Sales w/e 7/4/10	2,884.26	N
48	CR	1230	4000	CASH	14/04/2010	Sales w/e 14/4/10	2,915.74	N
49	CR	1230	4000	CASH	21/04/2010	Sales w/e 21/4/10	1,603.40	N
50	CR	1230	4000	CASH	28/04/2010	Sales w/e 28/4/10	1,944.68	N
						Total for Tax Code	15,047.66	
						Total for Vat Box 6	17,047.66	

Transactions Included In:
VAT Box   7   Purchase Inv   Tax Code   T0

No	Type	A/C	N/C	Ref	Date	Details	Amount	VR
17	PI	BTB01	5000	574	02/04/2010	Oven bottom loaves	70.00	N
18	PI	BTB01	5000	588	20/04/2010	36 seeded rolls	50.00	N
19	PI	BTB01	5000	591	25/04/2010	2 sponge cakes	47.00	N
20	PI	CCS01	5000	12/34-1	04/04/2010	32 mixed salads	40.00	N
21	PI	CCS01	5000	12/35-1	09/04/2010	1 box tomatoes	20.00	N
22	PI	CCS01	5000	12/38-1	01/04/2010	Assorted vegetables	39.00	N
23	PI	CHM01	5000	45301	05/04/2010	Cheese selections	70.00	N
26	PI	DFL01	5000	341	13/04/2010	2 fruit baskets	30.00	N
27	PI	DFL01	5000	344	20/04/2010	3 fruit baskets	45.00	N
30	PI	GFM01	5000	CF1460	02/04/2010	Beef fillet	167.00	N
31	PI	GFM01	5000	CF1478	13/04/2010	Free range chicken	190.00	N
32	PI	PPA01	5000	IT5748	20/04/2010	20Kg penne	150.00	N
33	PI	PPA01	5000	IT9387	29/04/2010	30Kg linguine	250.00	N
						Total for Tax Code	1,168.00	

Transactions Included In:
VAT Box   7   Purchase Inv   Tax Code   T1

No	Type	A/C	N/C	Ref	Date	Details	Amount	VR
24	PI	CHM01	5000	45378	12/04/2010	Fruit chutneys	20.00	N
25	PI	CHM01	5000	45399	28/04/2010	Crackers & biscuits	40.00	N
28	PI	EWC01	5001	3789	12/04/2010	Mixed merlot case	60.00	N
29	PI	EWC01	5001	3745	20/04/2010	Mixed white case	120.00	N
						Total for Tax Code	240.00	

Transactions Included In:
VAT Box   7   Purchase Crd   Tax Code   T0

No	Type	A/C	N/C	Ref	Date	Details	Amount	VR
34	PC	GFM01	5000	CF2201	29/04/2010	Credit bad chicken	-20.00	N

Date From: 01/04/2010
Date To: 30/04/2010

Inc Current Reconciled: No
Inc Earlier Unreconciled: No

						Total for Tax Code	-20.00

Transactions Included In:
VAT Box 7 Purchase Crd Tax Code T1

No	Type	A/C	N/C	Ref	Date	Details	Amount	VR
35	PC	EWC01	5001	C8894	28/04/2010	Credit corked merlot	-20.00	N
						Total for Tax Code	-20.00	

Transactions Included In:
VAT Box 7 Payments Tax Code T1

No	Type	A/C	N/C	Ref	Date	Details	Amount	VR
58	CP	1230	7300	CASHPAY	20/04/2010	Petrol	17.02	N
						Total for Tax Code	17.02	

Transactions Included In:
VAT Box 7 Payments Tax Code T2

No	Type	A/C	N/C	Ref	Date	Details	Amount	VR
56	CP	1230	7501	CASHPAY	03/04/2010	Postage	35.52	N
57	CP	1230	7100	CASHPAY	06/04/2010	Rent	600.00	N
						Total for Tax Code	635.52	

Transactions Included In:
VAT Box 7 Payments Tax Code T5

No	Type	A/C	N/C	Ref	Date	Details	Amount	VR
59	CP	1230	7201	CASHPAY	23/04/2010	Gas	42.86	N
						Total for Tax Code	42.86	
						Total for Vat Box 7	2,063.40	

The Orchard Bistro
Unreconciled Payments

| Date From: | 01/01/1980 | Bank From: | 1200 |
| DateTo: | 30/04/2010 | Bank To: | 1200 |

| Transaction From: | 1 |
| Transaction To: | 99,999,999 |

Bank 1200   **Bank Account Name** Bank Current Account   **Currency** Pound Sterling

No	Type	Date	Ref	Details	Amount £
41	PP	30/04/2010	102351	Purchase Payment	337.00
42	PP	30/04/2010	102352	Purchase Payment	400.00
				Total £	737.00

The Orchard Bistro

Audit Trail (Summary)

Date From:	01/01/1980		Customer From:	
Date To:	31/12/2019		Customer To:	ZZZZZZZ
Transaction From:	68		Supplier From:	
Transaction To:	71		Supplier To:	ZZZZZZZ
Dept From:	0		N/C From:	
Dept To:	999		N/C To:	99999999
Exclude Deleted Tran:	No			

No	Type	Date	A/C	N/C	Dept	Ref	Details	Net	Tax	T/C	Pd	Paid	V	B	Bank Rec. Date
68	JC	30/04/2010	0021	0021	0	DEPR APR	Monthly Depreciation - plant	250.00	0.00	T9	Y	250.00	-	-	
69	JD	30/04/2010	8001	8001	0	DEPR APR	Monthly Depreciation - plant	250.00	0.00	T9	Y	250.00	-	-	
70	JC	30/04/2010	0041	0041	0	DEPR APR	Monthly Depreciation - F&F	100.00	0.00	T9	Y	100.00	-	-	
71	JD	30/04/2010	8002	8002	0	DEPR APR	Monthly Depreciation - F&F	100.00	0.00	T9	Y	100.00	-	-	

The Orchard Bistro
Profit and Loss

From: Month 1, April 2010
To: Month 1, April 2010

Chart of Accounts: Default Layout of Accounts

	Period		Year to Date	
Sales				
Product Sales	17,047.66		17,047.66	
		17,047.66		17,047.66
Purchases				
Purchases	1,368.00		1,368.00	
		1,368.00		1,368.00
Direct Expenses				
		0.00		0.00
Gross Profit/(Loss):		15,679.66		15,679.66
Overheads				
Gross Wages	3,743.00		3,743.00	
Rent and Rates	600.00		600.00	
Heat, Light and Power	42.86		42.86	
Motor Expenses	17.02		17.02	
Printing and Stationery	35.52		35.52	
Bank Charges and Interest	37.58		37.58	
Depreciation	350.00		350.00	
		4,825.98		4,825.98
Net Profit/(Loss):		10,853.68		10,853.68

282

From:　　Month 1, April 2010
To:　　　Month 1, April 2010

Chart of Account:　　　　　　　　Default Layout of Accounts

	Period		Year to Date	
Fixed Assets				
Property	100,000.00		100,000.00	
Plant and Machinery	14,750.00		14,750.00	
Furniture and Fixtures	9,500.00		9,500.00	
		124,250.00		124,250.00
Current Assets				
Stock	2,500.00		2,500.00	
Debtors	2,350.00		2,350.00	
Deposits and Cash	8,705.48		8,705.48	
Bank Account	7,618.42		7,618.42	
		21,173.90		21,173.90
Current Liabilities				
Creditors : Short Term	345.50		345.50	
Taxation	865.00		865.00	
VAT Liability	2,939.72		2,939.72	
		4,150.22		4,150.22
Current Assets less Current Liabilities:		17,023.68		17,023.68
Total Assets less Current Liabilities:		141,273.68		141,273.68
Long Term Liabilities				
Creditors : Long Term	80,000.00		80,000.00	
		80,000.00		80,000.00
Total Assets less Total Liabilities:		61,273.68		61,273.68
Capital & Reserves				
Share Capital	50,420.00		50,420.00	
P&L Account	10,853.68		10,853.68	
		61,273.68		61,273.68

To Period: Month 1, April 2010

N/C	Name	Debit	Credit
0010	Freehold Property	100,000.00	
0020	Plant and Machinery	20,000.00	
0021	Plant/Machinery Depreciation		5,250.00
0040	Furniture and Fixtures	12,000.00	
0041	Furniture/Fixture Depreciation		2,500.00
1001	Stock	2,500.00	
1100	Debtors Control Account	2,350.00	
1200	Bank Current Account	7,618.42	
1230	Petty Cash	8,705.48	
2100	Creditors Control Account		345.50
2200	Sales Tax Control Account		2,983.34
2201	Purchase Tax Control Account	43.62	
2210	P.A.Y.E.		476.00
2211	National Insurance		389.00
2300	Loans		80,000.00
3000	Capital		50,420.00
4000	Bistro Sales		15,047.66
4001	Corporate Catering		2,000.00
5000	Food Purchases	1,208.00	
5001	Drink Purchases	160.00	
7000	Gross Wages	3,487.00	
7006	Employers N.I.	256.00	
7100	Rent	600.00	
7201	Gas	42.86	
7300	Fuel and Oil	17.02	
7501	Postage and Carriage	35.52	
7901	Bank Charges	37.58	
8001	Plant/Machinery Depreciation	250.00	
8002	Furniture/Fitting Depreciation	100.00	
	Totals:	159,411.50	159,411.50

THE INSTITUTE OF CERTIFIED BOOKKEEPERS

THE LEVEL III DIPLOMA IN COMPUTERISED BOOKKEEPING FINAL ASSIGNMENT - <u>MOCK</u>

This final assignment should be completed and posted to the Institute by the date at the bottom of this page. You are advised to obtain proof of posting from The Royal Mail.

Required:
Complete the various tasks and send all the required print outs to the Institute at the address below. Ensure that you include your ICB student/membership number on each section. Do NOT include your name. You may keep the question paper

(Peacock Couriers Ltd)
2012

Deadline Date...

The Institute of Certified Bookkeepers
Victoria House
64 Paul Street
London
EC2A 4NG

Assessment Criteria

This piece of work will be graded at Distinction, Merit, Pass or Fail. To pass, all candidates must achieve a minimum of 85% overall.

Pass: To gain a Pass, candidates must achieve 85-89% overall.

Merit: To gain a Merit, candidates must achieve 90-94% overall.

Distinction: To gain a Distinction, candidates must achieve 95-100% overall.

Fail: Candidates who achieve less than 85% of the total marks will be failed.

Any error will lead to a reduction in total marks. An error could include posting to the wrong nominal code, VAT being incorrectly coded, incorrect depreciation, accounts coded to the wrong section of the chart of accounts etc.

Note – it is important that you keep your own back-up of your data until you are informed that you have successfully completed this assignment.

Computerised section of the examination = 70 marks
Written answers = 30 marks

85% overall must be achieved to pass this examination

Peacock Couriers Limited
42, Sprint Lane
Anytown
Shireshire
AT24 9KP

The Situation

You are producing the company financial statements of *Peacock Couriers Limited* at the end of their trading year 2011/12. The company's year end is 30th November. At the beginning of the year there were 300 fully paid-up issued shares with a nominal value of £1. There are two directors, Karl Peacock who owns 200 shares and Harpreet Kaur who owns 100 shares.

Raising Finance

To raise some finance, on 1st March 2012 a further 100 ordinary shares were sold to Karl's friend Darren Rule for £4,000; and a 6% Debenture for £5,000 was taken out on 1st April.

Acquisition & Disposal

On 1st May 2012, the business purchased a new motor cycle at a cost of £8,400 including VAT by cheque. They sold an old motor cycle for £1,600 + VAT. The money for the sale was paid directly into the bank. The old bike was held in the accounts at a cost of £5,000 with accumulated depreciation of £2,625. The VAT rate used was 20%.

Depreciation

- Motorcycles are depreciated at a rate of 25% per annum on a reducing balance basis..
- Office Furniture and Computer Equipment is depreciated at a rate of 20% per annum on cost on a straight line basis.
- A full year's depreciation is to be charged in the year of acquisition and no depreciation is to be charged in the year of disposal.
- Depreciation charges are to be rounded to the nearest £5.

Accruals and Prepayments

There are to be accruals for accountancy fees of £1,500 and rent of £500.

In March 2012 £1,440 was paid for Vehicle Insurance for 1 year, starting from 1st April 2012.

In August, Harpreet entered into an agreement with the local bus company to display advertisements for the business on a selection of their buses for 1 year starting on 1st September. She paid £2,000 up front for this service.

Bad Debt Provision

The directors agreed that the provision for bad debts should be set to 2% of Debtors.

Corporation Tax and Dividends

Corporation Tax is estimated to be £1,200. £1,000 is to be transferred into the General Reserve. Before the balance sheet date, the directors declare that a dividend is paid of £7.50 per share and any remaining profit / loss be allocated to the "retained profit" account.

Peacock Couriers Initial Trial Balance

	Dr	Cr
Office Furniture	2,500	
Office Furniture Depreciation		1,000
Computer Equipment	3,000	
Computer Equipment Dep'n		1,200
Motor cycles	12,600	
Motor cycle Depreciation		5,900
Debtors	18,000	
Bad Debt provision		180
Bank		770
Creditors		7,500
VAT Liability		450
PAYE Liability		1,200
Share Capital		300
General Reserve		4,000
Retained Profit		2,500
Sales		100,000
Advertising	8,000	
Directors Salaries	60,800	
Rent	5,500	
Vehicle Insurance	1,920	
Printing and Stationery	6,300	
Electricity	600	
Postage and Carriage	60	
Repairs	550	
Telephone	1,200	
Petrol	3,400	
Bank charges	220	
Bad Debts Written Off	350	
Total	**125,000**	**125,000**

Section One

Task 1:

Post the initial trial balance shown above into your accounting software. (You may need to create new or rename existing nominal codes.)

Print:
- An Initial Trial Balance
- An Initial Profit and Loss account
- An Initial Balance Sheet

Label your reports with the task number.

Task 2:

Post the amendments needed to account for the finance raised through share dealing and debentures.

Print and label a report that shows the above transactions.

Task 3:

Post the transactions to represent the disposal of the old motorcycle and the acquisition of the new motorcycle.

Task 4:

Post the depreciation of the Fixed Assets for the year.

Task 5:

Post the necessary adjustments for the Prepayments and the Accruals.

Task 6:

Post the necessary journals for the change in bad debt provision.

Task 7:

Post the transactions to represent the payment of 8 months of Debenture interest due at 30th November.
Print:
- A draft Trial Balance
- A draft Profit and Loss account
- A draft Balance Sheet

Task 8:

Process the year end and then make the necessary adjustments to account for Corporation Tax, the declared dividends and the transfer to the general reserve. Assume that both Corporation Tax and the Dividend Payments will occur within 1 year. Ensure that a breakdown of Liabilities, Capital and Reserves is detailed on your Balance Sheet.

Print:
- An Opening Trial Balance for 2012/13
- An Opening Balance Sheet for 2012/13

This is the end of Section One (the computerised section) of the examination

Please go to page 8 for Section Two of the examination

Section Two

1. Using information from *the initial trial balance* of Peacock Couriers Limited *only* before any adjustments and showing your workings, calculate the current ratio. Based on this, provide a brief statement concerning your understanding of Peacock Couriers Limited's liquidity.

2. The table below shows the purchase date and cost of each motor cycle held by Peacock Couriers on 31st March 2012. Showing your workings, calculate the accumulated depreciation on the motor cycles if the residual value for each one is estimated to be 10% of its original cost after 4 years and depreciation is calculated monthly on a straight line basis.

Asset Description	Cost	Date of Purchase
Motor cycle A	£5,000.00	01/04/2010
Motor cycle B	£7,600.00	01/12/2009

3. Give a brief explanation of the differences that arise concerning business taxation with regard to a Partnership and a Limited Company.

This is the end of the examination

To Period: Month 12, November 2013

N/C	Name	Debit	Credit
0030	Computer Equipment	3,000.00	
0031	Computer Equipment Depreciation		1,800.00
0040	Office Furniture	2,500.00	
0041	Office Furniture Depreciation		1,500.00
0050	Motor Cycles	14,600.00	
0051	Motor Cycles Depreciation		6,105.00
1100	Debtors Control Account	18,000.00	
1103	Prepayments	1,980.00	
1104	Bad Debt Provision		360.00
1200	Bank Current Account	1,550.00	
2100	Creditors Control Account		7,500.00
2109	Accruals		2,000.00
2200	Sales Tax Control Account		320.00
2201	Purchase Tax Control Account	1,400.00	
2202	VAT Liability		450.00
2210	P.A.Y.E.		1,200.00
2230	Proposed Dividends to be paid		3,000.00
2240	Corporation Tax		1,200.00
2300	Debentures		5,000.00
3000	Ordinary Shares		400.00
3010	Share Premium		3,900.00
3100	General Reserve		5,000.00
3200	Profit and Loss Account		3,295.00
	Totals:	43,030.00	43,030.00

From: Month 1, December 2012
To: Month 12, November 2013

Chart of Account: Default Layout of Accounts

	Period		Year to Date	
Fixed Assets				
Office Equipment	0.00		1,200.00	
Furniture and Fixtures	0.00		1,000.00	
Motor Vehicles	0.00		8,495.00	
		0.00		10,695.00
Current Assets				
Debtors	0.00		19,620.00	
Bank Account	0.00		1,550.00	
VAT Liability	0.00		630.00	
		0.00		21,800.00
Current Liabilities				
Creditors : Short Term	0.00		9,500.00	
Taxation	0.00		1,200.00	
Proposed Dividends to be paid	3,000.00		3,000.00	
Corporation Tax	1,200.00		1,200.00	
		4,200.00		14,900.00
Current Assets less Current Liabilities:		(4,200.00)		6,900.00
Total Assets less Current Liabilities:		(4,200.00)		17,595.00
Long Term Liabilities				
Creditors : Long Term	0.00		5,000.00	
		0.00		5,000.00
Total Assets less Total Liabilities:		(4,200.00)		12,595.00
Capital & Reserves				
Share Capital	0.00		400.00	
Capital Reserve	0.00		3,900.00	
General Reserve	1,000.00		5,000.00	
Retained Profit	(5,200.00)		3,295.00	
P&L Account	0.00		0.00	
		(4,200.00)		12,595.00

To Period: Month 12, November 2012

N/C	Name	Debit	Credit
0030	Computer Equipment	3,000.00	
0031	Computer Equipment Depreciation		1,800.00
0040	Office Furniture	2,500.00	
0041	Office Furniture Depreciation		1,500.00
0050	Motor Cycles	14,600.00	
0051	Motor Cycles Depreciation		6,105.00
1100	Debtors Control Account	18,000.00	
1103	Prepayments	1,980.00	
1104	Bad Debt Provision		360.00
1200	Bank Current Account	1,550.00	
2100	Creditors Control Account		7,500.00
2109	Accruals		2,000.00
2200	Sales Tax Control Account		320.00
2201	Purchase Tax Control Account	1,400.00	
2202	VAT Liability		450.00
2210	P.A.Y.E.		1,200.00
2300	Debentures		5,000.00
3000	Ordinary Shares		400.00
3010	Share Premium		3,900.00
3100	General Reserve		4,000.00
3200	Profit and Loss Account		2,500.00
4000	Sales		100,000.00
6201	Advertising	6,500.00	
7001	Directors Salaries	60,800.00	
7100	Rent	6,000.00	
7200	Electricity	600.00	
7300	Fuel and Oil	3,400.00	
7303	Vehicle Insurance	1,440.00	
7500	Printing	6,300.00	
7501	Postage and Carriage	60.00	
7502	Telephone	1,200.00	
7601	Audit and Accountancy Fees	1,500.00	
7800	Repairs and Renewals	550.00	
7901	Bank Charges	220.00	
7903	Debenture Interest Paid	200.00	
8002	Office Furniture Depreciation	500.00	
8003	Motor Cycles Depreciation	2,830.00	
8004	Computer Equipment Depreciation	600.00	
8100	Bad Debt Write Off	350.00	
8102	Bad Debt Provision	180.00	
8200	Profit / Loss on Disposal	775.00	
	Totals:	**137,035.00**	**137,035.00**

Peacock Couriers Limited

Profit and Loss

Page: 1

From: Month 1, December 2011
To: Month 12, November 2012

Chart of Accounts: Default Layout of Accounts

	Period		Year to Date	
Sales				
Product Sales	100,000.00		100,000.00	
		100,000.00		100,000.00
Purchases				
		0.00		0.00
Direct Expenses				
Sales Promotion	6,500.00		6,500.00	
		6,500.00		6,500.00
Gross Profit/(Loss):		93,500.00		93,500.00
Overheads				
Gross Wages	60,800.00		60,800.00	
Rent and Rates	6,000.00		6,000.00	
Heat, Light and Power	600.00		600.00	
Motor Expenses	4,840.00		4,840.00	
Printing and Stationery	7,560.00		7,560.00	
Professional Fees	1,500.00		1,500.00	
Maintenance	550.00		550.00	
Bank Charges and Interest	420.00		420.00	
Depreciation	3,930.00		3,930.00	
Bad Debts (including Provision)	530.00		530.00	
Profit / Loss on Disposal	775.00		775.00	
		87,505.00		87,505.00
Net Profit/(Loss):		5,995.00		5,995.00

Peacock Couriers Limited
Balance Sheet

From: Month 1, December 2011
To: Month 12, November 2012

Chart of Account: Default Layout of Accounts

	Period		Year to Date	
Fixed Assets				
Office Equipment	1,200.00		1,200.00	
Furniture and Fixtures	1,000.00		1,000.00	
Motor Vehicles	8,495.00		8,495.00	
		10,695.00		10,695.00
Current Assets				
Debtors	19,620.00		19,620.00	
Bank Account	1,550.00		1,550.00	
VAT Liability	630.00		630.00	
		21,800.00		21,800.00
Current Liabilities				
Creditors : Short Term	9,500.00		9,500.00	
Taxation	1,200.00		1,200.00	
		10,700.00		10,700.00
Current Assets less Current Liabilities:		11,100.00		11,100.00
Total Assets less Current Liabilities:		21,795.00		21,795.00
Long Term Liabilities				
Creditors : Long Term	5,000.00		5,000.00	
		5,000.00		5,000.00
Total Assets less Total Liabilities:		16,795.00		16,795.00
Capital & Reserves				
Share Capital	400.00		400.00	
Capital Reserve	3,900.00		3,900.00	
General Reserve	4,000.00		4,000.00	
Retained Profit	2,500.00		2,500.00	
P&L Account	5,995.00		5,995.00	
		16,795.00		16,795.00

Date: 29/11/2011
Time: 17:08:10

Peacock Couriers Limited
Audit Trail (Summary)

Date From:	01/01/1980		Customer From:	
Date To:	31/12/2019		Customer To:	ZZZZZZZ
Transaction From:	57		Supplier From:	
Transaction To:	61		Supplier To:	ZZZZZZZ
Dept From:	0		N/C From:	
Dept To:	999		N/C To:	99999999
Exclude Deleted Tran:	No			

No	Type	Date	A/C	N/C	Dept	Ref	Details	Net	Tax	T/C	Pd	Paid	V	B	Bank Rec. Date
57	JD	01/03/2012	1200	1200	0	Share sale	Purchase of Shares by Darren Rule	4,000.00	0.00	T9	Y	4,000.00	-	N	
58	JC	01/03/2012	3000	3000	0	Share sale	Purchase of Shares by Darren Rule	100.00	0.00	T9	Y	100.00	-	-	
59	JD	01/03/2012	3010	3010	0	Share sale	Purchase of Shares by Darren Rule	3,900.00	0.00	T9	Y	3,900.00	-	-	
60	JD	01/04/2012	1200	1200	0	Debenture	6% Debenture	5,000.00	0.00	T9	Y	5,000.00	-	N	
61	JC	01/04/2012	2300	2300	0	Debenture	6% Debenture	5,000.00	0.00	T9	Y	5,000.00	-	-	

298

Peacock Couriers Limited
Period Trial Balance

To Period: Month 12, November 2012

N/C	Name	Debit	Credit
0030	Computer Equipment	3,000.00	
0031	Computer Equipment Depreciation		1,200.00
0040	Office Furniture	2,500.00	
0041	Office Furniture Depreciation		1,000.00
0050	Motor Cycles	12,600.00	
0051	Motor Cycles Depreciation		5,900.00
1100	Debtors Control Account	18,000.00	
1104	Bad Debt Provision		180.00
1200	Bank Current Account		770.00
2100	Creditors Control Account		7,500.00
2202	VAT Liability		450.00
2210	P.A.Y.E.		1,200.00
3000	Ordinary Shares		300.00
3100	General Reserve		4,000.00
3200	Profit and Loss Account		2,500.00
4000	Sales		100,000.00
6201	Advertising	8,000.00	
7001	Directors Salaries	60,800.00	
7100	Rent	5,500.00	
7200	Electricity	600.00	
7300	Fuel and Oil	3,400.00	
7303	Vehicle Insurance	1,920.00	
7500	Printing	6,300.00	
7501	Postage and Carriage	60.00	
7502	Telephone	1,200.00	
7800	Repairs and Renewals	550.00	
7901	Bank Charges	220.00	
8100	Bad Debt Write Off	350.00	
	Totals:	125,000.00	125,000.00

Peacock Couriers Limited
Profit and Loss

From: Month 1, December 2011
To: Month 12, November 2012

Chart of Accounts: Default Layout of Accounts

	Period		Year to Date	
Sales				
Product Sales	100,000.00		100,000.00	
		100,000.00		100,000.00
Purchases				
		0.00		0.00
Direct Expenses				
Sales Promotion	8,000.00		8,000.00	
		8,000.00		8,000.00
Gross Profit/(Loss):		92,000.00		92,000.00
Overheads				
Gross Wages	60,800.00		60,800.00	
Rent and Rates	5,500.00		5,500.00	
Heat, Light and Power	600.00		600.00	
Motor Expenses	5,320.00		5,320.00	
Printing and Stationery	7,560.00		7,560.00	
Maintenance	550.00		550.00	
Bank Charges and Interest	220.00		220.00	
Bad Debts	350.00		350.00	
		80,900.00		80,900.00
Net Profit/(Loss):		11,100.00		11,100.00

Peacock Couriers Limited
Balance Sheet

From: Month 1, December 2011
To: Month 12, November 2012

Chart of Account: Default Layout of Accounts

	Period		Year to Date	
Fixed Assets				
Office Equipment	1,800.00		1,800.00	
Furniture and Fixtures	1,500.00		1,500.00	
Motor Vehicles	6,700.00		6,700.00	
		10,000.00		10,000.00
Current Assets				
Debtors	17,820.00		17,820.00	
		17,820.00		17,820.00
Current Liabilities				
Creditors : Short Term	7,500.00		7,500.00	
Taxation	1,200.00		1,200.00	
Bank Account	770.00		770.00	
VAT Liability	450.00		450.00	
		9,920.00		9,920.00
Current Assets less Current Liabilities:		7,900.00		7,900.00
Total Assets less Current Liabilities:		17,900.00		17,900.00
Long Term Liabilities				
		0.00		0.00
Total Assets less Total Liabilities:		17,900.00		17,900.00
Capital & Reserves				
Share Capital	300.00		300.00	
Reserves	6,500.00		6,500.00	
P&L Account	11,100.00		11,100.00	
		17,900.00		17,900.00

Section 2
Question 1:

Peacock Couriers Current Ratio

Current Assets = Debtors – Bad Debt Provision: 18,000 – 180 = **17,820**
(or this figure may be taken from the Balance Sheet from Section 1, Task 1)

Current Liabilities = Bank + Creditors + VAT + PAYE:

Bank:	770
Creditors:	7,500
VAT:	450
PAYE:	1,200
	9,920

(or this figure may be taken from the Balance Sheet from Section 1, Task 1)

Current ratio = $\frac{\text{Current Assets}}{\text{Current Liabilities}}$ $\frac{17,820}{9,920}$ which gives **1 : 1.796** or **1 : 1.80**

A figure that is greater than one shows that the current assets exceed the current liabilities. This means that Peacock Couriers should be able to pay off short term debt without having to resort to selling fixed assets or taking out further loans. They can be described as being 'liquid'.

Question 2:

Motor Cycle A: Cost £5,000 minus disposal value of £500 means that £4,500 will be depreciated over 48 months. This equates to £93.75 per month. From its purchase date to 31st March 2012 24 months have passed so the total depreciation to 31st March 2012 on Motor Cycle A is £2,250.
(2 x the annual depreciation figure may be used in the workings instead).

Motor Cycle B: Cost £7,600 minus disposal value of £760 means that £6840 will be depreciated over 48 months. This equates to £142.50 per month. From its purchase date to 31st March 2012, 28 months have elapsed so the total depreciation to 31st March 2012 on Motor Cycle B is £3,990

The combined total depreciation of the motor cycles to 31st March 2012 is **£6240**.

Question 3:

A Sole Trader is subject to Class 2 (fixed) and Class 4 (based on profit) National Insurance Contributions and taxed as an individual based on the profits of the business. This personal tax is due on earnings above the individual's personal allowance and is based on the standard, higher and additional taxation rates depending on the amount of earnings.

Directors and employees of a Limited company are subject to PAYE whereupon they pay Class 1 National Insurance contributions on earnings above a threshold and the business pays Employer National Insurance at a higher rate on earnings as well as other taxable benefits enjoyed by the directors and employees above a threshold. Earnings above the individual's personal allowance are taxed at the same standard, higher and additional rates incurred by Sole Traders.

Profits of a Limited Company including dividends paid to shareholders are subject to Corporation Tax which, depending on the earnings of those receiving payment, may be taxed at a lower rate than the combined tax and National Insurance paid through PAYE.

CERTIFICATE IN COMPUTERISED BOOKKEEPING (C3)
Peacock Couriers Ltd

Signed Marker...............................
Grade   %

Name:	Number:

Task No	Poss Marks	Actual Marks	Comments
1. Initial Trial Balance and Reports	10		
2. Raising Finance	10		
Adjustments			
3. Disposal of Assets	10		
4. Depreciation	5		
5. Accruals and Prepayments	10		
6. Bad debt and bad debt provision	5		
7. Debenture Interest	5		
Print Reports after adjustments	5		
8. Appropriation of Profit	10		
Written Answers			
1. Current Ratio & Explanation	10		
2. Monthly depreciation with residual value	10		
3. Partnership & Limited Company Taxation	10		

THE INSTITUTE
OF CERTIFIED
BOOKKEEPERS

THE LEVEL III DIPLOMA IN COMPUTERISED BOOKKEEPING FINAL
ASSIGNMENT - <u>MOCK</u>

This final assignment should be completed and posted to the Institute by the date at the bottom of this page. You are advised to obtain proof of posting from The Royal Mail.

Required:
Complete the various tasks and send all the required print outs to the Institute at the address below. Ensure that you include your ICB student/membership number on each section. Do NOT include your name. You may keep the question paper

(Anytown Youthclub)
2012

Deadline Date..................N/A Mock..

The Institute of Certified Bookkeepers
Victoria House
64 Paul Street
London
EC2A 4NG

Assessment Criteria

This piece of work will be graded at Distinction, Merit, Pass or Fail. To pass, all candidates must achieve a minimum of 85% overall.

Pass: To gain a Pass, candidates must achieve 85-89% overall.

Merit: To gain a Merit, candidates must achieve 90-94% overall.

Distinction: To gain a Distinction, candidates must achieve 95-100% overall.

Fail: Candidates who achieve less than 85% of the total marks will be failed.

Any error will lead to a reduction in total marks. An error could include posting to the wrong nominal code, VAT being incorrectly coded, incorrect depreciation, accounts coded to the wrong section of the chart of accounts etc.

Note – it is important that you keep your own back-up of your data until you are informed that you have successfully completed this assignment.

Computerised section of the examination = 70 marks
Written answers = 30 marks

85% overall must be achieved to pass this examination

The Situation

You maintain the books for *Anytown Youth Club,* a not-for-profit organisation that provides a meeting area, social facilities and organised events for young people in the local area. The club is part funded by membership subscriptions to the Youth Club and the rest of their funding is raised through donations and by selling snacks and refreshments. Membership runs from 1st September one year to the 31st August the next year. The tasks that follow relate to the club's financial year 2011/12. The club is not registered for VAT.

Subscriptions

At the end of the year 2010/11, 5 members had still not paid their subscription for 2010/11, 3 members had already paid their subscriptions for 2011/12.

At the end of the year 2011/12 all 2010/11 subscriptions had been received, 6 were still outstanding for the year just ended and 8 had already paid for 2012/13. The total membership in the year 2011/12 was 80. The membership fee remained at £25 across all years.

Anytown Youth Club Initial Balances at the start of 2011/12

	Dr	Cr
Chairs	500	
Chairs Depreciation		400
PA Equipment	1,200	
PA Equipment Depreciation		300
Stock of Snacks (15 boxes @ £20)	300	
Stock of Bottles (8 crates @ £50)	400	
Bank	50	

Stock

Stocks of snacks and refreshments are purchased 4 times a year and used strictly on a First In First Out (FIFO) basis. Throughout the year 2011/12, the following purchases were made (inclusive of VAT):

Purchase date:	1/9/11		1/12/11		1/3/12		1/6/12	
Stock Type	Units	Cost per unit £	Units	Cost per unit £	Units	Cost per unit £	Units	Cost per unit £
Boxes of Snacks	20	22.50	25	25.00	15	33.00	10	30.00
Crates of Bottles	30	46.00	40	50.00	25	53.00	20	52.00

During the course of the year, 50 boxes of snacks were sold at a mark-up of 20% and 88 Crates of bottles were sold using a 20% profit margin. There were no returns of sales or purchases.

Donations

In March, the parish council had money left in their annual budget and donated £5,000 to *Anytown Youth Club*.

Acquisition & Disposal

In April, the club sold all their old chairs to a scrap metal merchant for £200 cash which was banked, and bought 50 new chairs by cheque for £12.50 each plus VAT at 20%. The old chairs were held in the books at a cost of £500 with accumulated depreciation of £400.

Depreciation

- Furniture is depreciated at a rate of 20% per annum on cost on a straight line basis.
- Public Address Equipment is depreciated at a rate of 25% per annum on a reducing balance basis.
- A full year's depreciation is to be charged in the year of acquisition and no depreciation is to be charged in the year of disposal.

Accruals and Prepayments

There are to be accruals for Bookkeeping fees of £400 and Bank Charges of £50.

Total rent payments on the hall of £4,200 were made and include all utilities and VAT. Rent is usually paid quarterly in advance with the most recent payment of £900 made on 31st July.

Section One

In completing the following tasks candidates should make every effort to configure their bookkeeping software to supply appropriately worded and named reports as well as accounts and headings within these reports. However candidates will not be penalised if their bookkeeping software does not facilitate all aspects of this configuration. **All candidates should indicate the software that they have used to complete this examination by writing a note on their Initial Balance Sheet.**

Task 1:

Ensure that a suitable chart of accounts is selected in your accounting software or edited to report on Accumulated Funds and Subscriptions.

Post the initial balances shown in the table above into your software together with your calculated figures that represent the status of subscriptions at the end of the previous year and the club's accumulated fund.

Print the following reports and label them with the task number:

- An Initial Trial Balance
- A Balance Sheet

Task 2:

Enter the subscriptions received during the year and make appropriate adjustments for those outstanding and paid in advance. All subscription payments received are paid into the bank.

Print and label a report that shows the above transactions.

Task 3:

Enter the purchases of Snacks and Bottles assuming they were paid for by cheque.

Calculate the yearly sales figures for Snacks and Bottles and enter these into your software. Assume all sales income was paid directly into the bank.

Task 4:

Calculate the value of closing stock at the end of the year and make the appropriate adjustments.

Task 5:

Enter the donation from the Parish Council then post the transactions to represent the disposal of the old chairs and the acquisition of the new chairs.

Task 6:

Post the depreciation of the Fixed Assets.

Task 7:

Enter the payment for rent and make the necessary adjustments for Prepayments and Accruals.

Print:
- A Trial Balance
- An Income and Expenditure (Profit and Loss) account
- A Balance Sheet

Task 8:

Process the year end

Print:
- An Opening Trial Balance for 2012/13
- An Opening Balance Sheet for 2012/13

This is the end of Section One (the computerised section) of the examination

Please go to page 8 for Section Two of the examination

1. Calculate the average number of days (to the nearest day) it takes *Anytown Youth Club* to turnover their stock. Show your workings.

2. Using only the stock purchased during *Anytown Youth Club*'s year 2011/12 and assuming there are 35 boxes of snacks and 35 crates of bottles remaining at the end of the year, calculate the total value of *Anytown Youth Club*'s closing stock using the Average Cost (AVCO) method. Show your workings.

3. If the new chairs that *Anytown Youth Club* purchased in April had been offered for sale with a discount of 6% provided settlement was made within 10 days, but instead of paying straight away the club made payment after 30 days, calculate the net book value of the chairs after adjustments at the end of the year 2011/12. Show your workings.

This is the end of the examination

Anytown Youth Club
Period Trial Balance

To Period: Month 12, August 2012

N/C	Name	Debit	Credit
0030	PA Equipment	1,200.00	
0031	PA Equipment Depreciation		300.00
0040	Furniture and Fixtures	500.00	
0041	Furniture/Fixture Depreciation		400.00
1001	Stock of Snacks	300.00	
1002	Stock of Bottles	400.00	
1100	Unpaid Subscriptions	125.00	
1200	Bank Current Account	50.00	
2101	Subscriptions Paid in Advance		75.00
3200	Accumulated Fund		1,800.00
	Totals:	2,575.00	2,575.00

Anytown Youth Club
Balance Sheet

From: Month 1, September 2011
To: Month 12, August 2012

Chart of Account: Default Layout of Accounts

	Period		Year to Date	
Fixed Assets				
PA Equipment	900.00		900.00	
Furniture and Fixtures	100.00		100.00	
		1,000.00		1,000.00
Current Assets				
Stock	700.00		700.00	
Subscriptions Owing	125.00		125.00	
Bank Account	50.00		50.00	
		875.00		875.00
Current Liabilities				
Advance Subscriptions	75.00		75.00	
		75.00		75.00
Current Assets less Current Liabilities:		800.00		800.00
Total Assets less Current Liabilities:		1,800.00		1,800.00
Long Term Liabilities				
		0.00		0.00
Total Assets less Total Liabilities:		1,800.00		1,800.00
Capital & Reserves				
Accumulated Fund	1,800.00		1,800.00	
P&L Account	0.00		0.00	
		1,800.00		1,800.00

Anytown Youth Club
Audit Trail (Brief)

Date From: 01/01/1980
Date To: 31/12/2019

Transaction From: 25
Transaction To: 33

Exclude Deleted Tran: No

Customer From:
Customer To: ZZZZZZZZ

Supplier From:
Supplier To: ZZZZZZZZ

No	Items	Type	A/C	Date	Ref	Details	Net	Tax	Gross
25	1	JC	1100	31/08/2012	Subscriptions	2010/11 Subscriptions Received	125.00	0.00	125.00
26	1	JD	1200	31/08/2012	Subscriptions	2010/11 Subscriptions Received	125.00	0.00	125.00
27	1	JD	2101	31/08/2012	Subscriptions	Previously advance payments transferred	75.00	0.00	75.00
28	1	JC	4900	31/08/2012	Subscriptions	Previously advance payments transferred	75.00	0.00	75.00
29	1	JC	4900	31/08/2012	Subscriptions	Further subscriptions for 2011/12	1,925.00	0.00	1,925.00
30	1	JD	1200	31/08/2012	Subscriptions	Further subscriptions for 2011/12	1,775.00	0.00	1,775.00
31	1	JD	1100	31/08/2012	Subscriptions	2011/12 Subscriptions Due	150.00	0.00	150.00
32	1	JD	1200	31/08/2012	Subscriptions	Subscriptions for 2012/13 Paid	200.00	0.00	200.00
33	1	JC	2101	31/08/2012	Subscriptions	Subscriptions for 2012/13 Paid	200.00	0.00	200.00

Anytown Youth Club
Period Trial Balance

To Period: Month 12, August 2012

N/C	Name	Debit	Credit
0030	PA Equipment	1,200.00	
0031	PA Equipment Depreciation		525.00
0040	Furniture and Fixtures	750.00	
0041	Furniture/Fixture Depreciation		150.00
1001	Stock of Snacks	1,045.00	
1002	Stock of Bottles	1,835.00	
1100	Unpaid Subscriptions	150.00	
1103	Prepayments	600.00	
1200	Bank Current Account	1,522.50	
2101	Subscriptions Paid in Advance		200.00
2109	Accruals		450.00
3200	Accumulated Fund		1,800.00
4000	Donations Received		5,000.00
4400	Fund Generation - Shop Snacks		1,350.00
4401	Fund Generation - Shop Bottles		5,387.50
4900	Subscriptions		2,000.00
4950	Sale of Assets		100.00
5400	Purchase of Snacks	1,870.00	
5401	Purchase of Bottles	5,745.00	
5500	Opening Stock	700.00	
5501	Closing Stock		2,880.00
7000	Rent	3,600.00	
7701	Bank Charges	50.00	
7901	Audit and Accountancy Fees	400.00	
8002	Furniture/Fitting Depreciation	150.00	
8004	PA Equipment Depreciation	225.00	
	Totals:	19,842.50	19,842.50

From: Month 1, September 2011
To: Month 12, August 2012

Chart of Accounts: Default Layout of Accounts

	Period		Year to Date	
Sales				
Donations	5,000.00		5,000.00	
Fund Generation - Shop - Snacks	1,350.00		1,350.00	
Fund Generation - Shop - Bottles	5,387.50		5,387.50	
Subscription Income	2,000.00		2,000.00	
Sale of Assets	100.00		100.00	
		13,837.50		13,837.50
Purchases				
Stocks for Shop - Snacks	1,870.00		1,870.00	
Stocks for Shop - Bottles	5,745.00		5,745.00	
Opening Stock	700.00		700.00	
Closing Stock	(2,880.00)		(2,880.00)	
		5,435.00		5,435.00
Direct Expenses				
		0.00		0.00
Gross Profit/(Loss):		8,402.50		8,402.50
Overheads				
Support Costs - Rent and Rates	3,600.00		3,600.00	
Management & Admin - Bank Charges and Interest	50.00		50.00	
Management & Admin - Professional Fees	400.00		400.00	
Management & Admin - Depreciation	375.00		375.00	
		4,425.00		4,425.00
Net Profit/(Loss):		3,977.50		3,977.50

316

Anytown Youth Club
Balance Sheet

From: Month 1, September 2011
To: Month 12, August 2012

Chart of Account: Default Layout of Accounts

	Period		Year to Date	
Fixed Assets				
PA Equipment	675.00		675.00	
Furniture and Fixtures	600.00		600.00	
		1,275.00		1,275.00
Current Assets				
Stock	2,880.00		2,880.00	
Subscriptions Owing	150.00		150.00	
Prepayments	600.00		600.00	
Bank Account	1,522.50		1,522.50	
		5,152.50		5,152.50
Current Liabilities				
Advance Subscriptions	200.00		200.00	
Accruals	450.00		450.00	
		650.00		650.00
Current Assets less Current Liabilities:		4,502.50		4,502.50
Total Assets less Current Liabilities:		5,777.50		5,777.50
Long Term Liabilities				
		0.00		0.00
Total Assets less Total Liabilities:		5,777.50		5,777.50
Capital & Reserves				
Accumulated Fund	1,800.00		1,800.00	
P&L Account	3,977.50		3,977.50	
		5,777.50		5,777.50

To Period: Brought forward

N/C	Name	Debit	Credit
0030	PA Equipment	1,200.00	
0031	PA Equipment Depreciation		525.00
0040	Furniture and Fixtures	750.00	
0041	Furniture/Fixture Depreciation		150.00
1001	Stock of Snacks	1,045.00	
1002	Stock of Bottles	1,835.00	
1100	Unpaid Subscriptions	150.00	
1103	Prepayments	600.00	
1200	Bank Current Account	1,522.50	
2101	Subscriptions Paid in Advance		200.00
2109	Accruals		450.00
3200	Accumulated Fund		5,777.50
	Totals:	7,102.50	7,102.50

Anytown Youth Club
Balance Sheet

From: Brought forward
To: Brought forward

Chart of Account: Default Layout of Accounts

	Period		Year to Date	
Fixed Assets				
PA Equipment	675.00		675.00	
Furniture and Fixtures	600.00		600.00	
		1,275.00		1,275.00
Current Assets				
Stock	2,880.00		2,880.00	
Subscriptions Owing	150.00		150.00	
Prepayments	600.00		600.00	
Bank Account	1,522.50		1,522.50	
		5,152.50		5,152.50
Current Liabilities				
Advance Subscriptions	200.00		200.00	
Accruals	450.00		450.00	
		650.00		650.00
Current Assets less Current Liabilities:		4,502.50		4,502.50
Total Assets less Current Liabilities:		5,777.50		5,777.50
Long Term Liabilities				
		0.00		0.00
Total Assets less Total Liabilities:		5,777.50		5,777.50
Capital & Reserves				
Accumulated Fund	5,777.50		5,777.50	
P&L Account	0.00		0.00	
		5,777.50		5,777.50

Section 2

Question 1:

Value of Stock at the beginning of the year: £700
Value of Stock at the end of the year: £2,880
Average value of stock = £700 + £2,880 / 2 = £1790

Total cost of goods sold: £5,435.00

Turnover = £5,435.00 / £1,790 = 3.036

Number of days to turnover the stock = 365 / 3.036 = **120**

Question 2:

Snacks
20 x £22.50 = £450
25 x £25.00 = £625
15 x £33.00 = £495
10 x £30.00 = £300
70 units cost £1,870 so average cost is: £26.71 x 35 boxes remaining = £934.85 (or £935)

Bottles
30 x £46.00 = £1,380
40 x £50.00 = £2,000
25 x £53.00 = £1,325
20 x £52.00 = £1,040
115 units cost £5,745 so average cost is: £49.96 x 35 crates remaining = £1,748.60

Total value of closing stock using AVCO: **£2,683.45** (£2,683 or £2,684 acceptable)

Question 3:

Net cost of each chair: £12.50.
After a discount of 6%, the discounted net cost would be £12.50 x 94% = £11.75.
VAT on the discounted cost of £11.75 at 20% = £2.35.
The gross cost of a non-discounted chair would be £12.50 + £2.35 = £14.85
50 chairs at £14.85 = £742.50
Depreciation at 20% = £148.50
Revised Net Book Value is £742.50 – £148.50 = **£594.00**

Note that as Anytown Youth Club is not VAT registered, the VAT cannot be reclaimed and the VAT element is included in the cost of the asset.

CERTIFICATE IN COMPUTERISED BOOKKEEPING (C3)
Anytown Youth Club

Signed Marker..............................

Grade   %

Name:	Number:

Task No	Poss Marks	Actual Marks	Comments
1. Initial Trial Balance and Balance Sheet	10		
2. Subscription adjustments report	10		
3. Purchases entry. Sales calculations & entry	10		
4. Calculation & Adjustment for Closing Stock	8		
5. Donation, Acquisition & Disposal	8		
6. Depreciation	4		
7. Rent entry, Prepayments & Accruals	10		
Print Reports after adjustments	6		
8. Year End & Opening Reports	4		
Written Answers			
1. Stock Turnover	10		
2. Closing Stock Valuation	10		
3. Calculation of revised net book value of furniture	10		

THE INSTITUTE
OF CERTIFIED
BOOKKEEPERS

THE LEVEL III DIPLOMA IN COMPUTERISED BOOKKEEPING FINAL ASSIGNMENT - <u>MOCK</u>

This final assignment should be completed and posted to the Institute by the date at the bottom of this page. You are advised to obtain proof of posting from The Royal Mail.

Required:
Complete the various tasks and send all the required print outs to the Institute at the address below. Ensure that you include your ICB student/membership number on each section. Do NOT include your name. You may keep the question paper

(Webfinity and Beyond)
2012

Deadline Date...............N/A - Mock...

The Institute of Certified Bookkeepers
Victoria House
64 Paul Street
London
EC2A 4NG

Assessment Criteria

This piece of work will be graded at Distinction, Merit, Pass or Fail. To pass, all candidates must achieve a minimum of 85% overall.

Pass: To gain a Pass, candidates must achieve 85-89% overall.

Merit: To gain a Merit, candidates must achieve 90-94% overall.

Distinction: To gain a Distinction, candidates must achieve 95-100% overall.

Fail: Candidates who achieve less than 85% of the total marks will be failed.

Any error will lead to a reduction in total marks. An error could include posting to the wrong nominal code, VAT being incorrectly coded, incorrect depreciation, accounts coded to the wrong section of the chart of accounts etc.

Note – it is important that you keep your own back-up of your data until you are informed that you have successfully completed this assignment.

Computerised section of the examination = 70 marks
Written answers = 30 marks

85% overall must be achieved to pass this examination

The Situation

You are producing the financial statements at the end of the trading year 2011/12 for *Webfinity and Beyond*, a partnership of web designers who also provide branded stationery to their clients. The company's year end is 31st March. There are two founding partners, Karl Shephard and Rosalina Thomas and, as the business has recently taken on more work, a new partner, Gehan Noel, joined the business halfway through the 2011/12 financial year and introduced a further £6,000 of capital.

Goodwill & Profit Sharing

At the end of September 2011 Goodwill was valued at £18,000. The partners agree that Goodwill should **not** remain in the accounts but should, instead, be apportioned appropriately to their capital accounts.

Profit sharing since the formation of the partnership had been in the ratio of 1:1. After the admission of Gehan it was agreed that it would become 2:2:1 with Gehan receiving 20% of the profits and a salary of £916 per month (paid out of the profits at the end of the year).

At the year end, a payment of 5% interest per annum is to be made on Capital into the partners' current accounts. Assume no changes in capital have been made throughout the year apart from apportioning goodwill when Gehan joined.

Acquisition & Disposal

When Gehan joined, the business required a new computer for him to use and as the 2 computers used by the existing partners were becoming dated, these were each sold for cash for £300 + VAT which was banked immediately. Three new computers were purchased on credit for a total of £1,800 including VAT. The original computers were held in the accounts at a net cost of £1,000 each with accumulated depreciation of £750 each. The VAT rate used was 20%.

Depreciation

- Office furniture is depreciated at a rate of 20% per annum on a reducing balance basis.
- Computer Equipment is depreciated at a rate of 25% per annum on cost on a straight line basis.
- A full year's depreciation is to be charged in the year of acquisition and no depreciation is to be charged in the year of disposal.

Accruals and Prepayments

There are to be accruals for Accountancy fees of £1,500 and Electricity of £300.

Last May £2,400 was paid for Insurance for 1 year, starting from 1st June.

Rent on the premises is paid quarterly in advance. The last payment of £2,100 was made on 28th February.

Stock

At the end of the year, the unused stock of stationery was valued at £2,500.

Bad Debt Provision

At a recent meeting it was decided that the provision for bad debts until this year had been rather pessimistic and that based on recent experience it should be reduced to 2% of Debtors.

Webfinity and Beyond Initial Trial Balance

	Dr	Cr
Office Furniture	20,000	
Office Furniture Depreciation		9,855
Computer Equipment	4,000	
Computer Equipment Dep'n		3,000
Stock of Stationery at 1st April 2011	5,000	
Debtors	40,000	
Bad Debt provision		1,250
Bank	11,100	
Creditors		12,000
VAT Liability		3,000
PAYE Liability		945
Karl Shephard Capital Account		10,000
Rosalina Thomas Capital Account		15,000
Karl Shephard Current Account	1,800	
Rosalina Thomas Current Account		2,500
Sales		84,250
Purchases of Stationery	12,500	
Advertising	10,000	
Staff Salaries	16,000	
Rent	9,800	
Insurance	2,800	
Printing costs	1,200	
Electricity	1,300	
Postage and Carriage	200	
Repairs	650	
Telephone	1,600	
Legal Fees	2,500	
Bank charges	470	
Travelling	680	
Bad Debts Written Off	200	
Total	**141,800**	**141,800**

Section One

Task 1:

Post the initial trial balance from the table above into your accounting software. You may need to create new nominal codes depending on your software.

Print the following reports and label them with the task number:
- An Initial Trial Balance
- An Initial Profit and Loss account
- An Initial Balance Sheet

Task 2:

Post the amendments needed for the admission of Gehan Noel into the partnership and taking into account the goodwill.

Print and label a report that shows the above journal transactions.

Task 3:

Post the transactions to represent the disposal of the old computers and the acquisition of the new computers. A general or sundry creditors account may be used instead of a purchase ledger account for the purchase on credit.

Task 4:

Post the depreciation of the Fixed Assets.

Task 5:

Post the necessary adjustments for Accruals and Prepayments.

Task 6:

Post the necessary adjustments for opening and closing stock.

Task 7:

Post the necessary journals for the change in bad debt provision.

Print:
- A draft Trial Balance
- A draft Profit and Loss account
- A draft Balance Sheet

Task 8:

Process the year end and make the necessary adjustments in accordance with the Profit Sharing agreements.

Print:
- An Opening Balance Sheet for 2012/13
- An Opening Trial Balance for 2012/13

This is the end of Section One (the computerised section) of the exam

Please go to page 8 for Section Two of the examination

1. Provide an appropriation account detailing how net profit has been allocated to *Webfinity and Beyond*'s partners at the end of their trading year 2011/12.
Note: Profit has been earned evenly throughout the year.

2. *Webfinity and Beyond*'s recent stocks of paper and envelopes had been made up from the following purchases:

Purchase date:	1st November 2011		1st January 2012		1st March 2012	
Stationery Type	Units	Net cost per unit	Units	Net cost per unit	Units	Net cost per unit
Paper (Reams)	20	2.25	15	2.50	15	3.25
Envelopes x 100	30	2.75	25	3.00	40	3.50

If 35 Reams of Paper and 60 Packs of 100 envelopes had been sold by the end of year stock check; showing your workings, calculate the total value of these remaining items of closing stock using:

- The FIFO method
- The AVCO method

3. If *Webfinity and Beyond* was a Limited Liability Partnership and assuming the founding partners had not guaranteed any loans and had not acted negligently; using the figures from the **initial trial balance**, state how much the partners could jointly have lost if their business was sued for £100,000. Give a brief explanation of your answer.

This is the end of the examination

Webfinity and Beyond
Balance Sheet

From: Month 12, March 2012
To: Month 12, March 2012

Chart of Account: Default Layout of Accounts

	Period		Year to Date	
Fixed Assets				
Office Equipment	1,000.00		1,000.00	
Furniture and Fixtures	10,145.00		10,145.00	
		11,145.00		11,145.00
Current Assets				
Stock	5,000.00		5,000.00	
Debtors	38,750.00		38,750.00	
Bank Account	11,100.00		11,100.00	
		54,850.00		54,850.00
Current Liabilities				
Creditors : Short Term	12,000.00		12,000.00	
Taxation	945.00		945.00	
VAT Liability	3,000.00		3,000.00	
		15,945.00		15,945.00
Current Assets less Current Liabilities:		38,905.00		38,905.00
Total Assets less Current Liabilities:		50,050.00		50,050.00
Long Term Liabilities				
		0.00		0.00
Total Assets less Total Liabilities:		50,050.00		50,050.00
Capital & Reserves				
Share Capital	25,700.00		25,700.00	
P&L Account	24,350.00		24,350.00	
		50,050.00		50,050.00

Question 1:

Webfinity and Beyond **Appropriation Account**
For 2011/12

	Net Profit	9748	9748
		Apr - Sep	Oct - Mar
Less Interest on Capital			
	Karl Shephard	(250)	
	Rosalina Thomas	(375)	
		(625)	
Less Interest on Capital			
	Karl Shephard		(295)
	Rosalina Thomas		(420)
	Gehan Noel		(60)
			(775)
		9123	8973
Less Salary for Gehan Noel:			
	6 Months x £916:		(5496)
		9123	3477
Profit for sharing			
	Karl Shephard (1/2)	4561.50	
	Rosalina Thomas (1/2)	4561.50	
Profit for sharing			
	Karl Shephard (2/5)		1390.80
	Rosalina Thomas (2/5)		1390.80
	Gehan Noel (1/5)		695.40
		9123	3477

Question 2:

FIFO Method

All the remaining paper is from the latest batch purchased. This is 15 x £3.25 = 48.75
Similarly all the remaining envelopes are from the latest batch. 35 x £3.50 = £122.50
The total value of these items of closing stock using the FIFO method is **£171.25**

AVCO Method

The average cost of paper is: 20 x £2.25 + 15 x £2.50 + 15 x £3.50 / 50 = £2.70
The remaining stock of 15 reams of paper is valued at 15 x £2.70 = £40.50

The average cost of the envelopes is: 30 x £2.75 + 25 x £3.00 + 40 x £3.50 / 95 = £3.13
The remaining stock of 35 packs of envelopes is valued at 35 x £3.13 = £109.55

The total value of these items of closing stock using the AVCO method is **£150.05**

Question 3:

As a LLP the partners are only liable for the total amount they have invested in the business.
In the initial Trial Balance this totals £25,700 for both partners.

Date: 05/12/2011
Time: 16:17:44

Webfinity and Beyond
Audit Trail (Summary)

Date From:	01/01/1980		Customer From:	ZZZZZZZ
Date To:	31/12/2019		Customer To:	ZZZZZZZ
Transaction From:	61		Supplier From:	ZZZZZZZ
Transaction To:	69		Supplier To:	ZZZZZZZ
Dept From:	0		N/C From:	
Dept To:	999		N/C To:	9999999
Exclude Deleted Tran:	No			

No	Type	Date	A/C	N/C	Dept	Ref	Details	Net	Tax	T/C	Pd	Paid	V	B	Bank Rec. Date
61	JD	30/09/2011	0060	0060	0	GOODWIL	Goodwill posted	18,000.00	0.00	T9	Y	18,000.00	-	-	
62	JC	30/09/2011	3001	3001	0	GOODWIL	Goodwill posted	9,000.00	0.00	T9	Y	9,000.00	-	-	
63	JC	30/09/2011	3002	3002	0	GOODWIL	Goodwill posted	9,000.00	0.00	T9	Y	9,000.00	-	-	
64	JC	30/09/2011	3003	3003	0	GOODWIL	New partner capital introduced	6,000.00	0.00	T9	Y	6,000.00	-	-	
65	JD	30/09/2011	1200	1200	0	GOODWIL	New partner capital introduced	6,000.00	0.00	T9	Y	6,000.00	-	N	
66	JC	30/09/2011	0060	0060	0	GOODWIL	Goodwill written out	18,000.00	0.00	T9	Y	18,000.00	-	-	
67	JD	30/09/2011	3001	3001	0	GOODWIL	Goodwill written out	7,200.00	0.00	T9	Y	7,200.00	-	-	
68	JD	30/09/2011	3002	3002	0	GOODWIL	Goodwill written out	7,200.00	0.00	T9	Y	7,200.00	-	-	
69	JD	30/09/2011	3003	3003	0	GOODWIL	Goodwill written out	3,600.00	0.00	T9	Y	3,600.00	-	-	

Webfinity and Beyond
Period Trial Balance

To Period: Month 1, April 2012

N/C	Name	Debit	Credit
0030	Computer Equipment	3,500.00	
0031	Computer Equipment Depreciation		2,375.00
0040	Office Furniture	20,000.00	
0041	Office Furniture Depreciation		11,884.00
1001	Stationery Stocks	2,500.00	
1100	Debtors Control Account	40,000.00	
1103	Prepayments	1,800.00	
1104	Bad Debt Provision		800.00
1200	Bank Current Account	17,820.00	
2100	Creditors Control Account		13,800.00
2109	Accruals		1,800.00
2200	Sales Tax Control Account		120.00
2201	Purchase Tax Control Account	300.00	
2202	VAT Liability		3,000.00
2210	P.A.Y.E.		945.00
3001	Karl Shephard Capital Account		11,800.00
3002	Rosalina Thomas Capital Account		16,800.00
3003	Gehan Noel Capital Account		2,400.00
3011	Karl Shephard Current Account		4,415.00
3012	Rosalina Thomas Current Account		8,965.00
3013	Gehan Noel Current Account		6,816.00
	Totals:	**85,920.00**	**85,920.00**

To Period: Month 12, March 2012

N/C	Name	Debit	Credit
0030	Computer Equipment	4,000.00	
0031	Computer Equipment Depreciation		3,000.00
0040	Office Furniture	20,000.00	
0041	Office Furniture Depreciation		9,855.00
1001	Stationery Stocks	5,000.00	
1100	Debtors Control Account	40,000.00	
1104	Bad Debt Provision		1,250.00
1200	Bank Current Account	11,100.00	
2100	Creditors Control Account		12,000.00
2202	VAT Liability		3,000.00
2210	P.A.Y.E.		945.00
3001	Karl Shephard Capital Account		10,000.00
3002	Rosalina Thomas Capital Account		15,000.00
3011	Karl Shephard Current Account	1,800.00	
3012	Rosalina Thomas Current Account		2,500.00
4000	Sales		84,250.00
5000	Purchases of Stationery	12,500.00	
6201	Advertising	10,000.00	
7003	Staff Salaries	16,000.00	
7100	Rent	9,800.00	
7200	Electricity	1,300.00	
7400	Travelling	680.00	
7500	Printing	1,200.00	
7501	Postage and Carriage	200.00	
7502	Telephone	1,600.00	
7600	Legal Fees	2,500.00	
7800	Repairs and Renewals	650.00	
7901	Bank Charges	470.00	
8100	Bad Debt Write Off	200.00	
8204	Insurance	2,800.00	
	Totals:	**141,800.00**	**141,800.00**

To Period: Month 12, March 2012

N/C	Name	Debit	Credit
0030	Computer Equipment	3,500.00	
0031	Computer Equipment Depreciation		2,375.00
0040	Office Furniture	20,000.00	
0041	Office Furniture Depreciation		11,884.00
1001	Stationery Stocks	2,500.00	
1100	Debtors Control Account	40,000.00	
1103	Prepayments	1,800.00	
1104	Bad Debt Provision		800.00
1200	Bank Current Account	17,820.00	
2100	Creditors Control Account		13,800.00
2109	Accruals		1,800.00
2200	Sales Tax Control Account		120.00
2201	Purchase Tax Control Account	300.00	
2202	VAT Liability		3,000.00
2210	P.A.Y.E.		945.00
3001	Karl Shephard Capital Account		11,800.00
3002	Rosalina Thomas Capital Account		16,800.00
3003	Gehan Noel Capital Account		2,400.00
3011	Karl Shephard Current Account	1,800.00	
3012	Rosalina Thomas Current Account		2,500.00
4000	Sales		84,250.00
5000	Purchases of Stationery	12,500.00	
5200	Opening Stock	5,000.00	
5201	Closing Stock		2,500.00
6201	Advertising	10,000.00	
7003	Staff Salaries	16,000.00	
7100	Rent	8,400.00	
7200	Electricity	1,600.00	
7400	Travelling	680.00	
7500	Printing	1,200.00	
7501	Postage and Carriage	200.00	
7502	Telephone	1,600.00	
7600	Legal Fees	2,500.00	
7601	Audit and Accountancy Fees	1,500.00	
7800	Repairs and Renewals	650.00	
7901	Bank Charges	470.00	
8002	Office Furniture Depreciation	2,029.00	
8004	Computer Equipment Depreciation	875.00	
8100	Bad Debt Write Off	200.00	
8102	Bad Debt Provision		450.00
8204	Insurance	2,400.00	
8300	Disposal of Assets		100.00
	Totals:	155,524.00	155,524.00

From: Month 1, April 2011
To: Month 12, March 2012

Chart of Accounts: Default Layout of Accounts

	Period		Year to Date	
Sales				
Product Sales	84,250.00		84,250.00	
		84,250.00		84,250.00
Purchases				
Purchases	12,500.00		12,500.00	
		12,500.00		12,500.00
Direct Expenses				
Sales Promotion	10,000.00		10,000.00	
		10,000.00		10,000.00
Gross Profit/(Loss):		61,750.00		61,750.00
Overheads				
Gross Wages	16,000.00		16,000.00	
Rent and Rates	9,800.00		9,800.00	
Heat, Light and Power	1,300.00		1,300.00	
Travelling and Entertainment	680.00		680.00	
Printing and Stationery	3,000.00		3,000.00	
Professional Fees	2,500.00		2,500.00	
Maintenance	650.00		650.00	
Bank Charges and Interest	470.00		470.00	
Bad Debts	200.00		200.00	
General Expenses	2,800.00		2,800.00	
		37,400.00		37,400.00
Net Profit/(Loss):		24,350.00		24,350.00

From:	Month 1, April 2012
To:	Month 1, April 2012

Chart of Account: Default Layout of Accounts

	Period		Year to Date	
Fixed Assets				
Office Equipment	0.00		1,125.00	
Furniture and Fixtures	0.00		8,116.00	
		0.00		9,241.00
Current Assets				
Stock	0.00		2,500.00	
Debtors	0.00		41,000.00	
Bank Account	0.00		17,820.00	
		0.00		61,320.00
Current Liabilities				
Creditors : Short Term	0.00		15,600.00	
Taxation	0.00		945.00	
VAT Liability	0.00		2,820.00	
		0.00		19,365.00
Current Assets less Current Liabilities:		0.00		41,955.00
Total Assets less Current Liabilities:		0.00		51,196.00
Long Term Liabilities				
		0.00		0.00
Total Assets less Total Liabilities:		0.00		51,196.00
Capital & Reserves				
Capital	19,496.00		51,196.00	
Reserves	(19,496.00)		0.00	
P&L Account	0.00		0.00	
		0.00		51,196.00

From: Month 1, April 2011
To: Month 12, March 2012

Chart of Accounts: Default Layout of Accounts

	Period		Year to Date	
Sales				
Product Sales	84,250.00		84,250.00	
		84,250.00		84,250.00
Purchases				
Purchases	12,500.00		12,500.00	
Stock	2,500.00		2,500.00	
		15,000.00		15,000.00
Direct Expenses				
Sales Promotion	10,000.00		10,000.00	
		10,000.00		10,000.00
Gross Profit/(Loss):		59,250.00		59,250.00
Overheads				
Gross Wages	16,000.00		16,000.00	
Rent and Rates	8,400.00		8,400.00	
Heat, Light and Power	1,600.00		1,600.00	
Travelling and Entertainment	680.00		680.00	
Printing and Stationery	3,000.00		3,000.00	
Professional Fees	4,000.00		4,000.00	
Maintenance	650.00		650.00	
Bank Charges and Interest	470.00		470.00	
Depreciation	2,904.00		2,904.00	
Bad Debts	(250.00)		(250.00)	
General Expenses	2,400.00		2,400.00	
Disposal of Assets	(100.00)		(100.00)	
		39,754.00		39,754.00
Net Profit/(Loss):		19,496.00		19,496.00

338

From: Month 1, April 2011
To: Month 12, March 2012

Chart of Account: Default Layout of Accounts

	Period		Year to Date	
Fixed Assets				
Office Equipment	1,125.00		1,125.00	
Furniture and Fixtures	8,116.00		8,116.00	
		9,241.00		9,241.00
Current Assets				
Stock	2,500.00		2,500.00	
Debtors	41,000.00		41,000.00	
Bank Account	17,820.00		17,820.00	
		61,320.00		61,320.00
Current Liabilities				
Creditors : Short Term	15,600.00		15,600.00	
Taxation	945.00		945.00	
VAT Liability	2,820.00		2,820.00	
		19,365.00		19,365.00
Current Assets less Current Liabilities:		41,955.00		41,955.00
Total Assets less Current Liabilities:		51,196.00		51,196.00
Long Term Liabilities				
		0.00		0.00
Total Assets less Total Liabilities:		51,196.00		51,196.00
Capital & Reserves				
Share Capital	31,700.00		31,700.00	
P&L Account	19,496.00		19,496.00	
		51,196.00		51,196.00

Practice assessment

Computerised accounting
Level 2 Certificate in Accounting

Assessment book

- This **practice assessment** is for familiarisation purposes only and **must not** be used in place of a 'live' assessment.

- When you feel prepared to sit the live assessment please contact your Training Provider who can schedule a live assessment for you.

Instructions to candidates

This assessment is in **two sections**. You must prove competence in each section to be successful.

- **Section 1** asks you to input data into a computerised accounting package and produce documents and reports.
- **Section 2** asks you to complete short answer questions.

The time allowed to complete this Computerised accounting assessment is **3 hours**.

Additional time up to a maximum of 1 hour may be scheduled by your tutor to allow for delays due to computer issues, such as printer queues and uploading documents to LearnPlus.

It is important that you provide all documents specified in the tasks so your work can be assessed. All printed material should be **titled** and be marked with your **name** and **AAT membership number**.

If your computerised accounting system allows for the generation of PDFs, these can be generated instead of hard copy prints. Screenshots saved as image files are also acceptable.

If you are using print-outs as evidence, the only document you will be required to upload at the end of the assessment is your assessment booklet. If you have generated PDFs or screenshots instead of printing, these documents should be uploaded to LearnPlus with your assessment book. Please ensure that your training provider is aware of which option you will be using.

Section 1

Data

This assessment is based on an existing business, Brookland Plants, an organisation that supplies ornamental plant displays and a maintenance service to local businesses. The owner of the business is Nadine Brookland who operates as a sole trader.

At the start of business Nadine operated a manual book-keeping system but has now decided that from 1 May 20XX the accounting system will become computerised. You are employed as an accounting technician.

You can assume that all documentation has been checked for accuracy and authorised by Nadine Brookland.

Sales are to be analysed in three ways:

- Plant displays
- Plant maintenance
- Cash sales, which arise from occasional sales of plant displays to friends.

Some nominal ledger accounts have already been allocated account codes. You may need to amend or create other account codes.

The business is registered for VAT. The rate of VAT charged on all goods and services sold by Brookland Plants is 20%.

All expenditure should be analysed as you feel appropriate.

Before you start the assessment you should:

- Set the system software date as **31 May of the current year**.
- Set up the company details under the name 'Brookland Plants'.
- Set the financial year to start on **1st May of the current year**.

This set-up does not form part of the assessment standards, so your training provider may assist you with this.

342

Task 1.1

Refer to the customer listing below:

- Set up customer records to open sales ledger accounts for each customer.
- Save your work and print a Customer activity list, which includes each customer's name, account code, credit limit and opening balance.

Customer Listing

Customer name, address and contact details	Customer account code	Customer account details at 1 May 20XX
Ennis plc 26 Highfield Road Ronchester RC17 1BG Telephone: 0161 876 4356 Contact name: Kelly Ennis	ENN01	Credit limit: £3,000 Payment terms: 30 days Opening balance: £1,698.70
Campbell Ltd 45 Green Lane Ronchester RC12 5FR Telephone: 0161 969 3221 Contact name: Matthew Jones	CAM01	Credit limit: £4,000 Payment terms: 30 days Opening balance: £2,100.00
MJ Devonish 27 Jurys Road Ronchester RC3 8HY Telephone: 0161 456 2874 Contact name: Usman Hussain	DEV01	Credit limit: £1,000 Payment terms: 30 days Opening balance: £352.50
Bell and Cooke Ltd 32 Forest Lane Ronchester RC9 7KJ Telephone: 0161 854 9327 Contact name: Jenny Holmes	BEL01	Credit limit: £3,000 Payment terms: 30 days Opening balance: £1,200.80

Task 1.2

Refer to the supplier listing below:

*   Set up supplier records to open purchases ledger accounts for each supplier.
*   Save your work and print a Supplier activity list, which includes each supplier's name, account code, credit limit and opening balance.

Supplier Listing

Supplier name, address and contact details	Supplier account code	Supplier account details at 1 May 20XX
Highdown Plants Ltd 26 Growcott Street Ronchester RC4 2JT Telephone: 0161 743 0097 Contact name: Hetal Patel	HIG01	Credit limit: £4,000 Payment terms: 30 days; Opening balance: £2,600.00
Lewis and Lane 45 Princes Street Ronchester RC18 7TR Telephone: 0161 834 0029 Contact name: Denise Lane	LEW01	Credit limit: £4,500 Payment terms: 30 days Opening balance: £1,800.00
Meadow Supplies 27 Jurys Road Ronchester RC3 8HY Telephone: 0161 738 2434 Contact name: John Black	MEA01	Credit limit: £2,500 Payment terms: 30 days Opening balance: £850.20
Broad Garages 32 Anderson Street Ronchester RC9 5DR Telephone: 0161 261 4486 Contact name: James Graham	BRO01	Credit limit: £1,000 Payment terms: 30 days Opening balance: £375.80

Task 1.3

Refer to the list of nominal ledger balances below:

- Enter the opening balances into the computer, making sure you select, amend or create appropriate nominal ledger account codes.

- Print a trial balance.

- Check the accuracy of the trial balance and, if necessary, correct any errors.

List of nominal ledger balances as at 01.05.20XX

Account names	£	£
Office equipment	3,189.00	
Motor Vehicle	14,500.00	
Bank	4,805.80	
Petty Cash	200.00	
Sales ledger control* see note below	5,352.00	
Purchases ledger control* see note below		5,626.00
VAT on sales		1,650.60
VAT on purchases	1,276.00	
Capital		24,300.00
Drawings	4,174.00	
Sales – plant displays		6,780.00
Sales – plant maintenance		3,460.00
Cash sales		460.40
Materials purchases	7,480.20	
Rent and rates	750.00	
Motor vehicle expenses	550.00	
* Note		
As you have already entered opening balances for customer and suppliers the software package you are using may not require you to enter these balances		

Task 1.4

You have received notification of a change of address and telephone number from a supplier, Meadow Supplies.

• Enter the new address and telephone number into the computer.

• Print a screen shot of the supplier's record with the new address and telephone number

The new address and telephone number are:

54 Sandy Lane
Ronchester
RC3 6RD

Telephone: 0161 456 1983

Task 1.5

Refer to the following sales invoices, sales credit note and summary of purchases invoices and enter these transactions into the computer.

Brookland Plants
46, Kirkland Street, Ronchester, RC4 0TS
VAT Registration No 476 3163 00

Telephone: 0161 743 5188
Email: N.Brookland@Brooklands.co.uk

S A L E S   I N V O I C E   N O   080
Date: 01 May 20XX

Campbell Ltd
45 Green Lane
Ronchester
RC12 5FR

	£
Supplying plant displays for reception area	900.00
VAT @ 20%	180.00
Total for payment	1,080.00

Terms: 30 days

Brookland Plants
46, Kirkland Street, Ronchester, RC4 0TS
VAT Registration No 476 3163 00

Telephone: 0161 743 5188
Email: N.Brookland@Brooklands.co.uk

S A L E S   I N V O I C E   N O   081
Date: 15 May 20XX

Bell and Cooke Ltd
32 Forest Lane
Ronchester
RC9 7KJ

	£
Supplying new plant displays	870.00
VAT @ 20%	174.00
Total for payment	1,044.00

Terms: 30 days

Task 1.5 continued

Brookland Plants
46, Kirkland Street, Ronchester, RC4 0TS
VAT Registration No 476 3163 00

Telephone: 0161 743 5188
Email: N.Brookland@Brooklands.co.uk

S A L E S   CREDIT NOTE   N O   016
Date: 18 May 20XX

Campbell Ltd
45 Green Lane
Ronchester
RC12 5FR

	£
Return of unwanted plant display	150.00
VAT @ 20%	30.00
Total for payment	180.00

Terms: 30 days

Brookland Plants
46, Kirkland Street, Ronchester, RC4 0TS
VAT Registration No 476 3163 00

Telephone: 0161 743 5188
Email: N.Brookland@Brooklands.co.uk

S A L E S   I N V O I C E   N O   082
Date: 25 May 20XX

Ennis plc
26 Highfield Road
Ronchester
RC17 1BG

	£
Maintaining existing plant displays	710.00
VAT @ 20%	142.00
Total for payment	852.00

Terms: 30 days

Task 1.5 continued

Summary of purchases invoices

Date 20XX	Supplier Name	Invoice Number	Gross £	VAT £	Net £	Plant supplies £	Motor expenses £
02.05.XX	Lewis and Lane	X204	2,400.00	400.00	2,000.00	2,000.00	
07.05.XX	Broad Garages	M145	216.00	36.00	180.00		180.00
12.05.XX	Highdown Plants Ltd	2010	960.00	160.00	800.00	800.00	
18.05.XX	Meadow Supplies	1904	1,284.00	214.00	1,070.00	1,070.00	
	Totals		4,860.00	810.00	4,050.00	3,870.00	180.00

Task 1.6

Refer to the following summary of payments received from customers and made to suppliers and enter these transactions into the computer, making sure you allocate all amounts as shown in the details column.

Cheque/BACS receipts listing

Date	Receipt type	Customer	£	Details
07.05.XX	BACS	Ennis plc	1,698.70	Payment of opening balance
24.05.XX	Cheque	Campbell Ltd	900.00	Payment of invoice 80 including credit note 16

Cheques paid listing

Date	Cheque number	Supplier	£	Details
11.05.XX	002365	Lewis and Lane	1,800.00	Payment of opening balance
18.05.XX	002366	Highdown Plants Ltd	1,500.00	Payment on account
23.05.XX	002367	Broad Garages	216.00	Payment of invoice M145

Task 1.7

(a) Refer to the following receipt issued for cash sales and enter this transaction into the computer.

Receipt Number 06
Date   06 May 20XX
Received, by cheque, from Fiona Wittin for a plant display:
£90.00 including VAT

(b) Refer to the following email from Nadine Brookland and enter this transaction into the computer.

Email
From: Nadine Brookland **To:**   Accounting Technician **Date:**   12 May 20XX **Subject:**   Drawings
Hello I have used the Company debit card to withdraw £180 in cash from the bank for my personal use. Please record this transaction. Thanks Nadine

(c) Refer to the following cash purchases listing and enter this transaction into the computer.

Cash purchases listing

Date	Payment method	Details	Amount
20 May 20XX	Debit card	Purchase of a computer printer, model number 45XK:	£108.00 including VAT

Task 1.8

Refer to the following petty cash vouchers and enter the petty cash payments into the computer.

Petty Cash Voucher	
Date 08 May 20XX	**No** PC28
	£
Emergency repair to lock on office door – VAT not applicable	38.87
Receipt attached	

Petty Cash Voucher	
Date 16 May 20XX	**No** PC29
	£
Taxi fare – VAT not applicable	22.00
Receipt attached	

Petty Cash Voucher	
Date 20 May 20XX	**No** PC30
	£
Paper for printer, envelopes and pens	27.60
VAT	5.52
Total	33.12
Receipt attached	

Task 1.9

Refer to the following email from Nadine Brookland:

- Make entries into the computer to write off the amount of £352.50 owing from MJ Devonish. (Ignore VAT).
- Match this transaction against the opening balance in MJ Devonish's account.

Email	
From: Nadine Brookland **To:** Accounting Technician **Date:** 10 May 20XX **Subject:** MJ Devonish	
Hello The above customer has ceased trading owing us £352.50. Please write this amount off as an irrecoverable debt. Thanks Nadine	

Task 1.10

Refer to the following journal entries and enter them into the computer.

JOURNAL ENTRIES TO BE MADE 12.05.XX	£	£
Motor vehicle expenses	65.00	
Rent and rates		65.00
Being an error in the opening journal entries		

JOURNAL ENTRIES TO BE MADE 28.05.XX	£	£
Bank	30.00	
Drawings		30.00
Being an error in recording the amount withdrawn from the bank by Nadine Brookland		

Task 1.11

Refer to the following email below from Nadine Brookland and enter this transaction into the computer.

Email
From: Nadine Brookland **To:** Accounting Technician **Date:** 31 May 20XX **Subject:** Petty cash
Hello Please transfer an amount of £ 93.99 from the bank account to the petty cash account to reimburse the petty cash float. The balance on the petty cash account should now be £200. Thanks Nadine

Task 1.12

Refer to the following bank statement:

- Enter the direct debit for rates (no VAT) and bank charges (no VAT) which have not yet been accounted for.
- Reconcile the bank statement. If the bank statement does not reconcile check your work and make the necessary corrections.
- Print the bank reconciliation statement.

North Bank plc
60 High Street
Ronchester
RC1 8TF

Brookland Plants
46 Kirkland Street
Ronchester
RC4 OTS

Account number 00678432   31 May 20XX

STATEMENT OF ACCOUNT

Date 20XX	Details	Paid out £	Paid in £	Balance £
01 May	Opening balance			4,805.80C
08 May	Counter credit		90.00	4,895.80C
10 May	BACS: Ennis plc		1,698.70	6,594.50C
12 May	Cash withdrawal	150.00		6,444.50C
18 May	Cheque 002265	1,800.00		4,644.50C
20 May	Debit card	108.00		4,536.50C
24 May	Direct Debit - Ronchester MBC - Rates	300.00		4,236.50C
21 May	Cheque 002366	1,500.00		2,736.50C
30 May	Bank charges	56.00		2,680.50C
31 May	Transfer	93.99		2,586.51C
	D = Debit C = Credit			

Task 1.13

Use the appropriate software tool to check for data errors and print a screen shot of the data verification screen. Make any necessary corrections.

Task 1.14

Print a trial balance as at 31 May 20XX. Check the accuracy of the trial balance and, if necessary, correct any errors.

Task 1.15

Back up your work to a suitable storage media and print a screen shot of the back up screen showing the location of back up data. Your assessor will tell you what storage media you should use.

Task 1.16

Print the following reports:

- The sales day book (customer invoices)
- The sales returns day book (customer credits)
- The purchases day book (supplier invoices)
- All sales ledger accounts (customer accounts), showing all transactions within each account
- All purchases ledger accounts (supplier accounts), showing all transactions within each account
- All active nominal ledger accounts, showing all transactions within each account.

Please note the accounting package you are using may not use exactly the same report names as those shown above, so some alternative names are shown in brackets.

Task 1.17

(a) Generate an aged trade receivables analysis and print a copy.

(b) Export the aged trade receivables analysis to a spreadsheet and print a copy. You do not need to make any alterations to the spreadsheet.

Task 1.18

Print an overdue account letter for Campbell Ltd.

Task 1.19

Use the relevant software tool to clear month end turnover totals and print a screen shot of the on screen instruction to clear month end turnover totals.

Section 2

Task 2.1

In a computerised accounting system the following data entry error message may sometimes appear.

WARNING	
Date entered is outside your current financial year. Are you sure you want to continue?	
Yes	No

(a)   Show the most appropriate response to this message by selecting **one** of the options from the table below.

Task 2.1	✓
Select the **Yes** button, continue to enter data and take no further action.	☐
Select the **No** button, check the accuracy of the date entered and if necessary change it before proceeding.	☐
Select the **Yes** button, continue to enter data and correct any errors later	☐
Select the **No** button, change the date to the current financial year and then continue to enter the data.	☐

Task 2.2

Several purchases invoices have been input into a computerised accounting system.

(a)   Which computer generated report would you use to review these transactions and identify any errors?

Task 2.2	✓
Trial balance	☐
Aged trade payables report	☐
Purchases day book	☐
Suppliers statements	☐

Task 2.3

It has been discovered that the rate of VAT on one of the purchases invoices in **Section 1** was incorrectly entered at 20.00% instead of zero.

(a) Show which **one** of the following sentences is correct.

Task 2.3	✓
In a computerised accounting system it is possible to use the software corrections tool to edit the error and change the rate of VAT.	☐
In a computerised accounting system it is **not** possible to use the software corrections tool to edit the error and change the rate of VAT.	☐

Task 2.4

Accounting information is entered into the computer from different source documents.

(a) Which source document is used to enter a regular monthly automated payment to a supplier?

Task 2.4	✓
Bank reconciliation statement	☐
Cheques received listing	☐
Remittance advice note	☐
Direct debit / Standing order schedule	☐

In a computerised system every credit customer is allocated an account code.

(b) Show whether the following statement is true or false.

'Two different customers **cannot** have the same account code because the computerised accounting system uses the account code to identify the customer.'

Task 2.4 continued	✓
True	☐
False	☐

Task 2.5

Data stored on a computer is at risk from various sources.

(a) Insert the appropriate risk number in the table below to match each risk to one of the situations described. You should identify the most appropriate risk for each situation and use each risk **once** only.

Risk number	Risk to data
1	Data may become corrupted
2	Data may be difficult to locate
3	Data may be lost
4	Data may be seen by unauthorised users

Situation	Risk number
There is no organisational policy for the use of passwords.	Choose option
In accordance with organisational policy back-up copies of data are taken every 2 months.	Choose option
In accordance with organisational policy back-up copies of data are stored on a bookshelf in a locked office.	Choose option
There is no organisational policy for the naming of files on the computer.	Choose option

A computer virus is a risk to data.

(b) Show whether the following statements about computer viruses are true or false.

	True ✓	False ✓
A computer virus is a piece of software that infects programs and data	☐	☐
A computer virus **cannot** enter the system as an attachment to an email	☐	☐

On 26 July 20XX an overdue accounts letter was sent to Jones Brothers, 27 The Parade, Wormley, WM7 4RD. You have now been asked to password protect the letter in accordance with best practice.

(c) Which **one** of the passwords in the table below is the most appropriate?

Password	Most appropriate ✓
Jonesletter	☐
WM74RD	☐
JB*let2607	☐
27Parade	☐

Task 2.5 continued

(d) When should a password be changed?

	✓
Once every twelve months.	☐
On a regular basis.	☐
If it is known to an authorised user.	☐
If it has been used on two occasions by one user.	☐

Task 2.6

(a) Match the accounting data shown in the table below, to the person or persons who require that data by placing a tick in the appropriate column. You should tick each column **once** only.

Accounting data	Sales Director	Credit controller	Customers	Suppliers
Aged trade receivables analysis	☐	☐	☐	☐
Statement of account	☐	☐	☐	☐
Monthly sales figures	☐	☐	☐	☐
Remittance advice	☐	☐	☐	☐

Task 2.7

Many computerised accounting software packages allow data to be imported from or exported to other packages.

(a) Show whether the following statements are true or false.

	True ✓	False ✓
Data cannot be imported into a computerised accounting package from a spreadsheet package	☐	☐
Data can be exported from a computerised accounting package to a word processing package	☐	☐

Organizations and professional associations

Information Commissioner's Office
Wycliffe House
Water Lane
Wilmslow
Cheshire SK9 5AF
Telephone: 0303 123 1113/01625 545745
www.ico.gov.uk
For the full text of the Data Protection Act 1998, go to
www.opsi.gov.uk/ads/ads1998/19980029.htm

Institute of Certified Bookkeepers
3 Minster Court
Mincing Lane
London EC3R 7DD
Telephone: 0845 060 2345/0207 7398 4440
www.bookkeepers.org.uk

International Association of Book-keepers (IAB)
Burford House
44 London Road
Sevenoaks
Kent TN13 1AS
Telephone: 0843 770 3523/International +44 (0)1732 808614
www.iab.org.uk

Publications

Marshall, P. (2010), *Mastering Book-keeping*, 9th Edition, Oxford: How To Books
Marshall, P. (2010), *Computerised Book-keeping*, Oxford: How To Books

Websites

www.masteringbook-keeping.com
www.bookkeepers.org.uk/forum